Some Write to the Future

Some Write to the Future

Essays on Contemporary Latin American Fiction

Ariel Dorfman

Translated by George Shivers with the Author

Duke University Press ■ *Durham and London* 1991

Previously published material in Spanish includes the
following: The chapters on Asturias's *Men of Maize* and
on Borges, from *Imaginación y Violencia en América*
(Santiago: Universitaria, 1970), © 1967 and 1968 Ariel
Dorfman; the chapters on Arguedas's *Deep Rivers* and on
Carpentier, from *Hacia la liberación del Lector Americano*
(Hanover, N.H.: Ediciones del Norte, 1984), © 1977 and
1980 Ariel Dorfman; the chapter on the testimonial
genre in Chile first appeared in a different form in
Ideologies and Literature, ed. René Jara, Monographic
Series 3 (Minneapolis: Institute for the Study of
Ideologies and Literature, 1986), pp. 170–234.

The chapter on Roa Bastos appeared as a foreword,
© 1982 Ariel Dorfman, to the English translation of Roa
Bastos's *Son of Man* (New York: Monthly Review
Press, 1988).

To my mother and my father

Contents ■

Note on the Translations

The essays on Asturias, Borges, Arguedas,
and the testimonial literature of Chile
have been translated by George Shivers
with the author. The essay on Carpentier
has been translated by the author directly
from the Spanish. The introduction and
the essay on García Márquez have been
written directly in English by the author
for this collection. The essay on Roa Bastos
was written in English as a foreword to a
second edition of Son of Man, *published*
by Monthly Review Press.

Twenty-three years have passed since I wrote the essay on Miguel Angel Asturias that opens this collection of my writings on contemporary Latin American fiction. The year was 1967, I was barely twenty-five myself, I did not have even one book published, my first son had just been born—but most important of all, I had no idea of what history was preparing for me, for my loved ones, for my country. The violence, the creative intervention of memory, the role of myth and language in resistance, categories which are all analyzed and dissected in that essay, would all too soon find their equivalents, their confirmation or their denial, in immediate political developments. I could not anticipate when I sat down in 1967 to explore in words the relationship in our culture of literature and hope, literature and repression, that three years later my country would elect Salvador Allende as its president in an attempt to give that hope a real historical chance of materializing. Nor could I have realized that three years after that a military coup would destroy that hope and the democracy which nurtured it. And I certainly could never have predicted that, included as a small part of the general disaster, I would be sent, with my family, into an exile which is only now, as I write this in 1990, coming to what I assume is a definite end.

In one sense, then, the distance that separates that first essay, written in Santiago in Spanish for a Chilean audience, from the last essay in this collection or from this very introduction I am composing right now, in English, in the United States, presumably for a predominantly North American audience, could not be greater. I am not, could not be, do not want to be, the young man who sat down in 1967 to write about Asturias, or the year after that about Borges, or ten years later from the distance of banishment about Arguedas and the *testimonio*. I would not today write those essays in the same way. This does not mean, of course, that I renounce their paternity or, for that matter, validity. What I feel, to the contrary, is that each one continues to open up authors and books and to challenge the readers to a more provocative understanding of literature and Latin America. And these diverse writings, organized in chronological order, can also be perused as signals of my own literary evolution and interests, the secret ways in which history forced me to deal differently and ever more deeply with obsessions that, expressed as well in my fiction, poetry, and plays, have remained with me through the years.

Which, naturally, brings up another sort of dilemma—or risk— of anthologies that span almost a quarter century of intellectual activity. Where is the unity in these writings, can a common thread be discerned and pursued through them all, can their inclusion under one roof be even remotely justified?

A tentative answer would affirm and point to one irrefutable constancy: all of these meditations stem from the same fierce belief that our literature has an important role, indeed an essential one, to play in the liberation of the people of Latin America. It was easier to hold that belief back in 1967 when it seemed that radical revolutions were about to sweep the South American continent than now in 1990 when the chances for significant change in our social and economic structures appear to be considerably reduced, but I still stubbornly proclaim that only an exploration of the ways in which our contemporary fiction subverts prevalent power, or submits to it, can reveal that fiction's true character.

It is paradoxical, of course, that this process of subversion (or of submission) must be carried out in a continent where the communication between the writer and the reader has not only been severely restricted throughout history but has, if anything, grown more regressive in the last decades. A series of barriers, each one more impenetrable, have been erected between those who denounce through their writing a world in dire need of citizen participation and the very citizens supposedly being stimulated and activated. To begin with, most Latin Americans are nonreaders: millions don't know how to read or write and the majority of those who do spend their intelligence on mass-produced, easily digested words that instead of impelling them to question their society tend to demand that they accept it. But there is also the succession of inquisitorial fires that have, in the last centuries, with a recent recrudescence, burned books (to say nothing of readers and writers) across our latino continent, there is the flagrant censorship of texts and the less visible, but equally implacable, censorship of the marketplace, an economic system that turns literature into a supreme luxury. The specialized communication that arises between a writer and a reader is not immune from the same chronic ills that afflict all attempts by inhabitants of our lands at connecting with one another in a dialogue: hunger, unemployment, lack of infrastructure for education, cruel and incompetent government officials, gross gender inequalities, and, of course, systematic violation of the basic human rights of anyone who dares to protest against this sorry state of affairs. If in the last fifteen years many eminent writers—whose faces are on the book jackets of novels translated into a variety of foreign languages—have "disappeared," what of the more voracious and less glaring extermination endured by those who would read the forbidden words but do not even have that pale, and it turns out useless, defense of being well-known? Not to mention the faraway brothers and sisters who, if they were ever to open a book, would see it as hardly more than a blank page.

And yet, this very absence of a real reader for the fiction that needs one so desperately, that desires so much an answer from reality to its echo of despair, implies a literary strategy that demands of that reader an unceasing birth, that calls for him or her to go beyond the enclaves of the past, the monoproduction of ideas and emotions, that urges the reader to leave behind passivity and apathy and to participate, to appear and—in a word—to develop. I have often wondered if the formal ruptures in a great part of our twentieth-century literature, its linguistic violence, its fractured levels of appeal and questioning structures, although undoubtedly the result of Western cultural modernist influences, do not profoundly owe themselves to the need to reach the blockaded readers gnawing at the shores of the text. Is it not possible that those nonreaders are our secret and omitted coeditors, white shadows that, however unseen, are always there waiting to materialize? Is the sheer weight of that unexpressed universe, of those millions of mute voices, not always silently present and intermingled in every cloistered word that is born in Latin America?

What I am suggesting is that, although a majority of those readers are constricted by social circumstances from an effective everyday interpretation of the books meant for them, they are, nevertheless, radically implicit in the structure and language of the books themselves, exercising a critique of, and longing for, those messages. Precisely because the world into which these words are born, with its prevalence of hierarchy and tyranny and enforced amnesia, the literature of Latin America tends, in general terms, to require what I would timidly call an anti-authoritarian reading and reader. Rather than establish with readers a relationship of propaganda or denunciation (though these are perfectly legitimate functions of the written word in a continent that cries out for liberation), most of the more interesting social literature in Latin America does not today circumscribe its political role to changing the immediate consciousness of the subject, verifying its effectiveness by measuring alterations in the behavior of the reader. This sort of aesthetic relationship would reproduce and preserve in the work of art the sort of unilateral verticality that is supposedly being attacked in the larger society where the writer must live and create. The authors I study in the following pages—and the very essays that study them—conceive of the reader in a more respectful way, as if she were a citizen of the future, trusting him to decide the multiple ways in which the work must be internalized in order to be fulfilled, giving to them the task of completing the fiction massively and plurally in the mirror or the window of their community.

Inasmuch as the works that we are going to examine purified our language, provoked the readers as mature and complex individuals instead of patronizing them, presented them with contradictions and dilemmas that refused to be solved in the literature itself, they are part of the slow—all too slow—democratization of Latin America. These meditations of mine, as well as the books that inspired them, are based on the hope, as alive now as it was in 1967, that the violence inscribed like a curse in our literature since its origins can be resolved, through action or compassion or doubt or rage or tenderness, in the lives of the liberated readers of today and tomorrow and beyond.

Durham, North Carolina, June 1990

Men of Maize: Myth as Time and Language

A strange fate has befallen Miguel Angel Asturias's master-piece, *Men of Maize*. Along with Alejo Carpentier's remark-able *The Kingdom of This World*, which was also published in 1949, it could well be said to inaugurate the extraordinary renaissance of the contemporary Latin American novel. And yet it has been consistently underrated by critics and neglected by readers.

Most critics seem to feel it to be a confusing, explosive splin-ter, not easily cataloged in Asturias's production. They prefer the dynamic coherence of the previously published and more famous *El Señor Presidente*, and would probably have liked to proceed in orderly fashion from that novel about the internal tyranny of a country to the Banana Trilogy with which Asturias, some years later, would portray the external tyranny of imperialism. They feel *Men of Maize* to be deficient, lacking in unity, unwieldy and frag-mented, a generic amalgam. Readers seem to agree, finding the novel boring or difficult—a conclusion I base on numerous con-versations and the even more telling fact of its three sparse editions (1949, 1954, 1957), until, after a ten-year delay, Editorial Losada, its hand forced by the Nobel prize, has finally brought out a fourth edition.

Even those few critics who recognize *Men of Maize*'s outstand-ing qualities, have had to accept the arguments of its detractors, affirming its greatness in spite of its defects. Giuseppe Bellini, for instance, who has given it the most affectionate consideration, as-serts that its unity is not to be found in the plot but rather in the "climate." In order to transmit the "spirit of Guatemala," he sug-gests, or because it is a "symphonic poem" which mixes the social and the mythic spheres, its structure is inevitably dispersed.[1]

If we are to rescue a work that has contributed so significantly to the founding of a new dynasty in Latin American fiction, a new way of transmitting and understanding our reality, we must go beyond such vague generalizations. Only a close reading of its six parts, attempting to find the novel's hidden unity, will allow, I believe, a real understanding of the significance and originality of *Men of Maize*, the reason why it should be considered a major source for the new forms of fiction that were to be written on our continent in the following decades.

Gaspar Ilóm

The first chapter tells how Gaspar Ilóm, the chief of the lands of Ilóm, begins a war against those who plant corn for commercial reasons. Señor Tomás Machojón, instigated by his wife, poisons the chief, and the latter, abandoned by his wife, la Piojosa Grande, drinks the river to pacify his guts, thus saving himself. But he gains nothing thereby, since Colonel Chalo Godoy has taken advantage of his absence to kill the Indian fighters. Gaspar throws himself into the river so as not to have to survive his warriors.

This action must be deciphered by the reader, who will find himself submerged in a buzzing swarm of words that float dream-like between the real and the fictional. One must interpret, break the linguistic spells, and uncover within that flowing cavern the profile of a meaning. This narrative method serves to indicate that we are confronting a moment, at the beginning of the book, in which dream and reality cohabit, in which the mythic is still fully incarnate in man, in which the human and the natural worlds are interchangeable.

Using certain magical, iterative formulas, the "ground" tries to awaken Gaspar Ilóm, who is sleeping, buried, "unable to break away from a snake of six hundred thousand twists of mud, moonlight, forests, springs, birds and echoes which he felt around his body." The earth "falls dreaming," but he cannot go on sleeping because there is no shade, no vegetation, "he awakens among what were once mountains, but are now the bare hills of Ilóm"; it (the earth) has been violated, snatched from its natural, sacred, state, thus making impossible the magical union of man and nature, the primordial link that is possible in a prelogical, unreal stage, where everything sleeps and everything dreams, not like now, a present in which there exists "corn-growing land filled with stagnant water from being awake so much." Provoked by the action of the corn growers who burn the vegetation in order to be able to grow corn for sale, offended by the destruction of her shade-filled forests which are converted into useless gold, desperately needing to go back to sleep and to make magic, nature orders Gaspar Ilóm to destroy the sowers, to install a symmetry of retribution, doing to them what they have done to the earth: "chop out the eyebrows of those who put axe to trees, burn the eyelids of those who burn the forest and freeze the bodies of those who stop the water." The cleansing from evil is proclaimed, and the return to balance, and revenge upon those who have separated man from nature. This loss of origin, a theme that runs throughout Asturias's work, necessarily brings oppression and exploitation in its wake, whether it comes from a local dictator, a Spanish conquistador, or the North American Empire. Corn "sown to be eaten is the sacred nourishment of man, who was made of corn. Sown for business it is the hunger of man who was made of corn." There are two types of men of maize, those who live in the magical plenitude of a sensual continuity with nature, the forms of a dream, of a sleep, and those who live in wakefulness, hunger, and death. The latter are uprooted, lose their roots, not only in a metaphorical sense, but also really and literally, becoming vagabonds upon the earth, deniers of the sacred vegetable growth. Therefore, the picaresque is ever-present in all of Asturias's production and in this work in particular: the directionless wandering in search of food, the absurd pilgrimage, a wind which passes again and again and brings ruin, which "will diminish the land and the corn grower will leave, taking his seed elsewhere, until he himself is finished, like a faded ear of corn in the midst of rich lands," with the nostalgia of rest in the wind of his eyes, the memory of the primal immobility that Gaspar Ilóm imitated and that is the equivalent of the lost paradise. As we shall see later, the novel is a tense dialogue between both kinds of men of maize, those who live the exile of never finding rest and those who become fixed in myth.

In his struggle, Gaspar has the aid of cosmic forces, the yellow rabbits for whom "there is no secret, no danger, no distance," the spirit of the fire which does battle beyond the death of the

chieftain himself and is an emanation of the natural order seeking permanence in its being. Everything that refers to Gaspar is
seen through whiffs of apparent chaos, which vibrate nevertheless
with the secret vertebration of ritual. The exaggerated language,
its serpentine, baroque syntax, a world that slithers forward like a
snake, the union of dissimilar elements, transfiguration by means
of the word, sacred, solemn, and distant, the inner vision of what
is happening: it all produces in the reader's mind the process of
enveloping primitivism that the character himself is living, and
forces the leveling of dream and reality, leading the reader to mix
fiction and fact without being able or wanting to separate them.[2]
The main theme of the novel, the relationship between myth and
reality, has its narrative and linguistic correlation in this fusion,
but it is only revealed fully in the first chapter, where the mythic
impulse transfixes everything. The fact that legend and reality,
word and deed, are the same experience for the reader and for the
character, will contrast with the remaining chapters, where it is
precisely the relationship between these dimensions, how near to
or far from each other they are, that is made problematic.

Take the poisoning of Gaspar Ilóm, at the beginning of the
novel. If we were to try to give a chronological or merely logical order to this chaotic moment (Gaspar is poisoned, the poison is made from two white roots, la Piojosa Grande flees), we
would find two successive, and perhaps parallel, sequences which
coincide in certain recurrences but whose linkage does not allow
us to exactly place each event nor to impose any order upon that
rush of images, prophecies, and foreshadowings. One of the two
sequences (Which of the two? And what if it were both?) is a pre-
monitory dream (or memory dream) of la Piojosa Grande. The
repetition, once in dream, again in reality, without being able to
define which is which, blurs and clouds the habitual way in which
things occur in this world. The reader must simply absorb what
happened, must interpret it, he or she suddenly transformed into
a magician. What is dreamed and what is lived are inextricably
bound together, and this means that any effort by the reader to
order that world will falsify it and end up in failure. Just as his
characters struggle against civilization and against cold, everyday
reality, Asturias will in the rest of the work, albeit in a more sub-
dued manner, continue to destroy all rational mentality, using,

although in a less exaggerated fashion, every viable means to make his language boil: tossing out time shifts, interweaving impersonal and subjective points of view, confusing colloquialisms and the thoughts of his characters with the supposed objectivity of actions, silencing men and personifying the animal and plant kingdoms, detaching all points of reference, sweeping away conventions. Fire, one of the protagonists of the novel, is also its formal principle: words are flames, they sputter, they refuse to be enclosed, they hop like gleaming yellow rabbits, they die down and then rise up again with an uncontainable rhythm of revenge, the consummation by the fire-grandfather-son, punishment, and we have reached the second chapter which narrates how those who betrayed Gaspar Ilóm are punished.

Machojón

When the chief died, the witch doctors of the fireflies had foretold the death of all the poison carriers and of their children, indicating that "su semilla de girasol sea tierra de muerto en las entrañas de las mujeres . . ." ("their sunflower seed will be a dead man's earth in the wombs of women . . ."). The curse begins to be fulfilled in the second chapter with the death of Señor Tomás and of his son Machojón, as also with that of Vaca Manuela.

The first to disappear is Machojón, who was on his way to ask for the hand of his girlfriend, Candelaria Reinoso, in marriage. No one knows what happened to him; only we, the readers, directly sense the supernatural wonder of his absorption by the fireflies, that fire that leaps from the words of the witch doctors: "From his hat behind his ears, along the collar of his embroidered shirt, down the sleeves of his jacket, along the hairy ridges of his hands and between his fingers, like a cold sweat the flickering gleam of the fireflies coursed, a light like the beginning of the world, in which everything was seen without any clear shape."

Suddenly the rumor spreads that Machojón rides each time the land is burned off, just prior to the sowing of the corn. This version originates in the visit of a mysterious woman to Candelaria Reinoso. Everything indicates that the woman is a semi-imaginary creature: we do not know who she is nor where she comes from; she is referred to as "ghost woman"; another customer does not see her; several times there is mention of her "teeth as white as lard" and "lard-like clothing," which is significant when we remember that it is precisely lard that Candelaria sells. What the woman affirms is also vague: "Yes, child, who would believe it, but the men who went out to burn off the land saw Don Macho mounted on his horse among the flames; they say he was dressed in gold." Lost in the gossip of others, anonymous, unknown, coincidental with what the narrator has already revealed, the legend of Machojón is born into reality. Immediately, "Candelaria Reinoso closed her eyes and dreamed or saw that Machojón was riding his wild stallion down from the top of the hill they were burning . . ." We are left in suspense as to whether she actually saw him or dreamed him.

In her turn Candelaria will transmit what she has heard, or what she has desired, or what she has imagined, to Señor Tomás, who will begin to give up lands for clearing, just to see his son who "appeared in the middle of the best fires, riding his stallion, bathed in gold . . . his spurs sparkling like stars and his eyes gleaming like suns." Señor Tomás consolidates the legend, trying to provoke the presence of the supernatural, while the corn growers take advantage of his weakness, since it is in their interest to obtain lands for their seed "without any formal arrangement"; they feed his madness, assuring him they have seen Machojón galloping among the flames, repeating the same words already on everyone's lips. Thus, this legend, which is of human origin and which has been invented out of the daily needs of each man and woman, will increase the action of the fire, more and more, until the night arrives when Señor Tomás, hearing the truth from the mouths of the children and the fools (who make fun of the story and transform Machojón into a scarecrow), decides to disguise himself as Machojón and imitates the appearance of his son as it is described in the popular tale; he sets fire to the dry corn field "in order to ride among the flames mounted on his stallion so they would believe he was Machojón." He wants that golden Machojón to exist (despite the fact that he cannot see him, he knows that he is real), and he wants the corn planters (who say they can see him, but do not believe in his reality) to be his witnesses. In a little while the fire spreads, the tone of the first chapter returns; Señor Tomás's fire becomes the mythic flame of the fireflies, the avenger who flows from the words of the witch doctors: "An immense firefly, as immense as the plains and the hills." First it is said that it is "like (igual a) the ears of yellow rabbits, in pairs, by the hundreds, baskets full of yellow rabbits, fleeing the fire, a round beast that was all face, no neck, a face rolling on the ground, a leathery-faced beast with an angry eye, among the heavy brow and the thick beard of the smoke." From the comparison "like" he goes to the metaphor and from there to the full and real narrated presence of the yellow rabbits, the mythological element: "the ears of the yellow rabbits moved among the sandy, deep-water streams without being extinguished." Thus, in one simultaneous instant, men create an action (setting a fire) and effectively provoke another (the revenge of the yellow rabbits); they are the servants of the fire and of the legend that has become reality. The origin of the fire and of the myth is found in human actions, but it has its foundation, its raison d'être, in the magical world, in the fulfillment of a curse. Señor Tomás, the corn planters, and also Vaca Manuela, are consumed by the fire that they themselves set, which is at the same time the cosmic fire punishing their betrayal.

It comes from Gaspar Ilóm who "had managed to hurl the lasso of his word around the fire that wandered freely in the mountains of Ilóm, and then to take it home and tie it up in his house, so that it wouldn't destroy all the trees, so it wouldn't work in collusion with the corn planters and merchants." The Indian's death means freedom for the fire, because "fire is like water when it is spilled. There is no way to hold them back." Men are transformed into "little fingers of a dark will that struggles, after millenia, to free the captive of the white hummingbird, prisoner of the man in the rock and in the eye of the grain of corn," the fire that sleeps there, ready to burst forth: "the captive can escape from the guts of the earth, into the heat and the light of the clearing fire and of war." When there is war (men destroy men) or there is clearing of land (men destroy earth), fire can escape, infected by human action, aided by the gestures of those beings who, without understanding the unlimited mythic power of their instrument, use it for their own ends, freeing the great, universal fire that seeks to wander free and destroy. "Its prison is fragile, and if the fire escapes, what brave, virile soul can struggle against it, when all flee in terror?" Therefore, because it is magical, only the *word* could bind the fire "so that it could do no damage." The supernatural cannot intervene arbitrarily; it must be invoked from the world of the human; it must originate in everyday events, just like the legend, that has its origin in small human words, and becomes gigantic because once man has hurled it out it begins to grow, to swell, on its own account. Myth, like fire, is held by fragile bonds, and it only requires a tiny spark to produce the final conflagration, a single word in an unknown mouth, a nothing that speaks, so that a story goes out victoriously to move around the world and take over reality. The words of the witch doctors are fulfilled. The legend of Machojón ends up being real, creating a fire, provoking an imitation that leads to the desired revenge.

It has been affirmed that Asturias's fundamental theme is free-dom.[3] It seems to me, on the contrary, that what most concerns him is tyranny, alienation, the grotesque presence of punishment, in any of its forms, in a decaying world. Dictatorship, which in *El Señor Presidente* manifested itself in the political realm, is now a dictatorship of fire and of the word, but always a tyranny that men themselves ask for, adore, and help to build. Just as el señor Presidente can exercise his mandate because he is sustained by fear and by the conscious or involuntary support of others, the legend is able to impose itself upon reality because men live it fully as a way to make sense of their humanity, and thus the cosmic fire can break out because men concur with its effort and thus free it. The "little human bundles" of Asturias's world end up destroying themselves, being disintegrated by the very forces they themselves released or supplanted by the words they themselves spoke. This tyranny of language perversely parallels the political oppression which is omnipresent in Asturias's world. Magic and the law both are born in that primitive universe from an original curse, an order which men cannot deny. The phantom of inhuman powers entan-gling mankind runs throughout Asturias's work, from *El alhaja-dito* to the victimization suffered by the characters in Tierrapau-lita, that magical and Pantagruelian dominion of *Mulata de Tal*. The consolation which Asturias leaves us is that human beings are responsible for their own condition.

And the revenge goes on.

The Deer of the Seven Clearing Fires

The brothers Tecún kill all the Zacatón family. Ostensibly, they do so to put an end to the spell by which the Zacatóns have harmed Señora Yuca, by "putting a cricket in her navel"; but in reality it is a matter of punishing the Zacatóns for having been the pharmacists who sold the poison used against Gaspar, as we will learn in the last chapter. Once again, a supernatural action is channeled through human hands. In order to discover who had caused the damage, according to the healer, the brothers needed "a fire of living trees so that the night would have a tail of fresh flames, the tail of a yellow rabbit," and we can guess that the Tecún will be the voice of the fire, the instrument of revenge: "The healer wedged himself in the doorway, bathed in crickets, a thousand tiny hiccups outside that answered the sick woman's hiccuping inside, and there he counted the fleeting stars, the yellow rabbits of the witch doctors who lived in the hide of virgin deer, those who offered and took away eyelashes of breath from the eyes of the soul." The hiccups and the crickets that the mother of the Tecúns has are, in fact, a part of nature, provoked by the healer in conjunction with the yellow rabbits. And the decapitated heads of the Zacatóns will be burned, consumed by the words, the verbal flames, of the witch doctors: "The flames, with the scent of human blood, stretched out, slipping away in fear, then they crouched for the attack, like golden tigers."

As a second part of the chapter we have the narrative of the death of the deer of the seven clearing fires, who in reality is the healer himself. It is the start of the theme of animal and man as a single entity: "They were one. The healer and the deer of the seven clearing fires, like you and your shadow, like you and your soul, like you and your breath."

But there is another focus of interest in this brief chapter. Seven years have already passed since Gaspar's death. Asturias has slowly distanced us from that moment, opening up a breach of time which will permit the creation of a legend. The entire book is full of dialogues in which the past is discussed and an event is ritualized as a way of molding its linguistic permanence. At times this event, already witnessed by the reader, is repeated just as it was before, word for word, narrating once again what happened. At other times, the exchange that comments on this previous event gradually deforms it, changing its meaning. In any case, the thrust of these dialogues is clear: the legend is created not just in its founding moment, in human action, but also in its transmission, which will determine what can be forgotten and what remembered of that instant.[4] As the pages unfold, intermingled with the life of the men of maize, stitched into imperceptible time, the myth gradually becomes residual, it becomes dynamic in the present and the future, it is remade, slipping into the future. And it is this presence of time, this basic dimension of all current Latin American narrative, which is going to change the interrelationship, distance and nearness, between myth and reality. For Asturias, time passes in the essential site where man becomes man, the fount of all lies and of all knowledge, the place where imagination and history touch: language.[5]

Colonel Chalo Godoy

In that world populated by sayings, by "the whys and wherefores of ancient speech," by events in process of becoming memories, the words of the witch doctors weigh ever more upon the memory of the last recipient of the curse, Colonel Chalo Godoy. During the entire horseback ride on the last day of his life, the light is playing with him, slowly surrounding him with signs of his approaching disappearance, worms of fire, "splendor of chaos," that he does not know how to interpret, until he is burned alive.

The way in which his death is narrated is striking and indicates another step in the evolution of the myth and of reality. We never see Godoy's agony as an objective fact; we are never sure how it happened; we are not supported by the omniscient knowledge of the narrator, who refuses to describe that death, surrendering his voice to one of his characters, Benito Ramos, who, because he has made a pact with the Devil, has the necessary prophetic gifts to tell us, even though he is far from the events themselves, how the Colonel died (or how he is dying at that moment, far from the place where Benito is riding). That event, at least in so far as we are concerned, never exists except in Ramos's words. The event becomes memory before it happens; it is an echo before it is a voice; and a legend before it is reality. The fantastic element, as it becomes more distant from its mythological origins with the passage of the years, fading into a post-arcadian world, becomes plausible, a full and integral part of reality, constructed from the perspective of a character. Immersed in everyday events, exiled from the realm of the magical, but still able to invoke its presence, the men of maize shape the legendary sphere that is always with them, as a continuous creation.

Through his version, Benito turns out to be a collaborator in the act of revenge. Those events could have originated in any of a number of human events that are mentioned, as if in passing, with hardly any attention given to them: Godoy's cigar was lit, the Tecúns trapped the Colonel and burned the forest where he took refuge, and many years—many pages—later we will learn: "In the report which the government made it said only that Colonel Godoy and his troops, while returning from an investigation, died in a forest fire."

And once again the fire is the center of the revenge, the element that unites reality and fiction: one of the circles that surrounds the Colonel and kills him "looks like a boiling pot, and is formed by an uncountable number of bear grass rounds of daggers made bloody by a fire . . . Their bodies are formed of fireflies and therefore, in the winter, they are everywhere, flickering their existence on and off." It is the seventh clearing, the epoch prophesied for Godoy's death: "and the seventh . . . will be of the fire of the golden owl which hurls owls from the depths of the pupils of its eyes." And this fire, creating a myth of itself from the inner eyes of man, from the tongues that slip like smoke and embers around its essence, is simultaneously the same fire with which the land was burned, the fire that was and is used to destroy and to make commerce, revenge of the fire that was the death of the land and now is the death of the man who betrayed Gaspar: "nevertheless, the smell was now that of fire in the air, the fire for clearing the land, for burning off the forest." This death is even more ironic when we realize that the Colonel was playing with the fire: "Fighting with guerrillas—he said a few moments before dying—is like playing with fire, and if I could do Gaspar Ilóm in, it was because from the time I was a child I learned to jump over fires, on St. John's Eve and the Eve of Immaculate Conception." His death coincides with the momentary resurrection of the healer, whose presence is nec-

essary for the deadly fire to begin: "I revived and only to get rid
of the one who had also reached his seventh fire." The fire is identified with time, it becomes ubiquitous, an element by which one
measures life: instead of years, clearing fires.

The first four chapters, therefore, demonstrate an evident cohesion, unfolding around Gaspar Ilóm's death and the revenge taken
upon his executioners, a punishment that is carried out by human
hands for superhuman reasons, a destruction that is at one and
the same time reality and legend. The passage of time will allow
each episode to be consolidated in a story, made myth for every
succeeding generation. The fifth chapter, nevertheless, seems to
escape this unity. Called a jewel within itself, it has been repeatedly
affirmed that we are dealing with an independent episode, bearing
no organic relationship with the rest of the book.

María Tecún

At first glance it would seem that the critics are right. What possible relationship between what precedes it and this story of the
blind Goyo Yic, who recovers his sight in order to be able to find
María Tecún, the woman who has abandoned him? Only vague
threads of plot unite this episode with the four preceding ones;
it seems to unfold in another period of time, almost in another
geographic space.[6]

Nevertheless, this story is essential to the profound development of the book. In fact, the chapter narrates a process of forgetting, the progressive loss of a woman along the pathways of
memory.

The herb seller operates on Goyo Yic so that he can under-
take the search for María Tecún; but when he recovers colors and
shapes and distances and light, he realizes that "his eyes were useless to him," because María Tecún was his "rubber plant blossom . . . a blossom invisible to the eyes that see outside but not
within, flower and fruit of his closed eyes, in his loving darkness that was sound, blood, sweat, escape, a vertebral jolt," and
the everyday world, which comes in through the eyes, substitutes
his inner, imaginative vision, his original relationship with that
woman who abandoned him. He had created her within himself,
in the conjunction of all his senses; as he becomes more like all

other men, he loses that experience that had connected him with María Tecún.[7] We see how he involuntarily betrays that real image, how as the days slip by, he loses his connection with that first vision, the one he had when he was still blind, when his world was still created like a ghostly but secure dream. "He was searching for María Tecún, but in the remotest depths of his consciousness he no longer looked for her. He had lost her."

One night he sees his shadow in the moonlight. It is the shadow of a *tacuatzín,* "with a pouch in front in which to carry its off-spring," his *nahual,* his protector animal, but more than that, it is his guardian essence, the fundamental aspect of his magnified soul, in animal form. Just as the deer for the healer, the tacuatzín is Goyo Yic's double, and the dominant passion of his personality: "You know that human beings carry their young in pouches like the tacuatzín." This little animal, which accompanies him everywhere, is the symbol of his need to find María Tecún and his children, so much so that "Goyo Yic was known more by the nickname Tacuatzín than by his own name." But when he has sexual relations with another woman, the tacuatzín disappears, along with the possibility of finding his wife in spite of having lost the Amate flower: "The Amate flower, transformed into a tacuatzín, had just left its empty fruit, escaping so that the blind man would no longer see it, just as he could not see María Tecún, the blind man who was now seeing other women. A truly beloved woman cannot be seen; she is the Amate flower, seen only by blind men, the flower of the blind, of those blinded by love and by faith, of those blinded by life." After the flight of his guardian animal, Goyo Yic wanders the land, falling into a state of oblivion tinged by memories, like doves in the smoke: "Only when he heard other women's voices did Goyo Yic remember that he was looking for María Tecún. Finally he didn't think about her much at all. He did think of her, but not as before, and not because that was his intent, but simply because . . . he wasn't thinking." It is time which is digging a pit between the woman and his memory: "He was gradually shrunken, to the point where there was almost nothing left, by the years and the grief that hangs a man without a rope, but hangs him none-theless, and by the bad climates in which he had been living, in his wanderings, searching all the towns and villages along the coast, and from drinking so much liquor to raise his spirits a little and to get rid of the bitter taste of his absent woman, until he became no one and nothing." And at the end of the chapter he will confess to his friend Domingo Revolorio, with whom he will go to jail as a supposed smuggler: "But so much time has passed that I no longer feel anything. Before, my friend, I searched for her in order to find her; now I search in order not to find her."

In fact, every human being lives the experience of Goyo Yic, his erased past, his necessary deformation of his life experience, his distancing from some obscure initial moment, and all of us, like him, go in search of that earlier purity, losing all trace of it, first drop by drop and then in cascades, as time intervenes. Goyo Yic gradually leaves behind his original identity, just as the other characters were separated from the events prior to their presence, those moments that they have not lived personally, but which they have heard about, that have remained in the form of the word, of spoken memory. Goyo Yic bids farewell to the first image he had of María Tecún; he loses the Amate flower, loses his blindness and the tacuatzín; he loses his archaic self, chews up his past and dimly remembers something that happened to another Goyo Yic, far from himself, and between one and the other there has been an accumulation of picaresque adventures, women, and roadways, all of what turns the men of maize into vagabonds. This inability to go on being himself, the break from his own continuity in time, simultaneously allows his life to become separated from the way in which it happened; that is the first step toward his deformation, his essentialization in the popular mind. What he does with the old Goyo Yic and with the old image of María Tecún is what the people will do with the story of his life; they will transform it into legend, and his mythification is possible and even necessary because it is the only way to recover through memory and through the word that original but lost self.

Thus, Goyo Yic experiences the same phenomenon that is presented in the rest of the novel, the same process of distancing from and loss of an earlier deed, except that here it is embodied in a specific man, in whom the psychological roots of a reality that seemed to be only social are examined. Goyo Yic lives a specific experience of forgetting, all subjectivity being absorbed by the picaresque action of time. It is the same thing that happens in the rest of *Men of Maize*, where something is lived through so that later it may remain encapsulated in the future word, distancing itself from its true form at the same time that it reflects it, a carnival mirror that deforms, but captures none the less the trembling essence of things through legend, thus transcending the sad certainty of everyday events. This chapter, therefore, allows us to discover how the foundation of legends is rooted in the individual human being's experience of time and in the internal disintegration that all human beings suffer. What happens to Goyo Yic in his mental transformation is what happens to humanity in its historical transformation. The ex-blind man's distancing from himself, this separation between reality and fiction in the life of the man who is depositary of that experience, is the first step toward the later legend. The first one to disturb reality and to transmute it is the subject himself, who becomes an accomplice in the process of conversion. In the earlier episodes those who deformed the original event were beings who had not lived that experience, beings who were not witnesses, but mere bridges of communication for that which they had not seen.

Of course, the psycho-biographical roots of the fictive do not occur just in this chapter, but are found throughout the novel. Uperto, one of the Tecúns, experiences a similar phenomenon: "With the eyes of his imagination he saw the deer killed by Gaudencio, in the darkness of the forest, yet far from the forest; and with the eyes of his face, the body of the healer, lying there before him." This difference between the eyes of the imagination and those of the face sustains the relationship, whether conflictive or cooperative, between what is real and what is imagined. In the case of Goyo Yic the eyes of the face displace the eyes of his imagination, an implacable corruption of his origin, the fount of all future truth, the window which will allow the world of myth to breathe into the vital center of every man. We can observe something similar in Señor Tomás: he doesn't see Machojón with his physical eyes, but he does see him with the eyes of his fantasy. He sees the profound truth, his punishment; he creates his destiny and his own death in accordance with that truth; he goes beyond the surface and forever after places the legend of his son in the trembling nucleus, the process of eternalization, which is everyday conversation, what people will say about him and his life.

By making the mythic phenomenon individual and personal in

this chapter, by making it coincide with the life cycle of every man, his irremediable distension and loss of himself, Asturias has explored, now from a new, oblique angle, the creation of the legendary, insisting upon using as his point of departure the concrete minute hand of the clock that tick-tocks away our lives, that which destroys by shaping the myth, a happening that goes beyond ourselves, a touching upon others from mouths which reproduce us and tongues that repeat us.

Correo-Coyote

We have established that, for these legends to acquire reality it is crucial that time pass, that men move away from that past, so that the action that occurred will not belie the word that transmits it. In this last chapter, many years have already gone by. One character mentions that "One of my grandparents used to say that he had plainly seen a healer who changed himself into the deer of the seven clearing fires; but all that happened so long ago . . ." and "There are more and more pieces of land being ruined by the corn growers." Always, when speaking of the past, when reestablishing the location and recounting the legends of Gaspar, of Machojón, and of Chalo Godoy, the characters try to give the impression of a vast distance, stretching backward in time, an uncrossable, irreversible abyss. The transformation of the past into myth hurls the characters into an incommensurable confusion of chronologies and distance from points of reference. The habitual duration of things is destroyed or ignored. The story of Machojón, for example, is not only spread from mouth to mouth, autonomous, altered ("He thought he saw fireflies, his memory of that horseman Machojón, who became a light in the heavens when he was on his way to lay claim to the future, was so vivid,"—a story that is repeated, with variations, some six times in the chapter), but also it has been fused with the popular vocabulary that is used to interpret reality, a word that automatically crops up when its use is suitable, a mental structure that man applies from his unconsciousness until the events that the readers witnessed persist only in popular sayings, that dictionary that is born out of everyday conversation: "transformed into a Machojón of hail" and a character goes through a harness shop where he sees horses "that move almost like fireflies . . . He thought he saw El Machojón, the way they say he can be seen whenever they are burning off the land. A pure light in the sky."

This incorporation of the past into the imagination of each present moment is emphasized by the frequent dialogues, as we have already noted, in which the legend is being formed from the words exchanged by men. That which seemed to be past is lived again, but changed ("hearing everything that happened before as if it were happening now"), in order to evade the prison of regular time ("maybe history has been invented for that reason, to forget the present"). It is the metamorphosis of the impersonal into an individual human voice: the event, which before existed as word on the level of the narrator, becomes a word in the mouth of the character. The "objective" knowledge, to which the reader had access while the characters suffered the tyranny of events, is integrated into the world, digested by a thousand anonymous bodies, returned to the realm of the concrete so that it can go on spinning. It has become independent of its factual situation and is living only in its linguistic situation, thus acceding in some way to the realm of the timeless.

But time is necessary in order for this other dimension, this realm beyond a communicative context which deceives the clock, to exist. In this sense, Asturias connects with Proust, Mann, and Joyce, who have demonstrated the appearance of the eternal, of the mythic, in the corrosion of each moment, in the minuscule death of each object.

It is therefore not at all paradoxical that in the face of that vague chronology and that shipwrecking of dates, there also appear concrete mentions of a regular, measurable time, just as in the face of magical and associative language we find the prosaic usages of everyday speech. It is in the great mosaic of what grows by aging, of unfolding lives, where legend can appear and be transformed. Between the first page of the novel and the last no more than fifty years have passed, although they also seem separated by an eternity. Candelaria Reinoso, the girlfriend of Machojón, is still of marriageable age at the end of the novel; Benito Ramos (who married María Tecún) is about to die; Musús, another of the Colonel's companions, has gotten married; María Tecún, who was only one year old when the Zacatóns died, is by now a mature woman with adult children; the blind Goyo Yic has been in prison for three years and seven months. Many of these statements contradict each other and would apparently even impede the establishment of the legend (for example, in the case of María Tecún, who is almost transformed into the word before she has lived), but they help us to enclose the characters within fixed, albeit fluctuating, limits, within which the mythic becomes at the same time both close and distant. This contrast between two kinds of time, living between one and the other dimension, which can also be seen in *El Señor Presidente* (as Ricardo Navas Ruíz has shown)[8] and in Asturias's other works, this thirst for eternity and this subjection to the present moment draw fiction and reality even closer together, duplicating the fundamental planes of the novel.

On the other hand, this sweeping prison in which the characters mature and decay is their punishment for having broken the repose in which the earth dreamed it was one with man, and became commercial men of once-divine corn. Theirs is a degraded world, replete with sickly beings, beggars, blind men, like so many others in Asturias's other books. Thus, the deformation of the world through language, the vortex of metaphors which press objects beyond all recognition, the grotesque mirror wherein time and the word come together in a monstrous copulation, is much more than a literary recourse or an influence of European Surrealism. It expresses the desire to shape the horror caused by the loss of the magical, so that a demoniacal reality can be shown through twisted, bestial lenses. Or perhaps it is a way of dealing with mysterious forces that control us, a spell that replicates the image of the hell it would like to exorcize.[9]

Magic still reigns in that world where the exiled wander without rest and with little hope, but it no longer shows any evidence of the primitive and benificent power which sustained the dream of Gaspar Ilóm. If, earlier, everything was linked by a great primordial and coherent animism, now it is the union of the dissimilar, the caricaturesque presence of missed meetings and howlings, a zone where the merely diabolical seeks to manifest itself. And nevertheless, in that continuing vestige of the magical, revenge on time which corrupts, decomposition of forms, death of the origin in the mouth without teeth, in the shadow left by the sun as its light is extinguished, in this punishment, man finds, at the same time that he finds his nothingness, his freedom. Myth, nostalgia of what has been lost, the falsification of what is original, is also a means of recuperation, a recovery perhaps for something better.

Is it possible, that this myth, which changes and rips apart what happened at the beginning, could at the same time be the depository of human truth? Can time and eternity meet in legend?

The answer Asturias gives to these questions can be clarified through an examination of the two most important episodes in the sixth and last chapter of *Hombres de maíz*.

The wife of Nicho Aquino, the postman of San Miguel Acatán, has abandoned him. Thus we see repeated the basic situation of Goyo Yic, whose story, now made legend, has undergone several variations. Any woman who runs away is called "tecuna," (just as in the case of Machojón, the proper name has become a common noun) and every abandoned husband is a "blind man": "remember what they say happened to the blind man who insisted on going in search of María Tecún. He heard her talking and at the moment when he was going to catch up with her, he recovered his sight, only to see her changed into stone and forgetting that she was on the edge of a precipice." This same version, adorned in one way or another, is repeated by many other characters, demonstrating that very little is left from the original story of Goyo Yic and María Tecún. The popular imagination has snipped away what was useless, the surface which does not represent the essential truth of the human experience and has left what can be remembered, although the final version (which will also change with time) is far from corresponding exactly with the actual facts. Man, in his turn, becomes trapped in the legend: his behavior is oriented by that story and he is attracted by it, until reality begins to imitate fiction.

We can see the most typical example of this in the survival of the witch doctors' curse. They had said that those responsible for the death of Gaspar Ilóm would be unable to have children. But what is significant is the form in which this is fulfilled: if the wife of Benito Ramos has a son, the only possible explanation is that she deceived him; when Musús has one, "it is his child by another." The legend cannot be placed in doubt, for it has become so real that it shapes men's conduct and their interpretation of it. By the mere fact of having been uttered, the curse produces its effect: given credence, it has already achieved its end. Everything that happens will take on certainty or will be invalidated according to the a priori conviction of men. "Those people sacrifice themselves to keep the legend alive," says don Déferic, and he adds: "The victims matter little as long as the monster of popular poetry is fed." Every archetype, which begins with an individual, almost insignificant situation, grows toward its justifying echo.

But this dictatorship ("The gods disappeared, but the legends remained, and the latter, like the former, demand sacrifices; the obsidian knives to tear the heart of the sacrifice victim from his chest disappeared, but the knives of absence, which wound the victim and drive him mad, remain") is possibly due to the existence of an internalization of that imaginary dimension, a fall toward deeper, universal regions of what is human: "The cry (of María Tecún) was lost with her name beneath a storm of accents in the depths of her ears, in the canyons of her ears. She covered her ears but she kept on hearing it. It did not come from outside, but from inside. The name of a woman that everyone shouts to call that María Tecún they carry lost in their consciousness." The supposedly arbitrary development of the legend is in reality a movement toward what is enduringly human; it gradually models what man should be, and through its imitation it sheds any contingent form that is not useful: "Who has not called? Who has not, at some time, shouted the name of a woman lost in his yesterdays? Who has not, like a blind man, pursued that being who abandoned his own being, when he was present, who went on leaving and who goes on leaving his side, fugitive, 'tecuna,' impossible to hold back, because if she stops, time will turn her to stone?" And at the end of the novel, after Nicho has descended to his nahual (the coyote) in search of his wife, the healer (deer of the seven clearings) will explain that the stone of María Tecún is in reality María la Lluvia, la Piojosa Grande, who "standing erect, will be present in the time that is to come, between heaven, earth and emptiness." Suddenly, we remember that other woman, the first to run away from her husband, Gaspar Ilóm; the same situation has circulated through the novel three times, in a different, disguised form each time, each time contributing to the legend, to the need to relate, in an atemporal form, the fact of separation, the loss of the past and of one's origins, the need to make oneself a stone against time.

One character, nevertheless, does not believe in the "tecunas" and in this way we come to the second sequence of the last chapter: the muleteer, Hilario Sacayón, has invented a legend, which has become independent of its creator, spreading on its own, objectified by the people. "Who hasn't repeated that legend that he, Hilario Sacayón, made up in his head, as if it really had happened? Wasn't he present during a prayer in which they asked God for relief and rest for Miguelita de Acatán? Haven't they searched in the old books of the parish registry for the baptismal certificate of that marvelous child?" It is the famous Miguelita, "whom no one knew and about whom everyone was talking because of the fame she had been given in places where mules and muleteers gathered, inns, taverns and wakes, by Hilario Sacayón." Here, for the first time, Asturias focuses on the problem of the legend from the perspective of the inventor, drawn from a state of anonymity in order to confront him with the extreme and autonomous growth of his own lie, the product of drunken sprees and highs. It is yet another angle for the binomial myth-reality. Hilario Sacayón does not accept the veracity of the stories that surround him because he knows that the origin of each legend (whether it be that of Machojón, or of a nahual, or of Gaspar Ilóm, or María Tecún, or Miguelita) resides in false clouds of alcohol.

It is in vain that Na Moncha explains to him that "one often believes he is inventing what others have forgotten. When someone tells what is no longer being told, he tells himself, I invented it, it's mine, this is mine. But what he is really doing is remembering what the memory of his ancestors left in his blood . . ." Hilario refuses to be the verbal bridge to communicate with a pre-existent past; he refuses to be the one who "saved (that story) from oblivion," so that it could "go on like the rivers." But one of the legends in which he does not believe will take control of his being, and will make him admit the reality of certain myths.

Nicho Aquino has left for the capital with the mail. Don Déferic, fearing that the former will fall over the legendary stone of María Tecún, contracts Hilario to catch up with him and to accompany him until he crosses the difficult area. Hilario does not find him, but he sees a coyote when he goes past the stone: "Therein was the doubt, because he saw it clearly, and saw that it was not a coyote, because when he saw it he had the impression that it was somebody, and somebody known to him." [10] And the idea that it is Nicho whom he has glimpsed gradually sinks into his being like a parasite, little by little, against his rational will, the realm of the magical takes over his mind and obsesses him with its possibility: "He almost knew it now and was now convinced of what he did not want to be convinced, of what his human condition completely rejected, that a being like that, born of a woman, nourished with a woman's milk, bathed in a woman's tears, could turn into a beast, could become an animal, put his intelligence into the body of an inferior being, stronger, yes, but inferior." Thus, the one who invented a legend must recognize that the imaginary or the impossible is true; he must in his innermost being accept the fact that he has not invented "his" legend, but rather that it belongs to other men and that no individual can deny his magical link with another world, not the everyday world, since the deep and authentic sense of history will correct that invention and man will use it to explore his own destiny. Hilario accepts, speaking for the author himself in a sort of *ars poetica,* being one link in a minute chain of true fictions: "he knew it, with all the powers of his soul that were not found in the senses, he knew it; his conscious mind had irremediably accepted as real what before, for his intelligence and conduct, had been a story."

The truth for Asturias is not found in the correspondence that can be established between a story and the factual events that it relates and that gave it its origin, but rather that something is more real when it more profoundly transforms those events in the direction of the unforgettable; it rescues the myth from its circumstantial beginnings, even though in order to do this, it must destroy and forget part of what apparently happened. Human beings, blind, lost in an under world, possess their myths only in order to orient themselves in the darkness, to understand their essence which is scattered in time. Reality begins to imitate that legend; man is transformed into the instrument which prolongs other beings, that touches other ears. Thus, in the poetic act, that of Asturias and that of his characters, the individual encounters his social self, he touches what is real and what is imaginary; time becomes eternal and eternity becomes mortal; there is a reconciliation of both kinds of men of maize, whose opposition and struggle have been shown at last to be an intense and solidary synthesis, two dimensions of one, unique, irreducible human being.

Myth and movement mutually support each other; they need each other in order to be able to exist: eternity feeds on the wandering mobility of human beings, imperfect fluctuations in the veins of time, and that movement is possible because it is supported by the enduring accompaniment of the imaginary.

This unity between men of maize has its correlative in the unitary evolution of this text: what seemed to be chaos is a deeper order; what was scorned as narrative irregularity is the inauguration of a new cosmovision; what seemed to be dispersed is really the temporalization of realities becoming words. Asturias narrated this experience (time, myth, reality, language, the interiorization of the social, the new ways of expressing our Latin America) in the only possible way in which it could have been narrated. Na Moncha never spoke so truthfully (and she was speaking with Asturias, who invented her as Hilario invented Miguelita) as she did when she explained that "If it hadn't been you, it would have been someone else, but someone would have told it so that it wouldn't be forgotten and lost completely, because its existence, fictitious or real, is a part of life and of nature in these parts, and life cannot be lost; it is an eternal risk, but it is not lost eternally."

1967

■ Borges and American Violence

The reaction of critics to the work of Jorge Luis Borges is like that of members of an audience to a great prestidigitator: they are so concerned with the disappearance of the rabbit and with the tricky hands that trace visible silhouettes in an invisible air that they tend to breathlessly miss the rabbit itself. When it has become a phantom, a meaningful emptiness where there was once a physical body, what matters in that event seems to be the magic of the disappearance, the game through which we have been deceived, the digital rhetoric which for an instant revealed to us the silent and marvelous possibility of other universes. But what happened to the rabbit?

The critics have allowed themselves to be mesmerized by Borges's masterful gamesmanship, by his verbal sleight of hand and his sinuous paradox of ideas, by the nihilistic intellectual game and the tethered emotive precision of his language, by the aestheticism of the metaphysical surprise, by his simultaneous, parallel, eternal, and vanishing temporal planes, his fragmented, repeating personalities, his annihilation of man into a quivering nothingness, his erudition and his ambiguity as weapons that produce ontological disarray, his convulsively changing perspectives. But the critics have given little attention to what happens *inside* that world, that is, who are the men (there are hardly any women) who suffer that bewildering imaginative chaos? Who are the ones suffering the labyrinth? Who is it that dies, devoured by that ingenuity? What did the rabbit feel as it dematerialized beneath the hand of the magician? The reason for this forgetfulness (or is it disinterest?) lies in the fact that most readers appear to be convinced—and

Borges himself assures them they are right—that what happened in that world is of no importance and, in fact (if we dare to utter the word "fact" here), is nonexistent. It is a dream, a delusion, nothing; the beings who inhabit that universe are in a state of disintegration; they are a reflection, "shadows of shadows of a shadow." Ana Maria Barrenechea has zealously studied the ways (ideological, semantic, syntatic) in which Borges erases that world and converts it into nirvana and illusion.[1]

But before becoming nothing, before dissolving and disappearing, those men have a face (although that face may be a mask). They have a purpose, a destiny, however false, absurd, annulled it will finally be. They have an anguish. Even before the disintegration, something—that something that will be abolished, whose very substantiality will be denied—must have existed. If that something turned out to be a dream, even dreams manage to entertain a shape and a development; they may have some meaning. Their appearance (a phenomenal being, from *phaenomenon*) will present some color, a false clarity, a dissolving kaleidoscopic structure. Even illusions might be made of a repeatable inconsistency. If we could glimpse that universe that Borges would annihilate with such slow and tender urgency, if we could discover what are the problems of those men who must vanish in his magical game, what are their projects (false or true), what laws they obey, what kind of life they lead, what death they seek out, then we might uncover one of the keys to the Borgean cosmos, and perhaps at the same time help to situate this writer in the Latin American context that has usually been denied to him.

Before their universe is extinguished, most of the main characters die[2] and, even more significantly, almost all these deaths are *violent*.[3] The characters, pursued and pursuer, executioner and victim, search for each other through labyrinths and mysteries; they communicate in the language of daggers, bullets, and fire. Death, for Borges, is almost always a murder; it requires another party; it presumes another hand and another face. Playing with these fictional deaths,[4] Borges shows a scholarly interest in violent themes (epic poetry, the detective novel, the first tangos, the outlaw companion, the duel on the outskirts of town, the cult of courage, the dagger, gaucho poetry) and an obsession, in his poems, with his ancestors who died fighting in Argentine wars (*Poema conjetural*

[*Conjectural Poem*], *Página para recordar al coronel Suárez, vencedor en Junín* [*A Page to Remember Colonel Suárez, Victor at Junín*], *Isidoro Acevedo, Al coronel Francisco Borges, Alusión a la muerte del coronel Francisco Borges* [*Allusion to the Death of Colonel Francisco Borges*], and the second of his *Two English Poems*),[5] all of which, added to all his statements in interviews,[6] gives us a rather strong indication that violence is one of the Argentine narrator's elemental passions.

This violence is, moreover, central to the very development of events: the presence of death coincides with the revelation, for the reader and for the dying character, of the true structure of the universe. The protagonist, sometimes the agressor, though generally the victim, experiences an almost mystical vision, which allows him *to understand* the meaning of his own selfhood or of reality. This illumination of the darkness proves to the character (and to the reader or a witness) that lived reality is fictitious, that he is an illusion, that concrete objects are clouds, that he never, in fact, existed. But that is irrelevant. In the act of understanding (in the act of dying), the man comes to know himself and transcends his blindness; he flows into the glittering and transitory eternity of absolute self-intuition: "Any fate," the narrator explains in *The Biography of Tadeo Isidoro Cruz*, "how ever long or complicated it may be, actually consists of a *single moment:* the moment when a man knows forever who he is." For the protagonist of this story, "there awaited . . . secretively in the future, a fundamental and lucid night: the night when at last he saw his own face, the night when finally he heard his name. In the final analysis, that night finishes his entire history; better yet, one instant of that night, one act of that night, because acts are our symbol."

Many of Borges's characters have this experience. Pedro Damián, in *The Other Death*, who acted in cowardly fashion during the battle of Masoller, in 1904, spends his whole life preparing for the possibility of being brave and achieves it by means of a dream which manages to change the history of that earlier cowardice. "He thought from deep within: if fate brings me another battle, I'll know how to deserve it. For forty years he waited with an obscure hope, and finally fate complied at the hour of his death. It complied in the form of a delirium, but the Greeks already knew that we are the shadows of a dream. In his final agony, he relived his battle and he conducted himself like a man and led the final charge and a bullet got him square in the chest. So that in 1947, by dint of a long passion, Pedro Damián died in the defeat of Masoller, which took place between the winter and the spring of 1904." In *The Circular Ruins* a magician dreams a man, creates a son out of the mist of his own imagination, only to realize at the moment of his own extinction, "with relief, with humiliation, with terror . . . that he was also a shadow, that another was dreaming him." In *The Dead Man*, Otálora becomes the recipient of the violence he wanted to exercise on others and discerns the meaning of the universe; he who believed he was in control of his own destiny understands that others, The Other, were determining his life and playing with him, "he understood, before he died, that they betrayed him from the beginning, that he was condemned to death, that they allowed him to have love, command and triumph, because they already considered him a dead man, because for Bandeira, he was already dead . . . Suárez fires, almost with disdain." Otálora's destiny is symbolic of every human effort in Borges's world: death, predetermined, wished for, almost an intimate desire of the protagonist (the case of Otto Dietrich zur Linde in *Deutsches Réquiem*), is omnipresent and guides us through the spider web of our own actions and illumines us in a petrified and perpetual intuition. The Minotaur awaits his redeemer and scarcely offers any resistance (*The House of Asterión*); Kilpatrick plans his own death, to redeem himself, in order to change his treachery into heroism (*Theme of the Traitor and the Hero*). Only at the moment of his execution, or the moment just prior to it, can Jaromir Hladík finish his masterwork, living in his own mind a secret year which takes place between the order to fire and the shot that kills him. The same thing happens in the case of Doctor Francisco Laprida in the *Conjectural Poem*, where he narrates his own death:

> To this disastrous afternoon I was drawn
> by the multiple labyrinth of steps
> woven by my days since one day in
> childhood. At last I have discovered
> the hidden clue to my years,
> the fate of Francisco Laprida,
> the missing letter, the perfect
> form that God knew from the beginning.

> In tonight's mirror I glimpse
> my unsuspected eternal face.

Therefore, when he speaks, at the end of the poem, of "the hard steel that tears my chest," he corrects that harsh impression by a more certain experience, one which is more his own, "the intimate knife at my throat." He transcends death, makes it his own, understands it. Death "made him a god," the "warm death" has enabled him to unify his experiences, become aware of himself, be eternalized in a definitive moment.[7]

This presence of a revelation, an intellectual companion of death, at the end of the narrative, can of course be related to the generic structure of the short story, with the necessity that in every aesthetic act there be "the imminence of a revelation, that is not produced . . ." (*Other Inquisitions*). The essential form of the short story often demands the moment of enlightenment at the end, the "surprise ending," the final sentence which confers fullness and clarity upon all previous meanings. The master stroke of Poe, of Maupassant, of O'Henry, of Chekhov, has left traces on the form of the short story developed by Borges. To this is added the idea that, for the Argentine writer, the reader is also pilgrim and brother in this labyrinth of words, and the presence of the fantastic as an integral part of the aesthetic act must uncover for him the being of the cosmos, making him doubt the rigid, constant, and invariable reality that hides the secret abyss that explains it all.

But if this particular configuration of the short story, which is meant to surprise and delight the reader and which coincides with Borges's own aesthetic quest, can determine the presence of a sudden revelation in text or require a change of rhythm and an opening toward other meanings hidden until now, what cannot be explained, in terms of literary form, the fact that such a revelatory act is synonymous with death, why this brilliant intuition of what is real arrives when man is in danger, when he is on the brink of killing someone or of dying himself.

Karl August Horst has suggested that this structure, the notion of eternity as negation of unreal time, was developed by Borges in "Sensing Oneself in Death" (*History of Eternity*): the reiteration of identical moments, as in Schopenhauer, is the proof that this reality is illusory and that eternity exists, since such repetition signifies the abolition of successive time ("Time, if we can intuit that identity, is a delusion: the indifference and the inseparability of one moment of his apparent yesterday and another of his apparent today, are enough to destroy it").[8]

But this interpretation, which reveals the epistemological co-ordinates of that final moment, and which establishes an interrelation between thought and action that is crucial to Borges, does not succeed in explaining why the death should be violent, or what this means to the characters themselves.

Violence operates in a very specific, peculiar and essential way in Borges's stories.

Man, for Borges, is trapped in an aggressive labyrinth, an enigmatic world where one being pursues another (*Abenjacán el Bojarí, Dead in his Labyrinth, Two Kings and Two Labyrinths, Death and the Compass, The House of Asterion, The Theologians, Deutsches Réquiem, The Secret Miracle, Three Versions of Judas, The Shape of the Sword, The Wait, The Garden of Forking Paths, The Babylonian Lottery, Emma Zunz, The Man on the Threshold*, etc.). The world—concrete, contradictory, and full of oppositions—operates under a sign of change and humiliating decay: for the future itself to be born requires violent struggle between hunter and hunted which ends with death or murder, natural and necessary acts, whose persistence Borges never attempts to explain. Fear and ambition, cowardice and dignity, greed, hatred, vengeance, treachery, all lead to conflict and to destruction. The characters face acts of aggression as something irreducible and undeniable, a given within the mutability of things; and rather than choosing violence, it would seem to choose them ("they noted that impetus that was deeper than reason" "that they would not have been able to justify," from *The Story of the Warrior and the Captive*).

If on the one hand they are in the grip of a force they cannot understand, on the other that force puts them on the path to their own liberation. One must live the violence, either given or received, in order to realize how fleeting it is. Like language, it is the frontier of their humanity and at the same time an instrument for their self-knowledge. Investigators of their own deaths, moving toward themselves at the very instant of their annihilation, they use violence to clear the darkness, so that each open wound may be a window upon the meaning that engulfs them and justifies them, so that the river of "sudden blood" which the dagger would shed may be a road to another world, more stable and essential. Between the destruction of outrageous time and the onset of oppressive nothingness, they manage to glimpse an infinite, frozen moment; although Borges, like Emma Zunz, has always declared himself opposed to violence, his characters, also like Emma Zunz, find in their personal violence, in their act of murder or in their own death, the revelation of an order in the obscure tangle of their lives, fixing all the previous chaos in an eternal, silent, and significant ice. Violence is an encounter, perhaps partial, with something greater than the individual human being, because it lets loose the fatal laws, draws man nearer to the divine, to the magic of death, the white lightening flash of understanding as a final step of consciousness and of growth.

Even if the protagonist later realizes that everything is fugacity and dream, that dream has assumed its shape in violent and inescapable situations; the shape of that deception that he himself has been appears as a tunnel of aggressiveness and of persecution. If life is a dream, for Borges that dream is a nightmare where men attack and hunt each other down in the middle of shadowy, internal cities. It is only by fully living and giving myself over to that nightmare, to my death in that dream (*The Circular Ruins, Encounter with the Enemy*), that I will be able to awaken from the dream, understand my death—which is the only way of comprehending my life—know that it was a dream, and that I am not nothing, but rather that I am *I,* at least to be fully that *ego* at the moment of my fading understanding. That is, revelation comes as I live the violence, however illusory or shadowy it may be, because it is the only way to fulfill a destiny, to exchange what has always been distant and impersonal for something that is nearby and my own, the only way to escape the dream, to break the mirror of my own eyes, to stop seeing myself in the mirror and to begin to see myself in death, in the flash of an instant to find the numberless keys to each door that opened and closed, leading me to this moment, the final one.

Death is the instrument of the character's self-realization, almost of his permanence; death is a linking point between dream and reality, a point that both differentiates them and draws them closer (*The Wait*), the intersection between eternity and temporality, the moment in which truth becomes incarnate in man or rises up from his inner being and must be faced. Experiencing one's death is a means of self-recovery, going beyond the absurd and fleeting world of the senses and of dreams, becoming part of a rite of passage that can be repeated by all human beings. Violence is the touchstone because it contains the key to approach that other universe, the possibility of evading that straight jacket of reality and of entering into the definitiveness of nirvana. It is the contact that men can establish with the hidden powers that govern their daily acts, whether these powers be divinities or mere, anonymous and cyclical laws, the key to all dreams, since they are the only permanent essence, however transitory, in the midst of so many illusions and pretenses. Exiled in a labyrinth whose only escape hatch is death, men like Lönnrot (*Death and the Compass*), like the true Abenjacán, or like Albert or Yu Tsun (*The Garden of Forking Paths*) must let themselves be trapped so that in the process of becoming cadavers, the universe suddenly takes on meaning, so that the arbitrary forms (only apparently arbitrary) may reveal behind, or beneath, or beyond themselves, the unity of a total meaning. It is in that way that the violence is denied, transcended, sublimated, essentialized, forgotten, understood, and explained. The surrender to illusion (violence is an illusion, perhaps the last one, to Borges) is the means to free oneself from it; it is the means of understanding oneself, of committing suicide at the hands of another.

But that instant in which dagger and flesh finally carry out their dialogue, that (momentary) exit which immerses man in nothingness after having enlightened him with an "an unsatiated immortality of sunsets,"[9] is not just the annihilation of what is human. It is also what gives him dignity. In that death there is the sign of other deaths, of numberless other similar agonies, which have occurred or will occur (it makes no difference) in a time which is parallel, anterior, fictitious, and a twin (it makes no difference). That is, this is the means through which we communicate with the species, with other human beings ("one man is all men," as Borges never tires of repeating).

Which means, of course, that pursuer and pursued are accomplices,[10] that this is, ultimately, an act of self-destruction, where both, executioner and victim, end up being irreducibly one.

The human personality, complex and tortuous, is divided into two components symbolic of two possible attitudes within the same man, of two opposing alternatives, a sign of the ambiguity found in every action, of the negation inherent in any affirmation; violence is the response to that split, linking both faces of the schizophrenia in one dangerous and aggressive confrontation. Quite often the difference that separates the *alter egos* is the courage of one and the cowardice of the other, the fact that one of them betrayed the other. In death, in the act of revenge, the man recognizes himself in the other, in the one whom he has just murdered or betrayed, and he assumes his personality; he becomes him, his enemy, and thus understands that he has killed himself.

Thus, we find the character who is assuming a personality: Zaid pretends to be Abenjacán, the courageous king whom he has betrayed; John Vincent Moon assumes the narrative role of the Irish conspirator whom he betrayed ("whatever one man does, it's as if every man did it"); Judas, pretending to be the Devil, betrays Christ, to be finally transformed, before the astonished eyes of the reader, into God, or into Christ; the false Villari takes the name of the man on whom he informed, the true Alexander Villari, who finds him and does him in; the black man becomes Martín Fierro, the man he has just killed ("He was the other. He had no destiny on the earth and he had killed a man"); Juan de Panonia is Aureliano, whom he has pursued to the death; Erik Lönnrot, the detective, is Red Scharlach, the murderer[11]; Otto Dietrich zur Linde is David Jerusalem, the man whom he tortures and kills in a Nazi concentration camp: "I don't know if Jerusalem understood that if I destroyed him, it was to destroy my pity. In my eyes, he was not a man, not even a Jew; he had become the symbol of a detested zone of my own soul. I agonized with him, I died with him, in some way I have been lost with him; that's why I was implacable."

This last quotation illustrates the internalization of violence in Latin America and its contemporary fiction, the splitting of the "I" into two seemingly opposite segments, man taking refuge in that bipolar insanity in order to be able to confront the contradictions of his immediate, concrete situation. It is death, the fear of death, which produces both this hero and this traitor; the moment of death will also be like a sword that will reunite the exiles, drawing together into a single, inner face, the two accidentally antagonistic masks.[12]

Kilpatrick pretends his own heroic death in order to make up for his treason, and thus, in fact, becomes a real hero; Otálora pretends to be Bandeira, until he suffers the death that he himself had planned for Bandeira; Pedro Damián lives twice, once as a coward, the other time as a man of courage, bringing together both personalities at the moment of his death; Dahlmann, on the other hand, dies twice, once without honor on the operating table, and later, again, as a brave man, on the field of honor. The desire for death is not grounded in the needs of metaphysical revelation in Borges: If the character desires that moment it is because in it he finds his own tearing apart, his other, the one who must kill him or make him die, the double who is both feared and loved, that being who is found deep inside each one of us, ready to destroy or be destroyed, Asterion and Theseus, Borges and the other.

Borges feels mired down in a miserable historical age where heroism and courage no longer exist; he feels the nostalgia—and the passion—for adventure; he remembers his ancestors and their memorable victories, their victorious deaths; he recalls bandits and duels at the edges of towns; he dreams about Homer, Troy, the Argentine civil wars, and Martín Fierro:

What does successive time matter if in it
there was a plenitude, an ecstasy, an afternoon.

And Quiroga reproaches Rosas in *Dialogue of the Dead*: "In 1852, fate, which is generous or wanted to probe you deeply, offered you a man's death, in a battle. You proved unworthy of that gift, because fighting and blood terrified you." The meaning of existence is offered to men at these moments; if a man rejects them (and there are as many cowards and traitors as there are brave men) he will have missed the opportunity to see himself in humanity, to achieve immortality, to become an archetype. Like Dunraven and Unwin, in *Abenjacán el Bojarí*, Borges is "fed up with a world without the dignity of danger" and through his characters he seeks the vicarious adventure that has been denied him, that he himself did not choose, that he now believes to be impossible, but which he can touch, as in transit, in the reality that surrounds him, in the Latin America that is his and that he denies, that he refuses to see, that rising, explosive Latin America that he interprets to his own chagrin and that he includes in his stories against his own rational will.[13]

Before elaborating upon this last affirmation, which does not stem from a whimsical desire to latinamericanize Borges, against everybody's will, including that of Borges himself, it is necessary to examine another possibility that is open to the characters, an attitude that is essentially the opposite of violence: that of contemplating the universe from a position of quietist passivity, doing away with any activity at all, since any action is absurd in a universe in which all that truly exists is the unitary center, God or eternity, where everything is ordered. The appearance of this sort of character (*The Aleph, The Zahir, The Writing of God, Funes the Memorioso*) is the exact reverse of the concretely violent man of the other stories. The meaning of this contemplative being is not only mystical, that is, does not just reside in his possibility of merging with the divine unity. He is the one who rejects the other pole, that of violence, and tries to avoid it not only by denying the risky and circumstantial world, but also his personal situation, his *ego*, rejecting all the contradictions in which the violent characters found an image expressive of their own internal selves. If one can live death fully, losing oneself in it until the revelation is reached, one can also simply deny the existence of that death, of such a universe and of the I itself.

This second alternative reaches its extreme in *The Writing of God*, where the character, having arrived at a magical formula which contains the totality of all that exists, is no longer concerned for the fate of his own I in that world, because that *I* is a matter of as much indifference and distance for him as any other object contained by and explained in his unitary contemplation. Tzinacán says: "But I know that I will never pronounce those words, because I no longer remember Tzinacán."

And: "Let the mystery, written in the tigers, die with me. Whoever has glimpsed the burning designs of the universe, cannot think about a man, in his trivial joys or misfortunes, even if that man is himself. That man *has been himself*, and is no longer important to him. What does he care about the fate of that other? What does he care about that other's country? If now he is nobody. That's why I will not pronounce the formula; that's why I let the days forget me, resting in the darkness."

All phenomenal form, then, is renounced; even any mental trace of the violence disappears, even its faint reproduction in thought. Paradoxically, we are dealing here with an Indian, imprisoned by the conquistadors. He rejects any rebellious action in favor of an absolute quietism. But in that rejection the reader can, if he wishes, draw closer to the situation that is rejected, the concrete, monstrous reality in which that I which "ahora es nadie" (now . . . is nobody) finds himself (or found himself), ask what that I would have done if it could have gone on being *I,* if it had accepted its circumstantially human condition: "It is a formula consisting of fourteen chance words (they seem to be chance) and all I would have to do to be all-powerful is pronounce them. That's all I would have to do to abolish this stone prison, so that the day could enter my night, to be young, to be immortal, to make the tiger destroy Alvarado, to bury the sacred dagger into Spanish chests, to reconstruct the pyramid, to rebuild the empire. Fourteen syllables, fourteen words, and I, Tzinacán, would rule all the lands that Moctezuma ruled." If he accepts his humanity, if he surrenders himself to the future, the only thing left will be violence, flight, or killing, searching for himself in the action that he suffers: he would, in fact, have to assume his identity in an anticolonial struggle.[14]

Many violent characters reached this same conclusion through their action: nothing exists; I am a dream. The contemplative characters come to the revelation that all things are illusory *before* taking action, *before* embracing violence, thus making relative and placing between parentheses all human possibility. That contradiction the violent man confronts, his need to kill or to avenge himself (*Emma Zunz, The Theologians*), his fear of being persecuted (*The Wait, Encounter with the Enemy*), his anguished desire to achieve permanence through action (*The Man on the Rose-colored Corner, The Garden of Forking Paths, The Other Death*), are false means, and it is preferable not to surrender oneself to any of these alternatives. That concrete situation is fraught with "fictions" and with "artifice"; the contemplative man destroys in advance all decision by denying that there is any substantiality at all in the world of decisions. On the other hand, for those who have chosen violence as an expiatory pilgrimage, as a quest for themselves, there are inevitable steps which the dream must fulfill in order to reach the state of nothingness; there are certain rites and configurations that must be repeated in order to be able to enter the realm of the infinite and to break the illusion. We reach the conclusion that Borges always tries to erase the world, whether through contemplation or through action, but that in both cases that unrealized phenomenological world, the one he is submerged in and the one he rejects as unreal, is described as violent and aggressive, populated by demoniacal darkness and blood. The world denied by Borges, the concrete situation that he rejects, is the reality that we have already described: savage phantoms that kill each other. This is the true, Latin American world described by Borges, the world he wishes to eliminate, the world he would like to change into one of those distant and controllable nightmares that we forget the next morning, but that will always be there, lying in ambush, inside, outside, identical to the night, identical to our real image, never completely forgotten, awaiting us there along the pathway among the days of our lives.

Whatever the disguise used to hide those violent situations, whatever the archaic costumes, the geographic past epochs, the Moslem, English, Chinese, or Persian locales, those who die and those who kill in the stories are Latin Americans, whether they call themselves Rufus, or Dunraven, or Dahlmann. Like the characters of Asturias, Carpentier, Fuentes, Vargas Llosa, García Márquez, Sábato, etc., through violence they search for the sign of their own essence or of the order of the universe. That violent situation has one primordial characteristic, present in all contemporary Hispanic American narrative: the fact that the violence is not chosen, but rather is assumed and accepted in order to find the characters' own identity. It never occurs to Borges's characters, any more than it would to those of Onetti, Droguett, Rulfo, etc., to reject aggression or to intellectualize it: They live it; they may choose the form of their violence, but not the fact of violence itself. It is in that way that they differ from characters in current Western European narrative: for Borges, as for the rest of our writers, the inborn violence offers an escape (momentary, to be sure) from the labyrinth, and that instant defines and forms the man. By killing or by dying, that Latin American man, sometimes the executioner, but generally the victim (Is this a pale Borgean recognition of oppression?), fulfills the underlying decrees of a given world, dying in the darkness, using his violence as an instrument of expression, to untangle himself from the chaos. Borges returns repeatedly to this situation, which is not found in the literary tradition which he claims to inherit. He masks his violence with his style and with the proud sophistication of his thought; he denies that reality, makes it transitory, but there can be no doubt that when he portrays a concrete world, he does so within the Latin American perception of violence as inevitable and a defining substratum of reality. He makes it blind and irrational as a means of liberation. Even though that wrenching experience signifies the destruction of what is human, as in the rest of our present-day narrative, it also constitutes an ambivalent escape from the maddening process in which we Latin Americans find ourselves. It is one of the keys to our understanding each other and communicating with each other, a solution that clarifies and frames the shadows among which we move. The inevitability of violence: because man is a fugitive, he will be killed; or he will search for his hunter, and by killing him he will foreshadow the liberation (collective) from those forces which have us trapped. Inevitability and liberating solution. Escape and loss. Aggression as a gnoseological act. Violence as companion to imagination. These are the characteristics of violence in Latin American literature and in Borges.

Yes, Latin American. But Borges's focus is singular, not to say original. The character surrenders to his own death or to the killing of another, because in this action (the only two actions allowed by Borges in his illusory world) man can free himself from the deception which he is living, free himself from his shadowy and fluctuating existence. He kills or dies to escape the labyrinth and, if only for a moment, to understand that violence and transcend it. It is the dream-like structure which marks these stories. But the basic problem in that world is very Latin American (very human): that inescapable violence may bestow a meaning, while bringing, at the same time, alienation, danger, and destruction. The difference between Borges and the other Latin American writers is not so much that they show Latin America and he does not, since all ultimately reveal the same internal structure of life and death on our continent, but rather that they tend to confront their own immediate, urgent circumstances; they do not need to invent eternal worlds outside of reality, because the eternal is found within what is real, social, and historical; while Borges, after hurling his characters into a world of violence and Latin American passion, prefers to disguise that world, to distort, deny, erase, and forget it.

Borges's Latin Americanism would seem to me to be undeniable. But so is his desire to turn his back on that reality equally undeniable.[15]

The Latin American world of violence exists in Borges, only to be dissolved into Schopenhauer's nothingness, Nietzsche's cyclical time, the avatars of thought, the Jewish cabal, Chinese labyrinths. The concrete world disintegrates and is absorbed by Borges's thought. As always in Latin American literature, we encounter the opposition between feeling and reason, America and Europe, barbarity and civilization, the two Borges.

Could his stories not then be seen as the literary and measured stylistic defeat of Latin American barbarism, its disintegration by the nirvana of idealism, its clouding over by the books and ideas and traditions that came from Europe, its absorption by perfect fiction, its conversion into a mind and (superior) civilization that thinks? One more Latin American utopian attempt at order in the New World? And could it not be that in this struggle, let us say (in Borgean fashion), that Borges destroys himself, searches for himself to destroy that dark sector of his soul, that "detested zone," that alter ego of which he has written so much, the enemy, the barbarian, the violent one, and that he finds him, finds himself, denies his Latin Americanness, the interweaving of his days and nights in the streets of Buenos Aires, that he defeats and transcends that being, believes that he defeats him, to understand at last (and it is he who relates this, not I) that in the eyes of history he has no alternative but to be Latin American?

It may be in that way, finally, that the drama unfolds: the scenario is Borges himself. He dissolves the world of violence, he civilizes the barbarism and pigeonholes concrete men in the hierarchies of European thought, all the while embracing the degraded world that secretly represents him.

All of which is a fiction, a rite that we presume to be inside Borges. One he would reject. *And yet, and yet. . . .* It could be the last game of the great Magister Ludi, the final trick, the way in which he rescues us (or believes he is rescuing us) from the barbarian hordes, the occult religion through which he at last defeats the disorder and saves his calm and uncompromised face.

Borges never ceases to proclaim that he is the other, his own double, and his stories show the silent signs of an intense internal struggle. It is this energy, this tension, this daily death and resurrection, which have made of Borges a fascinating writer, a secret fountain of inspiration, of experience and which, I believe, explain as well his need for such extraordinary, lucid, compact prose. In his battle is found the living process of our Latin American culture, the drama of our great synthesis of forms.

All repetition is significant. Borges's attempt to civilize the barbarians, to deny Latin America and to destroy it, although secretly in love with it all the while, has literary and historical antecedents. That coincidence with other works and deeds by other men must have some significance.

Perhaps, who knows, maybe, deception that we all are, Borges has after all succeeded in what he always desired: a wave of courage, an intimate dagger, a night beneath the lances, repetition, identity, time doesn't exist, perhaps Borges, dying in the living depths of a barbarism he has fought and succumbed to, is really none other than his illustrious ancestor, Francisco Laprida.

1968

■ Fathers and Bridges Over Hell: *Deep Rivers*

Growth. How does a child grow, how does a nation or a people grow? And can they grow together? That is the central question of José María Arguedas's *Deep Rivers*.[1]

Ernesto, the narrator of the novel, will tell the story of those crucial months of his existence in which he journeyed from childhood to adulthood, taking upon himself for the first time the complex responsibility of becoming "a man," a manhood that variously and conflictively includes being an adult, a member of the male sex, and a member of the human race. Even though he is accompanied by his father during the first three chapters of the novel, in the rest of the book he must accomplish that passage in solitude and helplessness, struggling with the infernal powers that govern the Andean people and the religious boarding school he is forced to attend.

Ernesto's problem, like that of any human being, is that growth is, above all, a concrete act of being integrated into an already functioning social structure: it is to elect (for those fortunate enough to have such a margin of freedom) a position, and therefore to make an ethical choice, placing oneself on one side or the other of the fight for power, wealth, and conscience. Before he renounces childhood, the protagonist must confront, within himself and in the world around him, the conditions which oppress him and which could twist even the most transparent destinies. He will also have to visit again and again those sources of natural and human solidarity which, like hidden springs, are the only ones that illuminate and guarantee a potential liberation, the only ones that can break the apparently infinite chain of betrayals and

despair. Therefore, Ernesto's fate will be determined by his necessary interconnections with other characters, mirrors and twins of
his own gaze, possessed by the struggle between death and love,
a savage dynamic whose terms and projections—as we shall see—
never cease to be social in nature.

The steps in Ernesto's growth will parallel, therefore, the evolution of his people—the poorest and the most abandoned of
Peruvians, the Indians.

Ernesto's Initial Situation

This youngster must try to reach maturity within the constricted limits of a boarding school in Abancay.

But before he is deposited there, the readers have been compelled to attest, along with Ernesto himself, that there is no other
place in the universe toward which he can emigrate; all other ways
and alternatives have been implacably and systematically closed
to him.

The novel opens in Cuzco, a city to which the protagonist and
his father, Gabriel, have arrived in search of El Viejo, an uncle, a
powerful and greedy landowner. Their purpose is to demand that
he fulfill some unnamed promise of help or work. They will fail.

El Viejo is at the apex of the political and economic hierarchy
of that world and is respected by the priests who monopolize the
categories of good and evil. Functioning as a mini-God in that
universe (owner of four haciendas and undisputed master of the
four cardinal directions), this patriarchal figure, the only relative to
whom Gabriel and his son can turn to, is at the same time, for his
visitors, the one who paradoxically occupies the lowest position in
their system of moral and religious values. For them he incarnates
the Antichrist, a perverse being, a hypocrite, who is lacking in all
humanity and is far removed from the true God. Indeed, he is the
opposite of all that is and will be seen as positive in the course
of the novel. This demoniacal and "damned" character, El Viejo,
is unequivocal: in his anti-Eden he stores up fruit only to let it
rot; he shouts in the "voice of a condemned man," frightening the
Indians with his ubiquity ("He is everywhere"). The child expects
a *huayronk'o* to appear next to him, "because these flying insects
are messengers of the devil or of the curses of the saints." El Viejo

is so evil he will not even reach the Final Judgment, which "is not for demons."

Therefore, from the very beginning, we have firmly established the problem of surviving (and growing) in a society constructed by men like this one: men who have appropriated all the power and who can, therefore, mold all the others in their own sub-image and likeness, but who, at the same time, are those with less "being," less humanity. The universe is inverted, and in such perverse, topsy-turvy circumstances being an adult means either incorporating oneself into the world just as it is or attempting to change it, subjugating oneself or rebelling, but inevitably learning that irrevocable apprenticeship of the distance that, no matter what one chooses, separates an authentic moral attitude from the need to earn one's living.

The fact, then, that the novel opens with this adult, male figure, who, in the case of some accident or other impediment to Ernesto's father, would replace him, is not fortuitous. Fed by hatred and by an incompatibility as much metaphysical as social, El Viejo will try to humiliate and to destroy the two "guests": he places them in a dung heap, the muleteers' kitchen; he dismisses them immediately before the mass is over; he tries to wear down Ernesto. El Viejo is always "above," at the highest point. He sees the world, and Ernesto and his father, as objects and would like to make them "pongos" (the lowest-ranking Indian servants).

Because in that lordly manor, neighboring the piss-stained and constrained Inca walls that still sing their song long after the deaths of their builders, there lives the most abject and lowly creature in all creation, descended from the Incas but having long forgotten his roots: the "pongo." He exists as the antagonist to El Viejo, while being at the same time, the unavoidable result of the old man's existence: when someone like the landowner has accumulated such power (economic and cultural) unfailingly there must be another, others, who have nothing. That Indian serf barely exists, separated from extinction and from nothingness by the shortest, whining thread of an abyss, the maximum marginality in an Andean world which is itself extremely marginal. Miserable, bent, and evermore bending, trying to become one with the ground or even to fall lower than the ground, fragile, barefooted, ragged, he defines himself as a negation, an "I don't want" ("manán," the first word he pronounces): "one could perceive the effort he was making to appear hardly alive, the invisible weight that oppressed his breathing." Thus, from the very beginning, both the reader (and Ernesto) are introduced to the two possible extremes of the Andean world: the oppressor and the oppressed, both carried to their ultimate and overwhelming consequences. In that totalizing, omnipresent relationship of exploitation, El Viejo interminably generates pongos and forces the rest of the inhabitants of that region to choose: either to be like the pongo or to be like the landowner, to be completely subjugated or to participate in the oppression of others, to ally themselves with the powerful or to suffer like the poor.

No one better illustrates this dilemma than the one person who would serve as a model for Ernesto or, at least, as his guide: Gabriel, at one and the same time the child's progenitor and his friend.

The narrator's father has been caught up by the in-between, hybrid culture of the mestizo, but cannot really establish his residence therein. The social contradictions in which this lawyer lives have turned him into an exile from the world of the whites and the landowners, yet have also alienated him from the Indian world.[2] Decidedly opposed to the established powers, despising the greed and the domination of the great feudal landowners, he has, nevertheless, been unable to consummate a complete break with the existing stratified order of things, to the extent to which he has not found anywhere an alternative class to which to adhere and to serve professionally. He vacillates between rebellion (grandiose projects to humiliate El Viejo and to overcome him, dreams of winning suits against some important landowner) and submission. Therefore his projects are unachievable or utopian. There are insufficient external forces (or perhaps internal guts?) to centralize, orient, give a greater meaning to that sense of isolated disenchantment, raising it to the level of a permanent act. A prisoner of his own marginality and insignificance, caught in the distant orbit of true power, like a comet that thinks it is free but which, in fact, always follows the path determined by the secret forces of larger stars, his fate is to wander. With an irrepressible stubbornness, he deludes himself with the idea of settling down and becoming independent, contradictory terms in a society as rigid as that one. To preserve some degree of autonomy in that suffocating universe, *mobility* is his only possible recourse, to migrate from town to town, searching for any tiny chance for power, sporadic instances of conflicts between the dominating forces and those opposing forces that might be able to call on his lawyer skills. Thus, he is the occasional ally of small landowners and "comuneros libres" (members of the Indian community who are not the serfs of any landowner), based more on the dispersed residues of former economic power than on any rising new social classes. His constant movement, his misrepresentation and self-deceptions, are the consequence of that unresolved and unresolvable conflict with the owners of the land. A fugitive from his own class of origin, he ends up running away from reality itself in an obsessive search for a perpetually postponed arcadia.

Since Gabriel's power is fictive, in the end his rebellion can only be partial. He incarnates a renewed tendency toward liberation within Christianity; he understands Peru; he loves nature, the Indians, and their culture; he idealizes the future and abhors injustice; and yet, when he tries to find a future for his son, Gabriel makes major mistakes. In the two most serious and critical moments in the novel (when his son must settle down to receive an education; and when, at the end, he needs to leave Abancay because of the devastation of an epidemic), the lawyer first chooses the same depraved school where he received his instruction, and then, finally, hands him over to the corrupt guardianship of his archenemy, El Viejo.

The precariousness of the father is underscored by the fact that he leaves Ernesto in Abancay with Alcilla, his ex-classmate, a man weak, sickly, and incapable. This guardian (the town notary), supposedly responsible for the well-being and health of the youngster during his father's absence, expresses the inevitable subordination and sterility that must be endured by such men when they do not manage to escape.

His father does not, therefore, serve Ernesto as a usable model in the world. He cannot offer a valid answer to the fundamental question: how do I grow up in an alienated society without changing or losing the humane values that I learned in some river of childhood? Gabriel has given Ernesto much: he has lighted his path with curiosity and legends and music; he has pointed out to him that there are moral values that must not be betrayed; he has kept him in touch with affection. But the novel opens at precisely the moment when this process can no longer continue, unless the child is to become a distorted and absurd replica of his father, a perpetuator of his failure and frustration. Ernesto has to settle down; his father has to keep moving. The trip to Cuzco will be the next to the last, and the one to Abancay the last, in an endless series of attempts to find a place where both of them, together, could resolve the contradiction between establishing a residence and earning a living, between settling down geographically and settling down morally. They spend enough time crossing each domain for the narrator to establish their hidden light in his memory, but not enough time to confront in that place what would have been the consequences of a prolonged stay. What is gradually running out, then, is not Gabriel's ever-renewable capacity to feed himself on illusions, but rather the possibility for Ernesto to go on accompanying him in that constant, bewildering flight. As the child grows, that tomorrow when everything will work out shows itself for what it really is, an illusion. The years of sterile migration have repeated over and over again "with an endless slowness" the same characteristics of cruelty and exploitation, forcing them to flee over and over again, until they end up in that final, closed space, the hell of Abancay, identical to the previous spaces, except that now, for Ernesto, there will no longer be any place to run to. There he will be beaten (let us note the passive, suffering sense of the word "golpeado") by the monsters and the fire (on the one hand) and by the great rivers that sing the most beautiful music (on the other).

It would seem to be fated, then, that Ernesto would end up alone and captive, as he confronts what his father cannot or will not confront: to live no longer in the constantly postponable purgatories of a town, a valley, a canyon, awaiting a salvation that never arrives, but rather to inhabit a hell with no evident escape. One must find those forces capable of changing the world, of opposing El Viejo and his class and his subordinates, here and now, in this valley, in this heat that undermines the will, and not in the other world of mountains and dreams. Gabriel is useless. His inconsistency becomes explicit when he leaves his son in the institution where one learns the machinery of domination, the institution where those who will be in control tomorrow (landowners, professionals, administrators, priests) are educated.

It is this absence of the father which provokes the double law upon which both the novel and the child's personality are constructed: on the one hand, the constant search for male allies who are adult or on the way to becoming so, who can point toward a path or exemplify a solution; and on the other hand, the tendency of the protagonist to look inside himself or in his past for the values that can save him.

This bifurcated spiritual movement of Ernesto is the means by which he attempts to defend those central, ethical objectives that, if one is to survive as a human being, require unswerving loyalty. The complication for him is that the models for the redemptive and free humanity he desires happen to be Indians, that is, beings who belong to a culture which is dominated and publicly despised. How is he to grow without distancing himself from that culture which has no power? But then again can he grow if he remains anchored to the past, gazing at the once-upon-a-time, determined not to move? [3]

In order to mature and develop, Ernesto has to avoid both temptations: the betrayal of the ideals that have nurtured him, as well as the passive adherence to them through a retreat or a self-absorption that precisely reproduces that tendency of the indigenous masses to a radical introspection which denies the world.

He must avoid both temptations, but when he arrives at Abancay, Ernesto is singularly ill-prepared to do so. [4] He carries with him experiences and ways of reacting in the face of adversity and humiliation, an already structured experience of how one overcomes suffering. When El Viejo exiles them to the kitchen, that act reminds him of a situation he had lived once before. On that occasion, his father had also left the child in a *strange* house, "always watched by cruel persons." The man who should have acted as his protector at that moment, the master of the house, enjoyed making "those who depended on him, whether servants or animals, suffer." It was then that Ernesto constructed the central way in which he confronts difficulties, based on two basic experiences: the first, the solidarity of his Indian champions, adoptive parents, at once both tender and strong, who replace his biological father, who care for him and keep him safe and sound; and the second, the fact that his real father, Gabriel, ended up rescuing him. In the face of the threatening and merciless world of adults, Ernesto has understood that there is a possible refuge, an alternative plain of human perfection, just as there exists, on the part of his progenitor, the almost chivalric capacity to come to his aid, intervening from without to put things in their proper place.[5]

To protect his identity, Ernesto will hold tightly to those two experiences; he will seek their repetition each time the world tries to bend him. Condemned to the satanical valley of Abancay, he will essay both solutions: a place where the values of solidarity will take sufficient root to keep on encouraging him, where they will take the form of some kind of power; and the appearance of a protector, an adult, male figure, who can put the universe in order and punish the guilty. The filiation of these two tendencies is found not only in Ernesto's previous personal history, but are also rooted in deeper aspirations of the species, especially in its more marginal, impoverished, and dispossessed sectors. Ernesto defends himself with the dreams that have given birth to myths, fairy tales, and mass media fiction, which reinforce in him a tendency toward the past, toward the once-upon-a-time, the certainty that one can resolve the howlings of the present by repeating the music of a successful yesterday. Several critics, and especially Vargas Llosa,[6] have called attention to this attempt on Ernesto's part to live in memory, running away from the pain of growth, freezing time with a leap outside present occurrences, daring to travel through the passes of the imagination, just as his father wanders the land. This preference reveals an extreme and virtual infantilization in Ernesto: of the two experiences with which he usually responds to helplessness, one corresponds to the maternal and the other to the paternal,[7] and both return him to childishness and dependence, an orphanhood which, after all, represents Ernesto's true state. He will have to learn the real dimensions of the world and at the same time the sense in which those dreams are true or false. That is, he must project himself beyond his own interior universe, objectify himself, without losing the dream of solidarity that allows him to endure reality; he must immerse himself in the real without denying the horizons of peace (the mythic or magical world) and of justice (someone, a man, will come to rescue the persecuted) which provide the foundation for hope.

It is no easy task.

While he was a child, those myths could be shown to be valid and valuable, as well as universally applicable, inasmuch as they corresponded to a great extent with his daily situation of helplessness and subordination, legitimately expressing the anguish of childhood. But when the one growing up is an adolescent entering the adult world, those myths may end up tying him to the past or demanding an impossible purity, desiring refuges and knights in shining armor, dreams as precarious as they are distant. Growing up is establishing a flexible relationship with power, with sex, with other human beings. To do that, one must put to the test not only the values but also the very myths according to which they function, and discover where one ends and the other begins. And that, in fact, means discovering the struggles around which the murky dynamics of life are entwined and constructed, discovering in the depths of experiences the why and the how, since those myths are only viable if they are put into motion by human beings. Of course, we are not dealing with the assimilation of something vague or conceptual or even with the elaboration of a theory with which to interpret reality and orient our conduct, but rather we are gropingly trying out the possible practice of liberation in a world of oppression. The eternal repetition of the childlike and primitive structure of magical hideaways and of messianic rescues crashes against the real interests that each person in that valley represents and exercises. To understand that is both to accept the complexity of those who commit themselves to the world of adults, the mixtures and impurities with which adult relationships are forged, and to allow one to gauge the fluctuating dividing lines between that which liberates and that which oppresses.

But this is a dialectical process, one of advance and retreat, of trial and error. Those dreams cannot be thrown away just like that, because they are the only protection that Ernesto has to keep from being shipwrecked in that dehumanized world, and because, for the time being, he does not have at his disposal any other means adequate to express the fundamental goals to which we all aspire (peace, justice, solidarity). To mature involves learning the limits of those dreams and simultaneously discovering what there is in them that is truthful, uplifting, and unchanging. Dreams must be used against the world and at the same time the world must be used against dreams. And one cannot remain attached to childish and passive regressions, nonexistent, manly bringers of justice or maternal bosoms of illuminated cornfields which have no permanent foothold in this world. That does not mean, however, that one should ignore the stubborn persistence of human beings who do struggle for liberation as well as for magical spaces that renew and calm and strengthen; but all of this as a means of activating the protagonist, of forcing him to grow up to the point where he knows that in the final analysis he is the only one who can choose, that none of his substitute parents (whether they come from society or from nature) can do it for him. There are, therefore, allies in this world, but they are not messianic saviors; and there are renewing spaces, but not to withdraw to, separating oneself from the day-to-day crossroads of life. Rowe[8] says that Ernesto must prove the universality of experiences that redeem, their objective validity for someone more than a subject, their application beyond a particular case. Although, in fact, this structure is similar to the one established in *El Quijote* (to be faithful to our dreams, we have to take the road to test them), a fundamental difference persists: deep down in Ernesto's redeeming experience the warm certainty germinates that *without others there will be neither liberation nor growth*.

We will attempt to demonstrate how Ernesto succeeds (not without ambiguity) in reaching what is his maximum aspiration: to grow because other human beings have done it, to link his destiny to the collective destiny, to transcend his private solitude in the vast solitude of the people.

And this deed, this interior epic, must be carried out in the worst place in the universe, the most aberrant of sites: Abancay.

The Demonic Space

From the first moment Abancay is seen as a hell. And this is no rhetorical assertion. The narrator takes great care to pile up images of external heat and internal ice: bodies boil and souls become petrified.[9] If in other places the birds were killed, here the crickets, the messengers of music, must be protected. Minstrels and saints flee that place, that is, if they are not taken prisoner. The dense, burning air, the fiery dust, the sun's flames, all bewilder, lead astray, and confuse whoever would seek a respite or a cooling brook. But these moral and climactic manifestations are nothing more than the dislocated and visible face of the social disorder in which the people exist: "it is a *captive* town, built on the land of *another,* on an hacienda" (emphasis is mine). Just like Ernesto, the town itself is *surrounded;* in the hands of others, it has no life of its own, depending entirely on the semi-feudal, backward, agrarian power of the landowner. These landowners exercise their dominion over horses (nature) and over Indians (human beings) in a brutal and humiliating manner.

In the face of this suffocating panorama, the narrator must seek out the sacred space of the Indians, repeat with them the past purification, when "they impressed upon me the priceless tenderness in which I live." But the Indians in that valley have also been contaminated by cruelty and poverty. Like El Viejo's pongos ("dirtier, scarcely upright"), whining, almost animals, more isolated from the world than Ernesto, their only words, always negative, are "manán" ("I don't want") and "Don't talk to me." This rejection of the boy who expects solidarity and openness is due to the fact that they have lost their memory ("they no longer listened to the language of the *ayllus*"); they have been unable to preserve their own identity. Thus, they symbolize the danger that pursues Ernesto: To absent oneself from the past, to accept the vision which the powerful have propagated with respect to that race (animals, cowards, defenseless children, drunkards) is to stop the flow of those potential waters of rebellion. And Ernesto goes back to the school, after his fruitless search for dialogue, "fearing I would not know the people or that they would deny me," that is, fearing that he too would become a laborer without a memory.

He will not, then, be able to turn back to experiences of the past, because those who should represent the liberating cosmovision, those who by their race are the brothers of the now so-distant Inca protectors, provide no model, offer no help. The workers, in fact, do act like children and are treated as such: they are victims, they weep, they do not develop nor grow.[10]

This relationship between childhood, the Indian race, and adulthood is central to José María Arguedas. His entire work, and life, are a courageous gamble: despite the fact that the world is dominated by structures that exploit and isolate, the need to exercise power and sex in direct opposition to a profound solidarity that resounds in the universe (in nature, in certain objects made by human beings, in people, in privileged communities), Arguedas believes it is possible to grow, as an individual and as a people, without betraying or forgetting those essential values. Even though the world may block the perpetuation of those values or may relegate them to the periphery and insanity, Arguedas is convinced that an inextinguishable liberating nucleus is constantly being generated. This nucleus or seed has two principal manifestations: in the first place, it is a constituent of every individual who is born, a biological tendency that is potentialized in each child; and in the second place, it is resplendently incarnated in certain strata of society which in Peru happen to be the free Indian "comuneros" who, collectively, best represent the social potential of this tendency. Arguedas assumes, then, that the Indian culture is sufficiently strong to go on coalescing in waves that are ever larger and ever more integrating (this is the evolution of his books, one after the other[11]), and this applies as much to the personality of those who live divided and torn lives as it does to an equally broken Peru. The longing for a liberating solidarity is not, in Arguedas's work, an appetite that is condemned to inevitable frustration or to an agonizing struggle in the interior of certain especially sensitive consciences (as happens in the great majority of European or North American novels in the twentieth century), but rather it is based on cultures, powers, life projects that are effective and socially functioning, objectively real and historical.

But this prophecy of victory would not be such were it not for the fact that Arguedas believes that in each individual there exists something that responds and vibrates with these social forces. Children represent the underdeveloped territory in which this is proven. Because they are marginal to the struggle for power and for sex, they have been able to communicate, to live in communion, with that harmonious, universal structure.

This theme, that the child lives closer to the truth, that he is uncorrupted and intuitive, has been much studied in Western literature (and in part in world literature) for centuries. Or, to put it in another way, the theme of childlike purity and its rebellion (Romanticism), of innocence as the companion of an immaculate nature (the pastoral myth, which culminates in the Renaissance and continues up to our own time, but which exhibits Greco-Latin roots) feeds this idea that Arguedas shares with his readers. In our own contemporary period a marginal element is added, that being who appears and remains on the fringes and who, therefore, from that position can observe the processes with greater care (the child as artist or as a borderline creature, overly sensitive, a witness, judge, and victim of what is happening).

If Arguedas thinks, then, as so many writers, that children have greater access to and contact with the depths of a confused and brutalized humanity, he certainly does not consider those values to be anti-adult or neglected by mature people. On the contrary, he is certain that there are vast adult sectors—especially those motivated by rebellion and poverty—who achieve that humanity. This is, in Peru, primarily but not exclusively the case of the comuneros, with their practice of a limitless brotherhood. And Arguedas definitely rejects our dominant ideology's primitivist trap, which identifies Indians with children, returning the natives to a preindustrial state of innocence, prior to modern man.[12] The fact that the Indians in that valley appear to be stagnating in a prepubescent age (the fact that society has succeeded in imposing that concept upon them), limits the possible parallel evolution of Ernesto. They are incapable of carrying forward the essential values that childhood illuminates and desires, precisely because they are passive victims, because they have not grown, because they are all "children" and none of them are "parents" who assume responsibility for things. On the other hand, the free comuneros have managed to preserve that childhood vision, while being fully adult themselves, having matured, being "taytas," "padrecitos."

In that hell, Ernesto must hold on to his central values without the Indian comuneros who could facilitate their preservation and passage. But at the end of the novel, having crossed on his own the evil and suffocating labyrinths, he will confront the sudden and surprising maturation of the Indian children, their immense growth to the point of no longer crying nor being afraid. And it will be that which will ignite, accompany, and guarantee the last spark of Ernesto's own rebellion. Groups have difficulties in changing similar to those of individuals. In his own personal biography Ernesto reproduces all the vacillations and potentialities of the Indian people with whom he wanted to join.

Arguedas also rejects the identification of childhood and arcadia. Childhood is exempt from terror, stains, and confusion. Children, rather than separating themselves from society, reproduce the worst vices of the system, carrying them to an extreme.

This is the reason that most of the novel takes place in a school. We are ready (we aesthetically and Ernesto from his existential point of view) to live with other children, who are no more than other probable projects of adult humanity. The novel's configuration, far from lacking unity, as some critics have suggested,[13] serves to *surround* the protagonist narratively: in the first chapter, it is demonstrated that there is no way of residing among his nearest relatives and that no benign, ordering center exists for the world (Cuzco can no longer fulfill that function); in the second,[14] we see the previous journeys that extend the suffering in space, their continued flight which does not resolve the problems; in the third, Ernesto bids farewell to his father, forced to assume in his extreme solitude the responsibility for that suffering; in the fourth, the existence of the hacienda and the nonexistence of the comuneros is established; and now, in the fifth, we are prepared to co-suffer with the narrator-protagonist, already knowing what he cannot do, where he cannot escape to.

The norms that govern that school are the same ones found in the society for which the children, defenseless without their parents, are supposedly being prepared: violence, degrading sexual practices, mutual recriminations, hypocrisy. What is basic for them is not *education* but *survival*. If the external world is one of struggle, where some (the landowners) exploit the others (the Indian workers), so is the school. Under the control of the Principal, of whom more later, there are endless war games in which the helpless destroy each other mutually. At night the combat goes on, no longer organized by the authorities, but revolving around sex with a demented woman, "la opa." In that in-between age of adolescent transition, the instincts and the need for growth are constrained by the weight of sin proclaimed by priests. The sense of guilt isolates them, converts them into mouthpieces of power, thus using against their classmates the same condemnatory formulas which their religion has taught them ("Antichrist," "damned," "All, all of you will squirm in Hell.") Instead of forming a common front, they are divided and waste themselves in discord, becoming fierce vigilantes of each other's conduct.

Two of the children carry this dismemberment to excess: Añuco and Lleras. Both, together with Antero later, will enter into a special relationship with Ernesto, representing three differing but equally frustrating and inauthentic directions in human development.

Añuco is Ernesto's alter ego. He has also been abandoned, but his father, a vice-ridden gambler who committed suicide, never obtained the protection of the comuneros, those guardians of the future. Thus, he has ended up being a small, treacherous animal, possessed by a rage that overwhelms him ("like a small animal, he growled, bit and scratched"). In Lleras he finds the male cohort he needs. Lleras is himself an orphan who was taken in by the priests. Being the strongest and the oldest of the band, he exercises in the school the sacred law of violence that he has observed in the world: in order to conquer, one must exaggerate brutality and terror among the weak. Thus, he is the incarnation and the expression of what is worst in that collectivity: he is its logical product, its almost natural culmination. The same arbitrariness which the official power brokers use *vertically,* from the heights of their social situation (exploitation and repression), is unleashed by Lleras *horizontally,* among his classmates.[15]

Both Añuco and Lleras are victims of the system. But instead of allying themselves with the other victims, the rest of the children, they try to increase the pain and the fear and promote the conditions for guilt and rancor. In a world so structured, the lack of unity and solidarity among the suffering almost means extinction. Lleras and Añuco unabashedly cultivate the values that prevail in the society that surrounds the school and into which the children are destined to enter when they are "men": the real anti-values that underlie the hypocritical words, the masks and costumes and empty comforts of that ruling Catholic institution. One can clearly read in their actions the cold and merciless laws that move men to scratch for success: domination, guilt, the law of retaliation, competition, solitude, and hatred. One is moved to pity them: they do nothing more than translate horizontally the violence that is vertical and resides in the world. And yet they are traitors, rebellious angels, demon-possessed in the Judeo-Christian sense of the word, because that struggle (horizontal) among equals, among members of the same social plane, is the prior condition necessary to prevent rebellion (vertical) in society. Lleras, then, represents pure vio-lence, without any institutionalization, without any self-justifying mediations, with no ideology to make it acceptable, breaking the minimum code of decency which allows mutual survival. The re-pression that the armed forces and the landowners (and the Prin-cipal) exercise comes accompanied by "beautiful words," military bands, awesome spectacles, and grandiose plans that, even though rhetorical in the mouths of those pronouncing them, are not in themselves (peace, brotherhood, charity) to be disdained.

If the school is an inferno within a valley that is already charac-terized as satanic, particularly demonic is the patio where the noc-turnal violation of "la opa" is perpetrated; she is another helpless soul who has been taken in by one of the priests (naturally to take advantage of her). Among the shadows of that filthy, dank, and dark place, the boys struggle with no sense of loyalty whatsoever to reach the denseness inside that woman, all of them turned into Añucos: "They never fought so fiercely: they even kicked their companions when they had fallen to the ground; they pressed the heel of their shoe into their head, in the most painful places." Whoever wins relegates the rest to the corner with the youngest boys. Being a man involves winning in the battle for a sick woman, forcing his defeated classmates into a childlike submission. All of them end up infected, possessed by a sickness and by a desire that springs as much from an inner dimension as from an outer one. Atrocious legends and myths are spun about that space, inhab-ited by monstrous beings, images of the solitary self-castigation by which they attempt to pay their subsequent sense of guilt.

"And we had nowhere to go."

What better definition of hell: immersed in heat ("the yellow, honeylike sky, seemed to be aflame"), those who should offer them guidance are too far away (their true parents) or too near (the priests), while their classmates are defined as enemies. It is as if all the negative aspects of Abancay and of the entire universe had been concentrated in that place, multiplying themselves in a com-pletely irrational way, to the point of perverting even the witness of that fratricidal struggle, turning him into an angry and lost soul.

Ernesto had earlier had a similar experience, in another dark zone: the Valley of Los Molinos. Also abandoned and in the care of someone almost crippled ("an old Indian, tired and almost blind"), he inhabited a world dominated by what was somber, yellowed, and narrow, by heat and by cold and by the dying. But hope had not vanished in him, because some signs of the world still reached his eyes (a ray of sunlight, a glimpse of river birds "inspired me to go on"). The school is even more degrading than the Valley. Back there the problem had been the lack of company, of other human beings to go out with ("and I needed companionship to overcome myself and to calmly explore"), to share his sorrow. In the patio and in the glacial atmosphere of the dormitory, the problem *is* the company; that is, what creates that abyss are the other human beings, their anguish and their guilt. Thus, the demonic is not inscribed exclusively in the landscape; it is also in the heart of the social community. The Valley of Los Molinos is terrible in that it foreshadows and symbolizes what is to come; it anticipates that future solitude, without fully reaching it. But there is no escape from the school, as there was from the valley, because the school is less a physical place than a spiritual one. Therefore the patio achieves a satanic power, which can even poison the magical power of nature that Arguedas, following Quechua civilization, has always affirmed as the potentiality to feel everything as one's own and not alien. The patio of the school alienates, makes reality a stranger: "the maternal image of the world disappeared from my sight."

Faced with this challenge, Ernesto seeks to renew himself, to return to his permanent self, visiting a positive and magical space which will annul the somber contagion of the patio: going through more fire in the valley, he will reach the waters of the great river Pachachaca, which serves as a natural and epic alternative to his problems, a model that strengthens him, a bridge that reconnects him with his roots, puts him in touch with his friends. It almost functions as Gabriel had, saving him from the dog-eat-dog environment, erasing "weeping images," clearing his heart and filling him "with strength and with heroic dreams."

But if the River holds out an *ought to be* which must be imitated, if it inspires and protects him, it paradoxically has limitations on its educative value, which are similar to those of Gabriel. The crazy woman and the patio have isolated Ernesto from the world; in its turn, the river isolates him from the patio and from the crazy woman, returning him to his own being ("For many days afterward, I felt *alone,* completely isolated"—emphasis is mine). Thus the two opposite and antagonistic experiences are complementary in that they offer no concrete orientation about how to act in daily life. Ernesto's ideal is to be like the river: to move "unstoppable and calm" or "unstoppable and permanent" or "imperturbable and crystaline like its victorious waters." To move and yet be permanent, to change and yet remain the same. To advance and yet stay behind, to live the future without having to cut his ties with the past—with which he will be in continuous communication. To inhabit the entire sweep of geographical space and yet not lose his sense of unitary coherence, to be like time which moves and like space which is permanent. The River is a traveler, like his father, and has greater depth, but it does not *resolve* the fundamental tensions to which the child finds himself subject. It is as though, for one ephemeral instant, he had the ability to prolong his past, to eliminate the school's malignant persistence.

The River may be an ally, but the solution lies elsewhere. He must confront those unsettling forces directly, along with the other children, and must combat the disintegration of that cosmos at its roots and escorted by its victims. In other words, he must find the objectivity of the River and its epic among human beings, the values of the water among those who surround him; he must test the validity of the Pachachaca and its teachings beyond his reinvigorated solitude. The repetition of the past can aid him in the harsh task of *surviving,* but not in that of really *living.* Armed with the power that nature has resown in him, he will have to dig deeper and break through the world that imprisons him, searching out the causes of that infectious core of evil. The Edenic temptation (to go back, to avoid the flames, to flee hell, purifying himself by withdrawing) would end up destroying him by making him incapable of growth, unable to know the true worth and solidity of his own convictions, occupying up until that moment invisible, underground, and obscure places. Because he is being pushed back into the past and becoming fixed eternally in an unchangeable, rigid, and dreamlike attitude, those values would cease to be positive or applicable, capable of *transforming* the world and not just of defending what is his own. He would be something like those Indians who cage themselves in their own culture and do not strengthen it by contact with the other, dominating culture, thus influencing it.[16] Therefore, at this stage, Ernesto says to the world the same thing the Indian workers reply to his urgings: "Manán," I don't want to. He doesn't want to be contaminated, but to be purified, to cleanse himself morally through the River. Of course, if he did not have this period of ethical restoration and repose, it would be impossible for him to take the next, inevitable step, the step toward others and solidarity. It is one more example of the parallelism between the child and the Indian people.

The River, for its part, has had antecedent rivers, like the Apurímac upon leaving Cuzco. Already in that experience of the Apurímac ("God who speaks"), in unitary opposition to the double face of the Christian God (who judges like a Father or suffers like a Son), that river sang of liberation, as other rivers will throughout the book like a leitmotiv and in its title, functioning as a redeeming space in contrast with the devil-possessed city of Cuzco. In effect, the land of Cuzco is poisoned by the great landowners; the colonial architecture oppresses the Inca walls; the cathedral was built to subjugate, to destroy, to make everyone weep. Everything foreshadows the suffering of the school: "It seemed like we had *fallen* . . . beneath the blankets of inextinguishable ice." The two poles of the Catholic world imposed upon the Indians—the Father and the Son, authority and affliction, the all-powerful and the all-victimized—are combined in the Crucified One, the Lord of Earthquakes.[17] The society of the oppressors finds in the Christian God the projection of its power and, at the same time, the justification for the suffering of the dispossessed. He is not seen as a liberating God (however much Gabriel may present another possibility), but as either Lord or He Who Suffers. The very plaza in front of the cathedral transmits their culture of imposing greatness and submission. Overshadowing trees and pilgrims, it forces people to their knees.

But this desolation that is Cuzco does not speak with only one voice. It is splintered by referents to other entities, which though tremendously relativized, are still capable of pointing in another direction. Confronting El Viejo and the cathedral is the Inca wall, very much alive, with flames that glimmer and whisper. The weight of the past that is sinking it, the dark, narrow, and silent street, the smell of urine, cannot suppress its message. And

in the patio of El Viejo's house, a rickety tree is trying to grow
and develop, scarcely able to survive in that air. Finally, in contrast
to the cathedral, there is another form of religious architecture, the
Company (a name full of symbolism) which sings, re-creates, and
does not inspire tears. This positive presence of something that
the white race built, in the name of the West and of Christianity
in its crusade, is central in the literature of José María Arguedas.
He does not present the total rejection of the dominating culture
of European origin, since in it the values of participation and of
solidarity can also be manifest.[18]

In Cuzco, in what was once the re-creating center of the world
and is now the center of betrayal, we can find three components
(Inca wall, tree, the church of the Company) which represent the
three elements that should come together in order to create a new
Peru, integrated and free: the Indians, nature, and that inalien-
able, humane part of the exploiting white race. The narrator guides
us; he needs these components. Later, in *All the Bloods*, Arguedas
succeeds in drawing the vast consequences from this sort of alliance, putting it in motion narratively and politically. But already
in the first chapter of *Deep Rivers*, the author anticipates, perhaps
unconsciously, the possibility of that alliance.

These three dimensions are all relativized, limited and oppressed
by structures which do not allow them to grow or to touch human
beings with all the positive influence of which they are capable.

The function of the River can now appear much more clearly.
Since it has not been enclosed, it can become a constant prolongation of these strangled attempts of the people to free themselves
from within the infernal enclosure. As far as values and models
go, it is the antagonist of El Viejo. The word "inspires" is used in
reference to the Apurímac, the same word with which the book
opens, referring to El Viejo ("he inspired respect") and is later
used on several occasions to define the Principal. But it is not respect that the River instills (which in the case of El Viejo means
inject, from above, the status quo, the established order, adap-
tation to what exists and is valid), but rather, "foreshadowings
of unknown worlds" and, therefore, the adventure of that which
changes and varies. The River exalts (heightens, elevates, raises)
and sings in the same way the Inca walls do, even though there

are now Viejos and pongos where there were once Incas. At the same time it foresees a curative function precisely in the face of the two ills which Ernesto will witness later, invading his body because of the violation of *la opa:* heat and terror. Because the traveler reaches the waters of the Apurímac "disturbed, feverish, with swollen veins."

There was a period when men and rivers flowed in harmony. The Inca carved rivers on their walls in that age in which art pervaded every object. Now the Incas, the protecting parents of an entire people, have disappeared, although their walls go on whispering what a few sensitive beings can still hear. Now the rivers carve out the message of human solidarity and of peace. They establish contact with "primitive memories, the most ancient dreams." And their mere existence makes transparent a demand for another kind of humanity, for a future that is renewed and clean. The walls contain promise and nostalgia, message and stone, nature and society, even in the name with which they have been baptized, "yawar mayu," river of blood.

Therefore, being faithful to the rivers cannot mean turning back toward a "natural" state, separating oneself from human conflicts. The guarantee that the rivers will go on singing for others, millennia away from us, kilometers of time, only persists to the extent to which we commit ourselves today to transforming the world (and the harsh, exhausting wall) which holds back the rivers we carry inside ourselves.

Therefore, it is not a matter of living in a "bridge *over* the world" (the title of the fifth chapter), but rather of discovering a bridge *toward* the world. The *zumbayllu* will fulfill that function in the next chapter.

The First Allies

Up to now (we are on page 73 of the novel), Ernesto has been the spectator and witness of what occurs. If he suffers more than others, it has been as part of a chorus or as a kind of passer-through. He has not developed a concrete, subjective relationship with any other boarder.

The zumbayllu is a marvelous toy top, which spins and rises

and dances, in which he will recognize an entire alternative system, almost religious, parallel to that of the school missionaries: it preaches, makes conversions, delivers messages, gathers the faithful, resurrects. Its joyous power is such that, like an anti-patio, it even infects Añuco ("he was like a new angel, recently converted"). From the beginning, the zumbayllu appears to be linked as much to magic (it breaks the ordinary categories of time and space, and a strange light descends whenever it appears) as to nature (rivers, trees, flying insects). But more important than all that: this toy that defeats those sent by death (beetles, spiders, and Lleras's monsters) with its ascending motion is an object made by human beings. We are moving (and Ernesto with us) from the natural world to the anthropological and sociocultural universe. Before we hear about the circumstances that introduce the toy, the narrator explains the etymology of its linguistic components, even going as far as to emphasize some Quechua derivations that have no scientific justification in order to suggest the top is an epic and luminous object. He steps outside his persona and becomes an anthropologist explaining everything in the native culture that gives the toy meaning, the entire linguistic structure that lies behind it, all the experiences and perceptions that those words evoke and unfold.

"For me it was a new being, an apparition in a hostile world, a bond that tied me to that hated patio, to that painful valley, to the school." The zumbayllu will force Ernesto to join the world, which means to struggle against old enemies and to discover new allies. Lleras recognizes in the toy implications of values which reject his violence. He intervenes to prevent anybody from selling it to Ernesto, so that the latter will remain isolated and defenseless.

But Antero, its maker, responds by taking a step forward, giving it to him for nothing, thus denying any commercial relationship.

Ernesto begins in this way his association with the life of that valley and with its habits, ceasing to be, albeit minimally, a stranger there. As if they were baptizing him, he suffers a typical rite of initiation. By demonstrating his ability to handle an object made in Abancay ("a natural-born *zumbayllero*") before the mocking children, he can also find happiness, unifying power, solidarity, in something and someone that come from a space until then unilaterally demonized. It is the start of a slow socialization process of the values of the River, as he finds its flow and song inside other generous human beings.

But, in addition, the magical object crystalizes a unity against Lleras, reveals a degree of resistance to his tyranny that from that moment on will go on growing. Ernesto's first act of rebellion, his quiet hatred of Lleras in order to protect that spinning, musical instrument, makes manifest attitudes which until then were hidden in the school and will finally blossom among the people of Abancay in the next chapter. This change of emphasis can be seen in the increasing preponderance of dialogue over subjective narration from this moment on: the weight of his relationship with others (expressed in words) will occupy an ever more important place in the character's life and, therefore, in the version of that life which he offers us, revealing the shift from enclosure to community, from solitude to the search for friends.

Nevertheless, Ernesto's victory is transitory. Añuco and Lleras prepare other assaults. They attack Palacios, the weakest of the students, the only Indian from an *ayllu*, "condemned to the torture of the boarding school." When this had happened before, Palacios had found a defender in Romero. This time it is Ernesto who comes out in the youngster's defense, and that leads him to confront Rondinel, incited by Lleras and Añuco, and later on Valle, who represents a kind of Europeanized pseudo-intellectual, a cold youth, with no feelings, who despises Quechua reality, collaborates in this spreading of hatred. If Lleras is the headless body of the beast, Valle is the head with no apparent body. They are two allies in underdevelopment, two complementary colonized territories, both sensing in Ernesto a formidable rival.

Ernesto is afraid, sure that Rondinel will beat him up. But Valle, mockingly, in order to intimidate Ernesto, has defined the conflict as one between races: the Indian (Ernesto) against the quixotic Spaniard (Rondinel). Ernesto turns the tables on these racist insults that are supposed to shame him: he will gain strength from his chosen race and his adopted religion, commending himself to Apu K'arwarasu, the mountain god, a father who will inspire him in combat.

Simultaneously, Lleras and Añuco attack from another side. The night before the duel between the two adversaries is to take place, they try to terrorize another child, Peluca, with spiders. Those tarantulas, which are terrifying and unsettling in themselves, are by their convulsive movements the symbolic continuation of the "sexual" monsters the children have become. But Lleras's power has diminished. On the one hand, Ernesto dares to warn Peluca that a plan is afoot, and on the other, Chauca, the child who is most desperate in his need for "la opa," is able to forget his guilt and hatred through helping another in need. This is one of Arguedas's basic moral laws: By being generous in offering solidarity to one's neighbor, one's own demons can be overcome.

And this time Ernesto has his zumbayllu and its magical music. The next morning he dances in the place where "la opa," on her back, was incessantly raped and degraded.

Now it is Rondinel who is afraid and who knows that Ernesto will bring him to his knees. But Ernesto need not use Lleras's arms; he must not direct the force of the Apu, the father-mountain, to dominate or control another. He has no desire to revive and spread the hatred and fear that he himself has felt. He controls his passions, offering peace out of the certainty that he is the strongest. From this episode it remains clear that Ernesto has truly grown: he has avoided the temptation to use his own anger or energy to fragment and divide, to cause others to cry. At bottom, what he is rejecting is becoming a petty dictator; he is refusing to grow at someone else's expense or to undo his own traumas by transferring the fear to someone weaker.

In this reconciliation, Ernesto is accompanied by his new friend, Antero, the Mark'aska, the first one to call him "brother."

Antero comes to the reader's attention together with the zumbayllu, and, like it, is surrounded by a magical atmosphere. He is defined as a messenger who brings together diverse mysterious and alternating currents: his hair is blond, but black at the roots; he is white but with freckles (that according to Quechuas reflect a non-solar light); his eyes seem to be, but perhaps are not, dark. This first strange appearance of Candela (as he is also called) contrasts with what will be his later, more gradual characterization. But this birth beneath the sign of mystery, being both dark and light at the same time, tells us that we are confronting someone who lives between two worlds and who can choose either road. Not everything in him is absolutely pure or sunny. Even his hair appears like "certain spiders" (which in the context of this chapter whispers terrible connotations). However, his alliance with Ernesto, which is cemented when the protagonist is able to help him communicate with the girl he loves (his queen) and as they exchange services and gifts, seems quite solid. Their union is based on three facets or aspects; as these crumble, so will their brotherhood. In the first place, the zumbayllu, which brought them together, symbolizes the ability that both of them have to perceive and to belong to the world of magic, childhood and Indian culture. The fact that they slowly come to understand solidarity in different ways will undermine this accord. In the second place, both of them are anti-Lleras, and therefore opposed to the unhealthy, criminal, cruel, and abusive violence he represents. In this they will continue to be united as long as Lleras remains undefeated. Finally, they share the same romantic, adoring attitude toward women. This will also be subjected to the wear and tear of growth, and will, in the end, lead to a definitive break between them.

The difference between the boys can be seen in the next chapter, "El Motín." Ernesto has hardly rejected the possibility of fighting with one of his schoolmates, when, almost immediately, another form of struggle appears, a much more open and directly social form of violence, that confronts the causes of the unjust condition of the world. The rivers, the mountain, even the zumbayllu, reinforce Ernesto's moral code and enable him to survive, keeping his hopes barely alive, but that is not enough: he must now go out into the world, outside the walls of the school. The rebellion of a group of *chicha* brewers, who distribute the salt stolen by the hacienda and challenge the spiritual director of the town, Father Linares, will provide the occasion for Ernesto to discover in Abancay itself other forces for solidarity, while at the same time suggesting his distance from Antero.

Both of them participate in the first step of the revolt. Ernesto becomes enthusiastic and feels like fighting, "advancing against someone," joining the chorus of the people's shouts. Antero, on the other hand, has defined his participation as a mere prank, something like a knight-errant's adventure. He doesn't understand Ernesto's conduct, "What's the matter with you?" he asks, and: "Who do you hate?" thus rejecting any complicity with the deep motives of the conflict, that is, the struggle against injustice. He wants to drag Ernesto away from that mob (not understanding that Ernesto has always been, by definition, outside the circle, always a passive spectator, and that it is truly transcendent that he be inside something, whatever it is), and finally deserts him. Besides having to take care of himself for his girlfriend and being tired of the game, he gives another reason, one which is social and racist in nature: "It's ugly walking with so many *cholas* (that is, lower-class women)." The way in which the narrator marks the physical moment of their separation underscores resonances that are not secondary: "He made his way through, *crouching*. I *advanced further*." (My emphasis.) The first incident outside the school propels them, at first subtly, later furiously, in different directions.

When they come together again, at the end of the chapter, Ernesto has now accompanied the rebellious women in a visit to the "colonos," has finally broken through the barrier of the hacienda, and has danced along the valley's roadways in a victorious march. These acts precede and explain the first discrepancies between them.

At the beginning of their conversation, it's nothing serious: merely opposing interpretations of the color of the eyes of Salvinia (the girl Antero loves), which can be defined with respect to the zumbayllu (Ernesto) or with respect to the hacienda's water (Antero). In this attempt to situate the woman's eyes in one or the other semantic field, the seed of the opposition that will divide them as the novel unfolds is planted. For the first time, Antero ceases being a kind of providential, angelic protector, maker of miraculous objects, and takes on a precise socio-economic outline. He places himself socially as the son of a landowner, and he brings his girlfriend not into the magical world of Indian and Andean camaraderie that forges the marvelous *yllu*, but rather into the world of submissive, superstitious, and terrorized Indians. At best, he admits the color "is also like the zumbayllu." An accidental connection.

His place in the cosmos of the "hacienda" will be increasingly accentuated in the course of the conversation. Antero understands the use of violence in an individual sense, for instance, to aid and defend his girlfriend from eventual rivals. But his courage, daring, and lack of fear are lessened by Ernesto having just had his first experience of another kind of violence, social violence, offered up to him by the women led by a doña Felipa dedicated to the struggle against inequality. It doesn't surprise us that Antero sees himself on horseback ("He would make him paw the air with his front hooves; with one blow to the chest he would knock his opponent down"), in terms which are almost symmetrical with those used to describe the landowners of Abancay some seventy pages earlier and used by the conquistadores four hundred years ago. Finally, he affirms, almost in passing, that women must be made *to cry*. This statement, which at first glance might seem insignificant, is central. Throughout the novel, making someone cry is equivalent to terrorizing and belittling. Crying is what the "colonos" and the pongos do, who are treated like children. Crying is what each boarding student does, when he is in an agony of fear, or knuckling under to Lleras's whims, or to the insanity of his own inhibited sexuality. Crying is what the Principal wants all the Indians and children to do; it is what the cathedral in Cuzco imposes upon their hearts. Therefore, making a woman cry is a way of affirming her in her role of passive object, a marginal being, subordinate to men, a mere instrument of their pleasure or prestige.

We shouldn't be surprised, then, that the chapter ends with Ernesto's affirmation that he didn't know Mark'aska well ("He no longer seemed like a student; as he spoke, his face hardened, matured . . . Where was the happy, skillful schoolmate, who had been the zumbayllu champion?").

Antero is the legatee of the social class that is responsible for all the misery and dehumanization in that world ("a small landowner, generous, full of ambition, feared by his Indians"). For him, growing and maturing are synonymous with betraying the zumbayllu and its message. In order to preserve those values sensed during his childhood, he would have to break with his father, with his origin, with his class, and with his future. Ernesto would like to be a zumbayllu turned into an adult human being, which means turning the violence back against the powerful and demanding a better world, a real earthquake in social relations, possibly a revolution. Antero does not feel abandoned. He is not, like Ernesto, in an intermediate position, a mestizo, caught between the points of conflict or social confluence, having to choose at each and every moment. Antero does not choose his destiny so much as follow it. Unlike Ernesto, he has no reason to test and feel out the validity of his roots in each one of the many concentric circles of which that society is formed.

Therefore, this brother of Ernesto's, who at first appears as a supernatural entity, outside of time and space, far from any social concretion, will become more social and more concrete as the novel progresses, impelling the narrator to judge him from his own new perspectives.

This process (moving from the magical to the precise social configuration) is the opposite of the road followed by doña Felipa, the gigantic figure who dominates the rebellion and who, while starting out as someone who is part of a clearly established multitude, will end up becoming a legend with the passage of time, a figure whose name and memory radiate solidarity with the weak.

Although the symbolic sense of that rebellion will only be measured later, it is clear that we are dealing with a categorical rejection of a society where animals have greater value than human beings (the salt has been sold for the cows on the estate and not for the Indians), and where the ones who are really stealing are the great landowners, not the *chicheras* who seek to redress that injustice.

But more important than all this, perhaps, is the way in which that first movement toward the social struggles is expressed in the novel: it is the dispossessed who rise up, and they do it in Quechua, in a joyous manner, well-disciplined, collective, and orderly. This will mark Ernesto.

It will be the first time that anyone has defied the Principal and placed his moral authority in doubt. He has monopolized the use of God and his word (the curse) to safeguard the established system of land ownership. Doña Felipa, in contesting the right of the church to judge who is a thief and who is damned, makes the priest's complicity evident.

But in addition, Ernesto comments on the order in which the salt is distributed: "Why didn't they scratch each other in the yard of the salt warehouse? Why didn't they insult and destroy each other shouting?" The chicha makers, then, establish an absolute harmony which is antagonistic to the insanity that reigns in the other patio, so nearby in space, where it is precisely a woman who is darkly violated. The women do not distribute the salt in the same way the boys share "la opa." From doña Felipa "there arose an organizing power that folded everyone in, that put an end to fear and drove it out." It is the first, but not the last, opportunity in which a parallel between doña Felipa and the crazy woman will be hinted at: one a woman who leads, elevates, orders, and the other, passive in the extreme, who drives the students to animal-like behavior.

This characteristic of the chicha maker doña Felipa has its logical continuation in her action: she does not forget the colonos, "the defenseless, the 'poor' of Patimbamba." It is not just a question of fulfilling her function as the Great Mother who distributes goods, but also that she must sense her rebellion is condemned to be ephemeral if it has no support among the majority, those who, if set in motion, could shake the entire social structure. Thence her mythic and prophetic dimension, the probable epic which she gestates and announces: the values in whose name she rebels are represented potentially by vast armies of the dispossessed and the marginal.

The future society that this and every rebellion foreshadows is expressed in that same moment in the march toward Patimbamba ("an immense joy and a desire to fight, even if it was against the entire world"). This matter of dancing toward the hacienda could not be more significant. The previous chapter had ended with Ernesto's solitary dance, driven by the zumbayllu, in the very spot where a woman had been violated. Now he is dancing along with other women, all on foot, wanting to restore to people as lowly as "la opa" the salt that has been stolen from them.

This discovery of forces in the world that are equal to his inner dreams and that, when pushed to their social culmination, would put an end to injustice, quickly clashes with the reaction of the authorities: the salt will be returned to the landowners, the Indians will cry, the chicha maker will have to flee, and Ernesto feels himself drawn back to the ice and the heat of his worst moments in the school patio ("I walked along in silence. The world was never sadder; hardened, hopeless, sunken into my innards like a frozen grief"). As always when things get hard, Ernesto prays for his father to come to the rescue—with no reply. The rebellion erupted in the exact middle of the novel. And beginning with

that commotion in the external world that is the (de) generator
of the school and of his own poverty and guilt, Ernesto leaps to
another dynamic in his development. On the one hand, he must
judge, confront, and criticize other characters (the process that
was initiated with Antero). On the other, without ceasing to con-
voke male models, the substitute fathers who could encourage him
in his quest, he will gradually discover the human values in other
people, generally those from the lowest and most repressed strata.
Finally, as if the social rebellion were the signal, profound changes
begin to occur in the school itself. It is a step toward definitions
and extensions of liberation, a step in which the groups in conflict
prepare and separate, and at the same time extend themselves. Who
are the dominant ones and what are they like? Who are the dominated, what are they like, and how are they dominated? Ernesto
can distance himself from the first group or he can witness the
gradual or sudden insurrection among the second that will change
sadness into an epic struggle, the multiple and plural insurrection
he may be able, someday, to call his own.

Definitions

Almost as an echo of doña Felipa's voice, what happens next
in the school is the expulsion of Lleras and a radical change in
Añuco. Lleras flees toward Cuzco after having beaten and insulted
Brother Miguel (who is defined as a true guardian for the children,
a saint who says "yes" when others say "no," one who recognizes
the value of the zumbayllu, and who comforts the boys), for reasons that are fundamentally racist ("he is black").

Lleras leaves Abancay two hours before the troops arrive, from
Cuzco precisely, to patrol the area after the rebellion. One could
almost deduce a kind of substitution: institutionalized, military
violence arrives, while the violence we have called horizontal disappears. This change coincides with an ever greater narrative emphasis upon Abancay and a reduction of the conflicts in the school.
In fact, the school occupies less and less space until it finally disappears, even physically, at the end of the book.

The elimination of Lleras seems to inaugurate a new epoch for
the school, expressed primarily in Añuco's profound transformation. When he finds himself without a protector, "suddenly dis-
armed," Brother Miguel, Palacios, Ernesto, and others incorpo-

rate him into a world of solidarity and affection. It is now Añuco who has been left outside the circle, a stranger, like Ernesto when he first appeared there. The children will not be vengeful with him. This is symbolized by a gift from Ernesto: a zumbayllu *layka* (that is, marginal, bewitched, reprobate), the most precious thing he owned (through which he believes he can send messages to his faraway father) and precisely one which would not be shown either to Lleras or to Añuco. The dialogue between the two indicates how far they have come:

"Shall we make it dance, Añuco? Shall we defend it if somebody tries to step on it?"

"Who would want to step on it?" he said.

"Let's go then! Let's go, *brother*." (My emphasis.)

Even Valle, Lleras's intellectual accomplice, allows himself to be convinced by the beauty of the zumbayllu, calling it a "graceful instrument" and begging them to make it dance again.

But that harmony is as transitory as the children's unity. Expelling Lleras from the inferno does not resolve the central dilemma: it is still an inferno, and the influence of the corruptor, real and symbolic, persists. Lleras may be condemned and damned (words that are generously applied to him until the end of the novel), the satanic qualities of Abancay fully incarnated in his pride; he may be seen as emanating the worst violence and sex of the repressed world; and the boys may exult imagining him far away, rotting. But all that is, ultimately, a fantasized comfort. The contaminating center remains in the oppressive structure of the social world; the evils that he exaggerated continue to rule and direct the human destinies in that valley.

Añuco therefore will be lost. The priests will not allow him to stay among the other children, the only ones who could have saved him. He will be sent to a convent in Cuzco, where he will be shut in to go on feeding the religious institution, living like another Brother Miguel. To grow he would need his new friends. To deny him that collaboration is to suppress light, air, and purification. He is described, shortly before he departs with Brother Miguel (who is also expelled), as unequivocally "dead." Those first signs of an agony, reiterated obsessively by the narrator,[19] not only push Añuco in the direction of descent (always downward), but also foreshadow the plague that will end up invading Abancay.

On the other hand, in parallel fashion, the one who does change and gradually saves herself is "la opa." Her last appearance had been the night before the rebellion when Lleras and Añuco plotted the tarantula attack. Now when she appears in the school patio the children pay no attention to her and go on playing carnival music ("This is fighting music."). When Peluca made his fleeting attempt to rape her, "she resisted" and immediately escaped. And Romero defends her. What has happened in the meantime is doña Felipa's uprising and Lleras's departure. Between them, the two incidents come together to open around "la opa" a space for movement and growth.

Just as Lleras has left his mythical curse behind in the city, doña Felipa has also undergone a similar evolution. After crossing the bridge and the river (and not in the direction of Cuzco), she changes into a legend, someone who is talked about and gives rise to reports, rumors, whisperings. Despite the fact that the soldiers try to degrade the chicha makers sexually ("These women should be on their backs, or with their behinds bare"), her power will go on growing in the popular imagination. Ernesto himself, with his zumbayllu, tries to protect the rebel, especially her body, so that she won't have to endure the sufferings reserved for that other woman, "la opa": "Perhaps they wouldn't be able to find her body. That was important, he thought. What wouldn't the police do, driven to a fury in the face of that wounded, hated and deformed body?" The story of her flight, miraculous and daring, soon makes her the talk of the town. Told by many, her story assumes a dimension of inextinguishable rebellion, becoming a fiery symbol in their daily life. Whenever they imagine doña Felipa returning to Abancay to burn it down bringing a ritual purification by fire from the jungle, the children enjoy thinking at the same time about Lleras being punished, melted by a merciless sun, crying ceaselessly to the mountaintops, begging for help, teeth chattering. "And no one, *not even his mother,* would forgive him now." (My emphasis.) This ardent, oral condemnation, in which the Indian, Palacios, outdoes everyone else, is a conversion that is just as mythic as the one suffered by doña Felipa. But instead of being elevated toward a memorable epic, Lleras sinks into his black legend, preparing his ultimate transformation into a legendary animal of evil, his final journey to the land of the dead, his identification with the plague.

Thus, although they both disappear from Abancay at the same time, departing in opposite directions, doña Felipa and Lleras continue influencing events. If Lleras's unhealthy violence has infected Añuco, dragging him down to condemnation, doña Felipa's heroic violence will gravitate over "la opa," raising her up from her enslaved condition.

Ernesto will be a witness to the exact moment when that transmutation occurs, and it mysteriously and symmetrically coincides with the hidden moment of the plague's arrival in the valley. Father Augusto and "la opa" bring typhus from the haciendas on the other side of the bridge. But she stays behind to rescue the shawl that doña Felipa had left hanging on a stone cross and which, until that moment, no one had been able to remove. This shawl is as orange as the polluted sunsets that followed her violations.

"La opa" carries out a truly epic deed. She climbs up, ascending in the direction that heretofore had been denied her. If, with this deed, the crazy woman is not magically converted into doña Felipa, she at least sets out on the road to that woman who is her opposite and perhaps her alter ego. At first, Ernesto does not understand what he is witnessing; he would like to fix the shawl in the past (always his temptation); he believes that it is a sacrilegious act that sullies the heroine. But later he understands the profoundly liberating sense of that act, when he sees "la opa" mooing happily, calling for "Father Augusto or perhaps Lleras." That act of climbing a sacred pole (a cross), above a raging river that drenches her, where no one else has dared to go, can be interpreted as a process of baptism, rebirth, an archetypal journey to the center of the universe.[20] And based upon this, Ernesto changes his relationship with the river, placing that experience in its adequate epic context: "You are like the river," he announces to the absent doña Felipa, giving a social and not a subjective sense to the enchanted waters. It's not necessary to be like the river; one can imitate real, larger-than-life people who are themselves already like the river. The river no longer isolates Ernesto from the world, and much less from "la opa."

The disappearance of Lleras, the magnificent legend of doña Felipa, and the ceremony that marks "la opa's" dawn, are interwoven to form the backdrop which allows Ernesto to change his attitude toward two male characters, his superiors in age and strength, who could have fulfilled the role of model and champion: the Principal and Antero.

Ernesto has always had ambiguous dreams with relation to the Principal. Much earlier than the period we are commenting on, he imagined him in a double vision: as a fish devouring small people (Indians, students, marginal beings) and as a father substitute reminding him of Maywa, "the Indian I loved most, hugging me against his chest at the edge of the great corn fields". Even though, as the book develops (and the narrator as well), the more negative perspective predominates, the Principal will always maintain a somber silhouette, correlative to a tormented inner life. In any case, learning to unmask this patriarch, this "santo varón," is to distance himself from Gabriel's interpretation of that ideological guardian of power.

After the rebellion, the Principal will adopt a more active role, which will make clear to the reader, and Ernesto, his true and hidden motives.

First of all, with respect to Ernesto himself. When the children had problems (terrible fights, masturbations and rapes, flagellations), he never intervened to prevent them. When a child *causes* a problem, he is instantly present to punish and repress. The first time Ernesto connects with him is to be whipped, to bend over (always a downward direction), so that the Principal can once again subjugate that which had escaped him. Even though those prayers and the punishment do not alter the protagonist's inner conviction, their result is evident: they serve to *belittle* that self which had grown big (become a man) in the liberating march.

In the second place, Father Linares treats the Indians who received the salt in the same way he treats Ernesto: he makes them cry and suffer "with the most beautiful words," thus prolonging the painful darkness of Cuzco.

And he also deals hypocritically with Brother Miguel. The Principal had punished Ernesto for joining the demon-possessed chicha makers, who affronted him. But when Brother Miguel punishes Lleras (no less!) for having insulted him as a man of God, the Principal reprimands the Brother, arrogating only to himself the representation of divinity. The parallelism between the two situations (two youths who rebel, one out of a desire for justice, the

other out of hunger for power; two punishments, one which succeeds in belittling, the other that fails to educate the violent one
but rather makes him run away) allows us to judge the incoher-
ence of the spiritual leader of that community. Within a short time,
Ernesto begins to insinuate a possible closeness between the Principal and El Viejo (the reception room "looked like El Viejo's . . .
I felt suddenly humiliated inside there").

Ernesto, of course, still needs to be protected. On two occasions
the Principal demonstrates his desire to help him by means of a
gesture: "The Father rested his hand on my shoulder, as if to protect me" and "He wrapped his arm around my neck." And the one
who will be described with similar words ("He wrapped one of
his arms around my neck," ten pages further on), is Antero. This
attitude underscores the paternalism of his friend, who, like the
Principal, treats Ernesto like somebody sick, delirious, and imma-
ture. Antero feels superior, because he is evolving toward the landowner who is his father, coming closer and closer to the world that
is inescapably that of El Viejo. Becoming a man, for both Ernesto
and Antero, means fulfilling a code of "manhood," of honesty and
decency, in the face of traitors like Lleras. But that definition is
insufficient for Ernesto, because it excludes the Indians and their
values (which we will call "maternal"). The Indians that Antero
knows in that valley and in the family hacienda are "crybabies,"
"sissies," "orphans" who "go about on their knees." They do not
constitute any possible model for an adolescent who wants to leave
his childhood behind. Ernesto places his own Indian protectors,
who are adults capable of pointing him in a responsible future direction, in opposition to these "babies" because he can't conceive
of being a man and forgetting them or not rescuing those others,
the ones who put "their mouths to the ground and weep . . . day
and night."

While Antero was a child, that is, while he was playing the role
of son, he was allowed to sympathize with those poor creatures.
"It's sad. And hearing them, you also wanted to cry like them;
I've done it, brother, when I was little. I don't even know what
I needed to be consoled for, but I cried for consolation, and not
even my mother, with her arms, could calm me." And also: "When
you're a child and you hear someone crying like that, when you
hear grown-ups crying, all together like an endless night, it tears

at your heart." But as he grew up, he had two patterns of conduct before him: he could cry like his mother or use the whip like his father ("My mother suffers for them; but my father has to carry out his responsibility"). Antero will follow the model of his land-owner father; he will be the Boss and not the Sufferer; he will pull the trigger instead of healing the wound; he will make others cry in order not to lament nor be overwhelmed himself. Growing up for that adolescent means causing others to suffer, becoming hard, in contrast to his mother, being a man and not a "woman": What can we do, kid? That's the way of the world.

But Antero, with his attachment to that social, vertical violence, gnaws at and assaults the foundation that would allow Ernesto to develop. Those beings whose maturation and transformation into a vast adult people, into heroic and not whining Indians, should accompany and generate the narrator-protagonist's pas-sage toward liberation (individual and collective), are treated like children and made to cry by Antero. The Indian-adults are capable of the greatest epic deeds, the basis for all volcanic and creative action: the transformation of sadness into struggle, of suffering into hope.[21] Antero, faithful to his class, which lives by converting the suffering of others into its own power and wealth ("The Indi-ans have to be kept in subjugation. You can't understand, because you're not a landowner"), establishes a definitive break between child and adult. Only women, who have, according to Antero, no reason *to take action in the world,* can afford the luxury of compas-sion.

The dominant class, therefore, wants to enclose the Indians in a childhood from which they will never escape, and correla-tively tries to make the children either dominators, like them-selves, (landowners, machos, soldiers, and priests), or subjects (like Añuco and the Indians) or marginal people (like Gabriel).

The deterioration of the relationship between the two friends, children of the River (but unalike in their interpretations of its qualities[22]), will be irrevocable. This process is marked externally by the changes in the way in which Ernesto refers to his com-panion: first as Mark'aska, later Candela, finally Antero—from the intimate and magical (Quechua), to the public and school-related (an affectionate nickname in Spanish) to his father's surname (the way it will someday be established legally).

More Walls and Expansions

All these changes in the characters take place in the two chapters that follow the rebellion ("Quebrada Honda" and "Cal y Canto"). The hesitant slowness with which the changes work themselves out contrasts with the speed that will overtake events as we approach the novel's denouement, preparing the reader for social and cosmic conflict. In the last two chapters of the book the plague and the rebelling Indians culminate and summarize the forces and tendencies in conflict in the months and pages that precede it.

The definitive break with Antero, which has been foreshadowed for us, is the most important of the transformations in the narrator's life and behavior. It is only when Ernesto returns the zumbayllu to his former friend, only when he can now see in it the demonic color yellow, that it will be possible for the plague, which has been incubating for weeks, to suddenly, like a deformed echo in a mirror, find the power to explode into visibility.

Their confrontation will take place around another definition of a "man," the last area of agreement that Ernesto and Antero shared. It is man as a sexual organism, the opposite of woman, the male who propagates the species, in contrast to those virginal beings who have not been initiated nor had any experience. The one who precipitates this falling out is Gerardo, the son of the colonel who is in charge of the regiment that has just arrived in Abancay, and who will substitute for Lleras (in the affection of the Principal, in sports events, and in leadership). But Gerardo, in contrast to his predecessor, does not abuse the other children ("He was happy and generous with the little ones"); he does not exercise an unhealthy, horizontal violence. The way in which Gerardo and Antero meet crystalizes this "nobility" of the new arrival (the word indicating both individual virtues and social advantages acquired by birth). Antero, possessed by the rage against the military that Ernesto has transmitted to him, challenges and insults Gerardo's brother, but Gerardo establishes between the two of them a chivalric code of honor, a series of rules that should not be infringed in the way Lleras had. From then on, they are to be inseparable, and Ernesto will be relegated to the sub-world of the younger children, thus marking the difference in age. Antero, "a grown-up puppy" confirms with Gerardo's presence that adult life

is a perpetual struggle which contrasts with the harmony of childhood, and that this struggle between equals should be governed
by minimal norms of honor, just as the struggle between those
who are superior and those who are inferior is governed by norms
of firm domination and paternalistic support. And "men" can recognize each other by their capacity to explore the pathways of sex,
disputing or sharing women, bragging to each other about their
conquests.

Throughout the novel, Ernesto has populated his dreams and
his failures with ideal women, the apex of an almost medieval and
courtly religion of love: with blond hair, pale skin, and blue eyes,
they are the counterpoint to his father's physical appearance. They
belong to Gabriel's "raza." These women are a priori unreachable;
they must be revered from afar, as above mundane vicissitudes and
wretchedness. They are myths, offering salvation by their mere
existence, untouched by the reigning filth and degradation that
Ernesto has encountered in his journeys and in the schoolyard.
Ernesto will never put to the test the sacred space that this type
of women offer him. Each time he tries to make contact with one
of them, who is flesh and blood, some external event or internal
crisis intervenes to prevent it: the suffering of another person dis-
tracts him; he perceives the painful distance between his idealized
memory and the concrete person (for example, noticing Alcira's
panties), and he runs away from the relationship; in spite of himself, he realizes the real attraction that women of another racial
appearance have (Indian women who correspond to the poetic
Quechua language which he uses to write "lyrical" letters for Antero). The ease with which such events keep him from confronting
what a woman means is symptomatic of a blind and deaf point
in Ernesto. Until the end, he stubbornly persists in defending,
sanctifying, and rescuing the pure female image, believing that if
he weakens in that enterprise, he is condemning women to the
ground on which "la opa" wallowed, to suffering sexual aggression.

Ernesto never overcomes this impossibility to enter into a normal relationship with a member of the opposite sex in *Deep Rivers*,
and one may conjecture that behind this impossibility lie the traumas that would continue to complicate the life of the author
himself. In any case, it was a theme which Arguedas preferred

to sidestep or, at least, not to make explicit.[23] Love's object was divided into two spheres which did not touch each other at all, a mutual and antagonistic sublimation of noncommunicating vessels: women are either like "la opa," suffering and grotesque, or like any of so many pale, redeeming ladies who populate his stories and other novels.[24] Even if this dichotomy can be traced to Arguedas's wrenching experiences during his own puberty,[25] it is remarkable that in a novel about how a child becomes an adult the author is unable to deal with the problem of how to communicate with those who are to be life companions, the mothers of future children.

The concept of femininity which Ernesto embraces does not change in the novel from beginning to end.[26] In contrast to the values of solidarity which he has learned from his Indian guardians and which have been strengthened through his contacts, both with human beings and with nature, the contradictory deification of woman will be neither confirmed nor denied at any time. Perhaps this is an indirect way of admitting that the foundations of that attitude have neither the strength nor the indispensable flexibility to survive if challenged in the future.

Ernesto's reaction, then, as he faces the arrival of the military (and their offspring), will be virulent. His ideal, perfect, immaculate women, who form his last link with Antero, will be taken advantage of by the soldiers and introduced to a world which he does not understand and which he defines as a "disguised" universe, as Cornejo Polar has noted. From now on, and before his astonished and pain-filled eyes, those women will become a part of the world of the oppressor, who comes and goes and lives and wins in order to kill and to conquer. Just as in society they impose order from above, so in love the men will prefer egotistical pleasure to the law Ernesto has tentatively established as the basis of his values and morality, the law that one should live to avoid causing pain to others. The military make the women weep, make them suffer, and in that way limit their possibilities for salvation or liberation. Through sex and deceit, women are turned into creatures like the "opas" or the pongos or the boarding students, robbed of the virtue of representing ideal celestial clouds and brought down to earth or to bed.

Gerardo teaches Antero that women must be punished, and

concretely that Salvinia must be enclosed within a wall. She must be dealt with just as the hacienda deals with the Indians, that is, not allowed to grow. Male adolescents must learn to do with females exactly what is done with children, Indians, peoples, and countries: frighten them into submission, overdevelop themselves at the women's expense.

Ernesto has dreamed of and prayed for a Bringer of Justice, someone to bring order to the chaos of the school. Earlier Gerardo would have surpassed his expectations. Together they could have set up an anti-Lleras student body. ("He was a strong and happy boy. He laughed with those who were excluded"). Gerardo's sincerity and honor are undeniable: despite the fact that Ernesto insulted him publicly, even going so far as to kick him, the commander's son will charge a sergeant with taking care of Ernesto during the plague. But Ernesto is no longer the person he was. He now senses that the school's problems stem from causes that go much deeper, located outside the school's walls. The struggle between the haves and have-nots has gone too far and the narrator has chosen the side of the colonos, doña Felipa and the poor, who are repressed by the army, commanded by Gerardo's father. At the same time, the newcomer represents the world of the coast which is attempting to culturally subjugate the Andean peoples, treating them as mental defectives and orphans. Even Romero, who plays wonderful native music, lets himself be guided and controlled by Gerardo.

So it is that Ernesto fights with Antero, the one who had come to his aid and linked him to Abancay during the hard times. Confronted by Antero's desire to postpone that break (he tries to turn Ernesto into a child again), Ernesto himself has no choice but to return the zumbayllu which had sealed their pact of friendship. For one instant that desperate act produces an effect, taking Antero back to "the pure water of their first days." It's as if time had not passed: "his face grew more beautiful, bathed from deep within by the light of childhood that was reborn in him. Whatever there was of cynicism, of animality, in his lips, disappeared." But it is only a temporary spark that soon burns out: they have grown in opposite directions. There is no longer anything to unite them. Gerardo and Antero are dirty and yellow ("I saw them, tall and robust, yellow in color"); they are "the devil's stepsons," condemned like Lleras or Peluca.

To Antero, Ernesto's motives are incomprehensible and perhaps ambiguous. It is true, no doubt, that Antero has now let his body be governed by his most primeval instincts. But it is equally true that Ernesto rejects his ex-friend's formula because he is afraid to grow, afraid to confront the contradictions and the authentic pain of the relationship between the masculine and the feminine. During his travels and in Abancay, the redeeming and distant women have been the only ones Ernesto could free from the meanness, sexual as well as social, that permeates and fills that universe. Unlike the case of the comuneros, his intransigent loyalty to them is not based on objective and historically provable situations, but rather expresses a desire to somehow and somewhere preserve ahistorical goddesses who redeem and inspire. But the goddesses are human beings, and they require an approach as flexible and as subtle as that required by men. Perhaps it is too much to ask of Ernesto to carry out all the battles at the same time. Perhaps, in order to cleanse the social world, he needs to preserve an enclave of redemptive imagination which does not obey the same merciless laws of reality and war. Perhaps. Nevertheless, it remains clear throughout the work of José María Arguedas that this exclusion of woman from the story, her condition as victim or as consoling mother but rarely as protagonist (doña Felipa is the only fleeting exception, and she is quickly made legendary), blocks out from liberation the area of relationships between the sexes. Though this is not the place to explore the problem at length, it is worthwhile to note that the novelist, like Ernesto, will carry this ambiguity with him, unable (rather than unwilling) to confront the swampland of its possible resolution. Arguedas does not subscribe to the reigning "macho" concept, but many of his valiant landowners (whom he does not entirely condemn), define themselves in terms of the rejection of any conduct that they (and the social code) attribute to women. Don Bruno in *All the Bloods* is a good example of this position, and Antero had already said that "outside of Romero and Lleras, it's as if the other children had been born sissies" which is almost identical to remarks made by don Julián, the landowner in *Yawar Fiesta* who distinguishes himself from the other men, those who in cowardly fashion submit to the mean authority of the Subprefect: "I won't be a part of women's nonsense." Arguedas tried to find some other basis for courage, being one of the first Latin American writers to deal with the very difficult relationship between tenderness and masculinity, between femininity and strength, taboo themes in our social structures and among the men of the continent, including those on the left. In any case, it is notable that in *Deep Rivers*, while the protagonist is constantly searching for adult, male companionship, it is two women, doña Felipa and "la opa," who represent two extreme opposite poles and allies in an insurrection that is long overdue. This unresolved tension cannot be understood only in psychological terms. We are not dealing just with the presence (or absence) of the mother or of women in Arguedas's work, but rather with the general problem of the feminine in Latin American culture and society.

In any case, with respect to *Deep Rivers*, we can say that this attitude of the protagonist is consistent with Ernesto's deepest character, and it is not just his passive adoration of women that demonstrates it. As we have already affirmed several times, Ernesto is "outside the circle"; he is a spectator who tends to isolate himself from the world, establishing an oblique dialogue with it, allowing certain actions or people to act tangentially upon his intensely subjective world. Faced with a reality formed of similar and virtually parallel experiences, metaphors which duplicate our condition or refute it, Ernesto's tactic for growth is to enter into secret contact with those close or distant currents where he can recognize, express, and accompany himself. The influence of certain events or human beings is verified indirectly, through mysterious means and methods. Each river which forms and crosses us is also a bridge, connecting us with others, a multiple bridge, like a star, crossing other people's sky and earth without their realizing it, but nonetheless shaping their destiny. This is true to such an extent that Ernesto will, in fact, never have exchanged a word with those who weigh most heavily upon his life and who decide, from their own autonomous passing, the protagonist's fate: the colonos, doña Felipa, "la opa," Papacha Oblitas (a wandering musician of whom we shall speak later); all of them pass through his life, profoundly moving it, without even knowing of his existence, without having engaged him even in a conversation.

Thus, the infectious nature of both evil and good act upon the child much as nature does, like a magical current. But we are not, as is generally repeated, dealing here only with a magical-moral contagion of nature acting on the human being (Ernesto's relationship with the River, the mountain, certain birds, or colors, or trees), but rather with a human being who acts and moves toward another. Each life, then, is a deep river which leads to or obstructs others. Ernesto is the meeting point, as narrator and as protagonist, of all those intersecting lives. Thus, the tender, distant style of *Deep Rivers* is not arbitrary. It expresses perfectly this being who both observes and empathizes, his urgency to see things personally and yet shared in some collective gaze. Perhaps the narrative voice of the protagonist, which is a product of the maturity of the author, has resolved what Ernesto still cannot get a hold of in his personal life: a vibrant unity that fluctuates between the lyrical and the epic, between the subjective and the objective.[27]

This process by which Ernesto makes contact with others is the key to his strength as well as to his fragility. In order to take action himself, he witnesses others taking action in the world, being able to identify with them or rejecting their behavior, and subjectifying or incorporating into his own private world those reverberating actions in order to give them a meaning. In the long run, this means that Ernesto is possessed by the tendency (or the aptitude, if you will) to *mythicize*. He submits almost all the other characters to this process, from Antero to Lleras, changing them into legends or symbols or projections of his own internal contradictions. He can relate more easily to myths (the hidden controllers of social or psychological phenomena) than to ordinary, concrete, honest-to-goodness human beings. Or can it be that the world is so constituted, with such fatal instability, that not one of his allies can *remain* at his side, that every ally is inevitably transitory, and that the only way to continue a dialogue with them is by setting them up as myths, establishing an influence of shadow and legend, breaking down the categories of rational classification in order to retain them?

Mythification seems on the one hand to be a defense of the psyche and on the other a dynamic which succeeds in internalizing and preserving the positive (and negative) actions of others in a world which is fragmented, confusing, and multifaceted. The conversion of the other into a word, which can be held on to, or into an overflowing image, at least guarantees the overcoming of the protagonist's isolation and permits the entry of others into the sanctuary of his conscience. Given his sensitivity, Ernesto has taken the only pathway that satisfies his desire to be a breeding ground of contacts with other human beings, even with those with whom he has never exchanged a word: this method allows him not only to incorporate and retain them in his world, but also presses his own trajectory to depend upon the direction that others will adopt. These currents of sympathy with others can be explained by the magical-natural roots of the Andean world, but I believe that they go far beyond that origin in their consequences. We are dealing rather with an entire theory of social interaction, attempting to determine the intersection where the individual as a social being can link himself to others, who are equally broken, in a vast and hostile universe, in other words, the manner in which one's internal struggle becomes a problem of the group and vice versa. Linked to others by secret passageways and messengers, the narrator is a sounding board for the world's actions, whether they be sympathetic or marked by hatred. The fact that *Deep Rivers* is narrated in the first person is no accident, nor does such a perspective constitute a drastic limitation on the knowledge that we will obtain (as might be supposed, for example, if we were to mechanically apply the categories established by Henry James and Percy Lubbock regarding point of view as the lens of a camera[28]). To narrate, for Ernesto, is consubstantial with his quest for a permanent residence. He must testify and accompany from his observation point; he must register and ripple with whatever is happening in a world which wants him to be indifferent and dominating. Others are not strangers. Rather, they portray the dilemmas and the developments that Ernesto himself suffers. They push aside his doubts and strengthen his options. There is one act, therefore, which, while being testimonial, is not passive. It is the aesthetic act. We might almost say that what Ernesto is searching for is an authentic language, a language which can serve as a coherent foundation for his existence, a language which potentially incorporates all interlocutors and receptors and guarantees a community and a communication, a language which functions as an act of social prophecy.

The process of criticizing Antero and the Principal stems from Ernesto's gradual awareness that, dissonant and inharmonious, they do not form a part of his community. At the same time, we have said, he is searching for, and finds, other human beings with whom he finds a surprising harmony, sensing how they broaden the meaning and the dimensions of the laws of solidarity which Ernesto has discovered, both inside and outside himself. We should not be surprised, therefore, that when this search, and this encounter, blossom in the next to the last chapter, "Yawar Mayu," they are linked to music and to dance as forms of human interconnectedness. This is expressed thematically: there is some musical expression associated with each positive incident. But it is more than that. It is that music, by the way in which it makes contact above and beyond verbalization, by the way in which it joins and penetrates and transcends and structures, is the artistic expression which, by definition, is best able to spin the secret web which will unite the dispersed and unknown fragments that lie from time to time in Ernesto's pathway, subreptitiously encouraging him in his journey to maturity.

The events of which we speak are condensed into a single day, the same day that Añuco leaves for Cuzco, the day after the protest. The military band is playing in the square and the children are enthusiastically strutting along behind. But Ernesto "could not be infected with that innocent joy." Even when Palacios comes upon Prudencio in the band, an Indian soldier from his village, a guardian and protector that Palacios has not lost, he remains outside, excluded, forgotten, conscious of his own abandonment.

Nevertheless, juxtaposed to the music of Palacios, as he goes to a *chichería,* he will come upon not one, but two musicians, who will be substitute fathers and models.

The first, a singer of songs dedicated to the Virgin Mary, is called Gabriel, like his father, and also like his father, is a pilgrim, has blue eyes, and a blond beard. Ernesto saw him sometime many years before. We witness the child's meeting with a small zone of his own past, with an Indian, who, unlike those on the hacienda, does not reject him and who strengthens him with his tenderness. This guide, who wanders the world alone with his memories and with his song, escapes from Abancay, the "cursed" place, that "is no good for anything," that does not pay homage to the Virgin.

Ernesto asks the singer to pray to the Pachachaca River to help him to get away soon. "You will tell Our Father [the River, it is understood] that I will go to say farewell to him."

The second is called Tayta or Papacha (Great Father), a harpist whose music is like a river. He will be taken prisoner for playing a song about doña Felipa, and the singer of songs to the Virgin will take his place, seeking to rescue him with the same music. Ernesto, who has never spoken with him, goes to the jail looking for him, asserting that he is his *godson*. The meaning of the relationship is understood: when he asks if the harpist is crying, the guard whispers: "Don't be an idiot. Why should he cry . . . He's just messed up his hands, beating on the wall."

But perhaps more important is the revelation that Ernesto has during the music that Tayta is playing. "Who can mark the limits that separate what is heroic from the ice of a great sadness? With music like this, a man can cry until he consumes himself, until he disappears, but he could just as well fight against a whole legion of condors and lions and against the monsters they say live at the bottoms of the lakes up in the highlands and on the shadowy slopes of the mountains. I felt more like fighting against the devil as I listened to this song . . . I would go against him, sure of winning."

Music (like nature) is made up of opposites. It is possible to disappear and to be consumed, or to rise up and struggle. Both attitudes are possible and are born from the same root and situation. This closeness of sadness and heroism, of suffering and of epic action, is fundamental to a liberating perspective, because it is symptomatic of the fact that beneath the almost geological layers of sorrow, there persists, is re-created, develops, and emerges, the opposite conduct: struggle. The dominated have before them the options of being heroes or victims, of suffering or of fighting, because within each of them contradictory dimensions touch and are juxtaposed. Music and nature reveal and express this unstable mixture. It is for that reason also that so many "fathers" so many "educators" and so many "guides" are needed: because of the enormous number of heavens and hells that populate the planet as well as the interior land of which we all are formed.

Growing up well consists of passing through the apprenticeship of that limit between the ice of intense sadness and the heroic, of finding beside suffering and within it, in its very veins, the possibility of happiness, of struggle, of dance, which is nothing more than encountering another human being, a companion, a brother or sister. To mature one must grow through struggle, and not be diminished by anguish nor underdeveloped by sadness. Even if this process is quite long, and in Ernesto's case it is an arduous task, it can also come about instantaneously, in flashes of insight. Such is the case of a soldier in the chichería who starts to dance to doña Felipa's song, a song which mocks nothing less than the armed forces themselves, in effect, mocking that soldier's own service to the dominant class. By dancing he frees himself of his military condition, turns back to his origins and his indigenous self. He dances against himself and against his comrades in arms. The day before, Ernesto had seen another soldier, identical to this one, who was walking along crying like an orphan. Downtrodden, kicked by his sergeant, devoured by a sense of abandonment, he was singing, "Alone, all alone, in a strange town." Ernesto had said that if that soldier should see the bridge over the river, "this Rukana Indian would perhaps stop crying, or howling, would hurl himself into the current, from the cross." The next day, music accomplishes what the bridge might have done. That miserable wretch has within him the same defiant power of the dance as his alter ego in the chichería. They are the same (archetypical) person taking different directions. Beneath the surface of domination are the deep rivers which liberate. In this case, and in others, Arguedas touches upon the themes of his Latin American generation, and especially of Julio Cortázar, with whom he had unfortunate differences and misunderstandings.

The soldiers, therefore, described as "motherless people, born of the wind," can recover the land through music, and become the fathers of themselves.

Of all the arts, it is music which best reveals what it means to be human. Even earlier, in Cuzco, a hell bedecked with suffocating signs of minimal splendor, the narrator was able to see the same characteristics in the María Angola bell, which produced two apparently incompatible phenomena in him. On the one hand, he and his father are *"enteramente felices"* ("completely happy"), because that tolling of the bell reminds him, from the center of the world, of the most jubilant moments from the past. On the other hand, that resonating sound digs at him and makes him suffer terribly, taking him back once again to the cruel house in which he was abandoned.

Cuzco itself illustrates this union of opposites within the same object. Things, cities, rivers, and especially people seem to inhabit the confluence of different, and at times, antagonistic, streams. They are submitted to the irrefutable influence of opposite tendencies or perhaps it is that they are capable of functioning in two entirely dissimilar directions. "And where no one except the water moves, *peacefully or violently*." This potential of water, which contains within itself two facets or emotions, is repeated throughout Arguedas's work. It reveals the world's brokenness, its being radically divided, and at the same time the unending attempt at unification. (Put at another level, the question is really about the viability and the survival of fractured Third World nations and cultures in this second half of the twentieth century.) The savage coherence of Arguedas's vision at this profound, material, and territorial level of language no doubt obeys its most mysterious and concrete level. According to him, things possess a potential duality, a basic disjunctive, which nonetheless is incessantly resolving itself into a real unity. The ability of something or of someone to have within itself or himself a state and its opposite (for example, heat and cold, peace and violence), is possible because people are always involved in tension, in a dynamic process, moving in a still indefinite way, influencing each other mutually. People are in a state of becoming, they are a "this" and an "almost that." Language, the fruit of that terrible and agonizing struggle of which Arguedas spoke,[29] accompanies, anticipates, and gives expression to that major dilemma in its most mundane, least conscious form. We have already noted how the word "inspire" can represent two morally antagonistic elements. Even the color yellow, whose negative use in the novel is extensive (the patio, the Valley de los Molinos, Añuco before his conversion, the color of fear and of sickness after the salt is returned to its owners, Gerardo's and Antero's complexion, the plague itself), can and must have another potential which is magical and positive. The point of the zumbayllu itself is yellow. Beneath the Manichean antagonism, beneath a merciless economic and class struggle, beneath all the division, it is as if material reality and Ernesto's conscience were attempting to harmonize and point toward a subterranean foundation for community among men.

This may help to explain another characteristic of Arguedas's style. He never describes things in a static way, but prefers to set what is observed into motion narratively. The landscape, for example, is not just there for contemplation. It is something that is happening to someone, which already contains a glance, which intervenes or calls into action. We are not dealing with a scene, but rather with a process of movement. Like the Inca wall itself, which seems to be made of stone, but really is not: the number of verbs used proves that those landscapes are anything but inert matter waiting to be molded or commented upon. So much attention has been drawn to Arguedas's lyrical descriptions that we often do not notice that we are not dealing with a "literary" quality or with technical ability. One could even argue the opposite: these descriptions function, and elicit emotion, to the extent to which they do not establish a unilateral, external relationship with reality. They do not reproduce reality or even an atmosphere, but rather are a form of dialogue, of mutual interaction with it.[30]

José María Arguedas's style, therefore, cannot be separated from the liberation which he desires for his characters. He conceives his books as a prolongation, on another plane, of the emancipating attempt at communication which drives his fictitious Indians and mestizos. In the world of readers it ought to function like the music which is propagated and diffused in *Deep Rivers*.

The fact that music, and therefore art, including literature, in a context of underdevelopment should produce an *ascension* among human beings, intensifying within them the need to resolve the distance between sadness and struggle, is confirmed by the evolution of "la opa."

Ernesto remembers her on two occasions linked with the dance. First, when it becomes known that Añuco will go to Cuzco, lost and crying along the feverish banks of the Apurimac, Ernesto conjures up the image of "la opa": "at this hour she would be contemplating the shawl, laughing to herself . . . She had climbed up the slope, almost dancing, with the shawl on her back. She did not go to the patio." Almost dancing. The chicha makers danced as they marched in search of the colonos. Ernesto himself danced with the zumbayllu in the patio. The Indian soldier will dance to doña Felipa's song, which passes from mouth to mouth and from town to town, evoking her memory, converting her deed into an enduring and inspiring myth. And "la opa" does not go to the patio that night.

The second occasion is even more significant. The Principal preaches a sermon at the school against doña Felipa, praying to the

Virgin to forgive those who have been led astray and to cast out "the devil from their bodies." While the others, on their knees, repeat the prayer in Spanish, Ernesto rebels internally. In Quechua, he directs himself to the rebellious woman: "Doña Felipa: La opa has your shawl; dancing and dancing, she went up the slope with your castilla over her breast. And at night she didn't go to the dark patio anymore. She didn't go!" Originally, "la opa" was described as running and mooing with happiness. Nothing was said of dancing. Later, the first reminiscence presents her as "almost dancing." Now, sure that she has not returned to the patio, he twice repeats the certainty that she was dancing. The imaginative accommodation of the past is a way to read its deepest meaning. Doña Felipa, "la opa," and Ernesto support each other mutually in the face of official ideology and religion, without ever having spoken to each other, the struggle of each one having repercussions in the resistance of the others.

The process of "la opa's" purification continues. She climbs the tower, facing the public square, and from there she laughs at the official world, mocking the authorities, the women who pass by, the soldiers, etc. She who is the lowliest and the most violated, pulls herself up and, from on high, celebrates herself as a child, an innocent. Ernesto, who witnesses this victory, defines it as epic and as the second step in the climbing of the cross of the previous day ("But her deed tonight was greater"). In both deeds she makes use of religious architecture (the cross on the bridge, the tower of the church) to invert the function it has carried out in the subjugation of the Indians: instead of suffering or sinking, she climbs up and celebrates. As in a fairy tale the possession of the heroine's shawl is enough to achieve her transformation.

But the past continues to operate, and doña Felipa has not succeeded in changing the world. "La opa" will be the first victim of the epidemic and, appropriately, its carrier. Nevertheless, in her very death one can already see her change and prior rebellion. Ernesto will sit up with her and care for her as though she were his mother, without fear of contagion. It is here that he gives her a name for the first time, calling her Marcelina instead of "la opa." That baptism, equivalent to the water with which the river drenched her when she climbed up to get doña Felipa's shawl, coincides with the certainty expressed by Ernesto of "la opa's"

salvation and her ascent into heaven. In her agony, he sees her becoming more at peace and more beautiful. In the end he calls her
"doña Marcelina," which to the priests seems a further indication
of the boy's dementia. Even the Principal refers to her as "the unfortunate one, the animal." So this conversion by Ernesto of the
raped woman into a lady, into *a person*, is one step more in her
transformation into guardian angel, almost a deus ex machina, in
the fight against the epidemic. She "will be praying for me there
in glory. She will burn the wings of the lice; she will save us."

This movement of "la opa," the most abject being in the school
and in the galaxy, Indian, woman, and idiot, is what foreshadows
what will be the transformation of the Indians-colonos-children.
Beginning with doña Felipa's insurrection, "la opa" slowly rises
up, achieves some form of identity, manages to advance. All are
part of the same victory march. It is the "yawar mayu," the river
of blood which stirs in the Inca wall. It is the turbulent river that
sparkles in the sunlight. It is "the violent time of the war dances."
It is the shout—or rather the hymn, or dance—of the colonos.
They will be able to destroy the epidemic, because earlier, during
the novel, Ernesto himself had struggled and had witnessed other
equally redemptive conflicts.

The Epidemic and the Colonos

The yellow death arrives.

The epidemic has all the characteristics with which Lleras infected the world or, if you will, with which the sick world infected him.

It is a fever that is propagated like light from a fire, that pierces
to the very marrow of the bones like the dark ice that grows from
the demonic possession of "la opa." It isolates, silences, disperses,
corrupts ("they covered their heads with blankets and immediately
fell silent; they isolated themselves. I remained alone, as the others
must have been"). It has accumulated earlier in the foreshadowings of the heat and of the cold, in the filth, in the orange-colored
and sickly twilights, in the spiders, the lice and the flies, to burst
forth in the most hellish of forms, one which summarizes them
all: death.

But it is not just that the epidemic is the continuation of earlier leitmotivs and situations. It exercises a violence and a destructiveness like that of war, the sort Lleras would have dreamed of: it dominates each one of them, makes them flee. It is a much more powerful army than the one commanded by the colonel, and has, additionally, sexual connotations, due to the fact that it was spread in that way (from the Indians to "la opa," from "la opa" to the janitor) and because the Principal associates that fever with sex when he interrogates Ernesto: the epidemic acts in the same way as the infectious focal point of sex in the earlier chapters (seen as a sickness that is contagious, raises the temperature, confuses and leaves the victim senseless).

Therefore, it is not possible to understand this epidemic as something external, something that comes from outside Abancay, but rather as a curse which has always been festering and gestating in the town and in the school, like a tortured and bloody egg. It is Lleras's contaminating strength, raised to the level of an apocalyptic natural law, scattering the same destruction that certain human beings have imposed on the world. Rather than sudden, it is born of the overaccumulation of demonic residues in American and Peruvian history, having manifested itself through other means, voices, penalties, deviations, throughout the course of the novel. Just as the Pachachaca River is nature's equivalent of the Indian comuneros, rebellious and unified, and of the epic that dwells even in the most beleaguered of us, so the epidemic is, in nature, the equivalent of Lleras, who degrades, dominates, and destroys. But unlike the case of Lleras, it has no social limitations on its actions: it saturates every stratum with its injustice, internal and external, rich and poor. Like Lleras, the plague does nothing more than apply the existing laws in the world. But it is sufficiently all-powerful to apply them without limitation, in depth, doing away with everything.

How then can one combat such power? How can it be combated, when we are no longer dealing with the miserable criminality of a Lleras, or with the unchallenged military, ecclesiastical, and economic powers, but rather with nature itself, which objectifies and universalizes death and Hell? Who can do it? Who can kill death?

The answer seems to be: no one. The army can't control it; the priest doesn't make it retreat.

In these circumstances, the last thing one would expect would be for the hacienda Indians to assume such a struggle. They have been defined (in the book and also in the centers of power that monopolize the right to give names) as passive, damned, mute, useless, whining, timorous to the hilt. Eternally.

But typhus has transformed everyone (students, soldiers, landowners, priests) into pongos, timid and terrified creatures.

It is only in this Judgment Day atmosphere that the fine line which separates heroism from extreme misery and whining can be crossed, that fine line Ernesto had discovered in the effects of music, in the transformation of "la opa" and in the soldier who danced.

Because the Indians do rebel. They cross the river to reach Abancay, demanding a mass. The explanation given by Arguedas for this phenomenon is well known: if these submerged classes are capable of being stirred into action for that immaterial, religious reason, what will they not do when they have something more real and more concrete, such as land, to motivate their advance.[31]

But we are more interested in emphasizing the sense of growth which that change implies. When Ernesto informs the sergeant, who is guarding the road to Abancay, that he was brought up by Indians "more manly than these colonos," the soldier, with everything that that condition implies with regard to machismo, courage, and will to power, replies dryly: "More manly, you say. It would be for something, but not to challenge death. There they come; neither the river nor the bullets have stopped them."

The colonos are finally "men." They are not afraid and they have stopped crying. Inspired by their joy, they begin to sing the call to emancipation which they have always nourished inside themselves. It is as if the values represented by the river have become incarnate in a human alternative at the moment when Lleras's values, which are anti-community, have been made intensely physical in the ferocity of the fever and of nature. These "children" who can be heroes to the point of confronting death itself, demonstrate by *their very transformation* that it is possible to destroy the totalitarian power of the disease, that there is a place which the epidemic has not and cannot reach. In this way, the colonos become the Indians, parents, protectors, and models that Ernesto has searched for throughout his time in hell. The sobbing orphans whom Antero was to whip to prove his own "manhood" realize an almost ontological leap forward. And not in the direction of nostalgia for some memory that we try to grasp in the middle of the mist, nor in the direction of a faraway and unreachable utopia, but in the here and now. Crossing the threshold of terror, singers and dancers, climbing upward instead of coming down, they actively embody all the values which Ernesto has been nourishing and guarding throughout the novel and which have had only a sporadic corporality so far, a "once in a while" which is more individual than collective. That will to fight, therefore, is near, very near, in fact, at hand ("it's enough to have the courage to reach out your hand in the darkness," are words whispered in Cortázar's *Hopscotch*). From the river, they triumphantly climb the mountain, challenging and berating the plague. No image, in my judgment, underscores as well as this one Latin America's distance from Western and European culture in the twentieth century. It is enough to compare it with the Algeria of Camus's *La peste*, that Third World country where the French writer sees no social or collective salvation.

And although it may seem strange, the moment of the fever's annihilation is ambiguously described as an oddly sexual act, masculine, almost virile, like a cosmic insemination: "Perhaps the shout would reach the mother of the fever and would penetrate her, making her explode, turning her to inoffensive dust that would disappear beyond the forest." Men and women, the entire Indian population, will inseminate death, destroying its malignant mother, thus becoming, with that germinating act, procreators of the world and of life itself. Just as the sickness is propagated by secret and dark sex, so this act, both musical and sexual, the reproduction of life as struggle and music and joy and challenge, can, like a father, impregnate, when it is in the hands and the mouths of the oppressed Indian people.

It is this growth, this sudden leap to the other shore, which Ernesto has been unconsciously preparing throughout his exile in Abancay. The one who is most oppressed, homeless, and abandoned, the one whom everyone calls demented, crazy, Indian, sick, and disturbed, will be the only one in the school who will also not be afraid. Every time he had visited the hacienda without being able to contact the Indian men (he does not look for the women), he would come back sad and dejected. This time, with Abancay reeling with fear, and knowing that the colonos are on the point of descending on the town, of invading that satanical space, he can, for the first time, *sing* along the road returning from the hacienda.

We have reached the moment when Ernesto too must decide, when Ernesto too will have to determine if he has become a man or if he will go on being a child forever.

His father will not come to rescue him. Far from it. Demonstrating his impotence, he will hand him over to El Viejo, returning him to the barbarous kitchen where the other substitute father and relative had enclosed him, but this time in a more definitive way, because in the haciendas of El Viejo there will no longer be anyone who can revive him. His father asks Ernesto to fall back toward a deeper hell, toward the hacienda which surrounds the villages, ruled over by the Anti-Christ, the torturer of trees and the ruler of pongos. He instructs him to set out for Cuzco, the center of contagion, the place from which the army (carriers of repression and of coastal civilization) came, the place chosen by Lleras, by the defeated Añuco, and by Brother Miguel (frustrated by racial prejudice): the place of death.

Ernesto is alone. Accompanied by "la opa" in death, by doña Felipa in memory and by the Indians from the suffocating streets of Abancay, he must decide whether or not to obey his father and the Principal. Of his scattered and defeated classmates, only Palacitos, the Indian, has remembered him, giving him some gold with which he will be able to transform himself into a traveler either of death or of life. Ernesto fantasizes: "They will think I am the wandering son of some prince or a messenger of the Lord, who is going about testing the honesty of his children." And, in effect, the Principal accuses him of having stolen that money, avarice shining in his eyes, just as earlier those eyes were hardened by the "nasty fire" and "hell" of sex ("a repugnant tension that made him seem like a hot-blooded animal").

Ernesto feels that he must reject the Principal, possessed as he is by the desire for money and by the ashes of sexual contagion, just as he must challenge El Viejo, who treats the priests (the subjectors of the Indians) like princes, while he treats the Indians like beggars (and not like true children of the gods).

There is another possible direction, the one opposite to the one leading to Cuzco. It is the one taken by his father, by doña Felipa, and by the singer don Jesús Gabriel; it is the direction from which the Indian colonos are coming; it is the direction of the bridge and of the river. But it happens that this is also the direction of risk, the uncertain road to probable death, the road that is swollen with disease. It is the direction that leads to the dawn of the rivers which are himself and the others—even if that direction means death.

"We will see each other."

Those had been El Viejo's words as they left Cuzco. Thus had he threatened Ernesto, smiling.

Because El Viejo knows that it is he who holds the power and that, even if the adult Gabriel does escape his nets, he does it by fleeing within the borders of a world where what persists as law is El Viejo's filthy and subjugating image, where everything is molded in his destructive likeness. Gabriel's child Ernesto will not be able to escape. El Viejo is like God the Father, a deformed and satanical male-paternal figure who inhabits each one of the other men whom Ernesto has met. He holds the angels prisoner, accumulating and concentrating all the evils of a society. The circle which Ernesto must describe is already marked out by El Viejo: it begins in Cuzco and runs from there only to end up, apparently, on the four haciendas that belong to El Viejo himself, where the same conditions of humiliation and destruction will be repeated.

When Ernesto decides, on the last page of the novel, to disobey his father and the Principal, to rebel against El Viejo, what he does is to break this circle, give the lie to this "we will see each other," this cyclical fatality that awaits him (and to which so many characters in other Latin American novels have succumbed). Unlike his father, he chooses the values of liberation instead of those of economic security. Such a break was anticipated in the progressive distancing of himself from Antero (who was becoming El Viejo). But it is not just a matter of separating himself from an authoritarian father figure (the Principal), but rather also of rejecting the weaknesses and limitations of his real father. With his attitude, Ernesto breaks with the idea of the son who is "good and Christian," submissive and defenseless, just as the colonos have done. Perhaps with this resolution, Arguedas was subconsciously remembering the Quechua myth of a possible third humanity, winged and wandering, which will ascend higher than sin, and which must be the product of a God who transcends the earlier dichotomy, the Father and the Son.[32]

How can such a rebellion, equivalent to the miracle of the regeneration of all humankind, an unceasing resurrection, become really feasible?

Hell-like circumstances, with only a few glimpses of freedom or of opening, have been emphasized as much in Abancay as in Cuzco. But both places are no more than secondary circles within the wild, central orbit, the hacienda, that axis of Hell which contaminates everything, where the anti-values of a Lleras can command without any counterbalance. It is this entanglement which Ernesto rejects, denying its inevitability.

At this point, it is worthwhile focusing our attention on an extra-literary testimony of Arguedas himself which, as far as I have been able to determine, has not yet been used to illuminate this denouement of *Deep Rivers*. In the prologue of the book *The Singing Mountaineers, Songs and Tales of the Quechua People*, in English ("On Andean Fiestas and the Indian"), José María relates,[33] among other autobiographical experiences, the treatment the Indians received on the four haciendas of someone called El Viejo, no less. Everything approximates the version of him given by Ernesto in the first chapter: they feared him like the Devil because of his shouts; anyone who dared eat bananas was punished; the Indians had no land of their own. But more important than these and other characteristics reproduced by the fiction are the following words that were not transferred to the novel:

> These Indians did not know how to sing. The hacienda Indians never made noise . . . On that hacienda there was not one *quena* nor a small band of bronze instruments. When they came in (from work), they were given *lawa*, a soup made from frozen potatoes, and whatever was available to drink, and then they went to bed, whether they were married or single. Why don't they sing? I asked. I was tormented. Some nights I went to visit them and I sang *huaynos* from Ayacucho, Abancay and Coracora. But they didn't seem to listen. "Sweet little boy," they said, but (the song) made them sleepy. And I had to go. Later, the foreman's cook told me that one night El Viejo had heard a flute being played in the main house of Karkeki and he had gone to the hacienda, sneaking up to the door of the room where the flute was being played, and he

had entered the house, saying, "Indians, this is the time to pray." He asked for the flute and broke it on the floor with his feet.

Every morning while it was still dark, the peons went first to the hacienda chapel, where they prayed with the foreman and then they went out to work. All that regimentation had been established by El Viejo. During the Carnaval season, all the Indians came down to the hacienda. The foreman gave them several barrels of cheap rum, and both women and men drank the liquor; they all got drunk right there. By nightfall, almost all the Indians were fighting, throwing stones at each other, kicking and beating each other. The women fought among themselves or joined in the men's fight. The foreman stood watching them calmly from the hallway. At night they slept on the ground, men and women together, no one remembering who was a husband, a brother or a sister. An Indian carnaval with no *tinya*, no flute, no songs! But only in that place! In the other towns where I lived, the Indians always had a song, whether for sad occasions or for happy ones."

In these evocations, we possess what has to have constituted the heartrending secret image which holds together and feeds Ernesto's terror. The colonos of those lands combine, in a single group, both the characteristics of the patio and those which infect the fiery canebrakes of Abancay. Therefore it is here that we find the central axis, point zero, absolute Hell: because the two worst, most negative spaces become one space, solitary and infinite. The school's incestuous and fratricidal chaos takes up residence in the heart of the Indian. It is there, and only there, that no one sings and there is no music. There can be nothing lower than this.

For Ernesto to go there is to abandon all hope. He will not need to. When the peasants cross the city of Abancay, in reality they come to wash the patio where their younger brothers (the boys) scratched and cursed each other, all for the favors of a poor, worn-out Indian woman. Only the rebellion of the Indians, a distant product and at the same time an echo of other small advances which Ernesto witnesses and participates in, a rebellion against death, can point the protagonist in the direction of a divergent adventure: it is preferable to die rather than to see the Indians acting like the schoolboys, rather than keeping silent and killing the music.

The march by the Indians turns into a model, a river that is intangible but unique. Ernesto will not see them. He will hear them, carrying to the limit, one final time, his marginal and enclosed condition, becoming a mere listener of events instead of a spectator. But sound is enough, for sounds have always drawn human beings together more than light in Arguedas's works. The next morning, when Ernesto leaves the town, he discovers that the Indians have marched in perfect order, without trampling on the flowers, just as the chicha makers had when they distributed the salt. Thus they once and for all give lie to the way in which El Viejo prophesied that they would act.

The last view we have of Ernesto, the one he gives us of himself, is crossing the Pachachaca River in his imagination, climbing up into the mountains, seeing the epidemic carried off by the waters of the river.

"The river will take it away to the Great Jungle, the land of the dead. Like Lleras!"

Thus ends the novel. A few days earlier the narrator had imagined the Apurímac, God who speaks, cornering Lleras, rotting him in "some miry shore where devilish, colored worms would wriggle in and out, devouring him." Now the other river, which has acted as Ernesto's father and is simultaneously a relative of the Quechua hymns that have penetrated to the very roots of the trees to cast out the fever, the other river which is like the body of the Incas and of their stones that sing as they seek out and demand cosmic reintegration, that river Pachachaca will participate in the cleaning up of the world. Accentuating its dependence on the actions of men, the river will be able to carry the sickness far away, once the colonos have exterminated it. Only then will it be able to serve as a link with and a means of passage to the land of the dead. Only when the child-Indians grow up to occupy the city where the patio of "la opa" is shining with its dark moon-like light. Only when the poor have become mobilized.

As in the case of Lleras, the already legendary representative of the social and moral sickness that convokes and opens the door to physical disease.

Growth of a child; growth of a people.

Arguedas wants his readers to understand that both forms of growth are one and the same, that the song of one multiplies and guarantees the song of the other, that without both dimensions (the individual and the collective, the external and the internal), there is no way out of underdevelopment. *Deep Rivers* demands a deep revolution. But will it come? Is it even possible?

What lies beyond the bridge that Ernesto is on the point of crossing, the bridge that, in the novel, Ernesto crosses in his imagination?

For Ernesto, we have no way of knowing. It could be death. Or a way of life that the author cannot yet anticipate with words, since it would depend on changes that the people would have to achieve in order for the child to go on growing.

On the other hand, for Arguedas himself, we do know what was on the other side of the bridge. It was the savage and half-lighted jail in *El Sexto*, the all-encompassing epic of *All the Bloods*. And later there would be *El zorro de arriba y el zorro de abajo*, that farewell work which attempts to resolve, through a synthesis, a world which, vast and extensive, was overflowing into a contemporary chaos that would, in a merciless fashion, put to a final test those values that Ernesto had never doubted.

Beyond the bridge, then, is the magnificent risk of living and dying like a human being, facing forward and standing upright, singing far from the silence.

Ernesto took that risk and he took his father, and our own spiritual father, José María, with him.

Perhaps they discovered that, together, it was possible to overcome the demons and to do away with the geological layers of human misery as well.

Let us hope that one day, one year, one century soon we will be able to discover that, yes, as they crossed the bridge, they were finally right.

1977

■ Sandwiched Between Proust and the
Mummy: Seven Notes and an Epilogue on
Carpentier's *Reasons of State*

■ *"We have called at all the doors which lead nowhere, and the only one
which would have worked and which we have vainly knocked at during one hundred years, opens before us when we happen to stumble on it by
accident . . ."* —Marcel Proust, *A la recherche du temps perdu*

I

The most revealing episode of Alejo Carpentier's *Reasons of
State*[1] comes toward the beginning of the novel when the central
character, a dictator, fresh from a great military victory against an
upstart general, escapes into a cave from a tropical downpour and
finds seven mummies from pre-Columbian America. One of them
seems more important than the others. Chieftain, high priest, warrior—whatever his original stature, it is clear that once upon a
time, many millenia ago, he was also, in this same geographic location, a Head of State.

He who was once a king in America is today eminently dead.
Not even his name is known. Nor will his culture and civilization
(*sic*) be called the way he used to call it, but will circulate as Rio
Verde—in commemoration of the current Head of State's recent
battle. His mummy's final destiny is to be shipped to Europe to
be exhibited in the Trocadero Museum. Worse still, that ancient
monarch will be used in a publicity campaign ("the Grandfather
of America is about to arrive") organized to divert public attention from the denunciations by the French press of the massacres
carried out in the Head of State's country, New Córdoba. For a
while the old relic will even get shuffled from port to port awaiting the end of the First World War, when he can finally find some

peace—but alas no quiet—in the museum. He has been reduced to less than ashes, an extreme of helplessness and passivity. This existential impotence contrasts with another public figure who is mentioned at great length in the same chapter, a warrior who, unlike the American monarch, is not exactly on the margin of universal history: Julius Caesar. The Head of State explains to his two acolytes (his secretary Peralta and Colonel Hoffmann) that the previous battle was won by following, step by precise step, the tactics suggested by the Roman general in his *Commentaries*. The Head of State's readings have allowed him to apply lessons written more than two thousand years ago, perhaps in the same epoch when the man who is now less than a rotting skeleton in a forgotten cave reigned over his tribe or nation.

The contrast could not be more heartbreaking. Julius Caesar has managed to subsist and impose himself far beyond his physical disappearance. His influence, indeed, is so vigorous that even the battles in Latin America are determined by his recommendations and memories. Caesar was the dictator, the center of an empire, the owner of the known universe. His "culture" is the seedbed of the very language that the Head of State is speaking and of the language in Paris that experts will use to discuss the life of that other pre-Columbian king. The juxtaposition of the mummy and Julius Caesar is not a coincidence. The author is offering us two possible paths and directions that a ruler can take after his death, two alter ego ways in which to persist. Both of them contemplated thousands of years later by another sovereign, a man who has also orchestrated his life in order to achieve power, swearing that he will be able to endure and remain. This is the essence of the novel: Carpentier's perpetual president believes he is, wants to be, like Julius Caesar and will end up being, and secretly already is, the mummy. Though it will take us the whole narrative to realize it, the Head of State is dead and stagnant at the very opening of the book, he is already an unrecognizable statue at the bottom of the sea, a caudillo whom everybody will soon forget. The most peripheral of human beings. His fate is like that of the mummy: to be exhibited in Alejo Carpentier's Museum of Never-ending and Identical Dictators.

Rather than an arraignment against the tyrannies we Latin Americans have suffered for so long, *Reasons of State* is the slow, sarcastic exploration of the exercise of power—a power inevitably bastardized, secondary, illusory—in a misdeveloped continent. The Head of State will try to persist, only to realize—and half-realizing, at that—that power was never really his but belonged to the real owners of the world: the Juliuses and Caesars of now, the proprietors of the twentieth century's emporium and empire, the United States of America. The way in which the Head of State conceives and develops his authority leads him irremissibly to the ignominious fate of the mummy, in the best of cases a mere asterisk at the bottom of a page in a history manual for European schoolchildren. The book is therefore not a pamphlet or a piece of propaganda which informs us about horrors which our unfortunate bodies know all too well, nor is the Head of State a mere figure in effigy that we can comfortably burn with our indignation: we are going to cohabitate with his desire to survive in time, we shall be blind like him, trapped in the idea that he is able to impose his will on history. But because he will participate in history-as-oppression, a minor screw turning in a vast machine, he will be condemned to be a fossil, a mere reflection in a museum window.

Fourteen years after the battle of Rio Verde, the Head of State, who has finally been overthrown and no longer has a country to command, will go to visit the mummy. This will be his last act, an obscene voyeuristic ritual, before dying.

"Don't complain, you sonuvabitch," he says to the mummy, "I took you out of the mud to turn you into a person . . . Into a per—". The Spanish is "hacerte gente," to turn you into "somebody," make "somebody" out of you. Thus does the former dictator address the heap of bones a few days before he himself will follow that same fate. He still sees himself as a superior being who was able to extract certain lower entities from the dirt and elevate them, place them among the "gente," those who made it. This transmutation from unformed earth to the supreme status of being "somebody," a "person," represents the Head of State's life project, not only for himself but for his whole country.

But what does this mean, to be turned into "somebody"?

II

The phrase, "hacerse gente" has been used twice before in the novel.

The first is when the Head of State, lamenting the rebellion by his protégé, General Ataúlfo Galván, bitterly proclaims that he had "dragged him from the dirt of a provincial barracks, . . . taught (him) to use a fork and pull the lavatory chain, and converted (him) into somebody (*haciéndolo gente*), a gentleman." The second is when the opera arrives to that "backward" American country and the protagonist observes that his compatriots are beginning to adopt the customs and schedules of the Old World: "We're becoming real persons, Peralta, we're starting to become real persons" ("Nos estamos haciendo gente"). The mummy, Ataúlfo Galván, the opera-lovers: all rise from the filth and backwardness of ignorance to the clean luminosity of power and civilization. The Head of State's politics will be determined by his quest of the dynamic duo that confers perdurability to human beings: Latin American power and European culture. One might even dare to suggest it this way: Latin American power in order to possess European culture.

Hacerse gente. To be turned into somebody, a real person. That was the dream of a poor, forlorn journalist living in a small Pacific port, significantly called Surgidero (Launching Place): to be accepted as a coequal in the European salons, to converse with the patrons of the verb and the dispensers of the latest refinements. Even if it meant stealing the elections and taking over the government of his republic. Even if, once admittance had been obtained to those cultural sanctums, it means having to return from time to time to suffocate insurrections by mutinous military men, irate professors, refractory workers. Even if it means, now back in Latin America, that he must continue to dream of returning to Paris, of a tranquil old age among paintings, music, literature and—what is more essential—high class gossip, "somebody" in the eyes of those who matter, the "real persons" who have the right to talk about others and classify them. The Head of State is, therefore, essentially colonized: his deepest desires are to leave behind his original earth and interfuse with the values of those who are "superior," to be a conspicuous member of the select group of humanity who happen to own the cannons, the factories, and the phonemes and who can guarantee him a place in their dictionaries.

What is interesting in his case is not, of course, the project in itself, which we suffer daily in less sophisticated versions in TV,

movies, and comics, but rather his failure, the reasons why he fails
that reveal, through the novelist's critical eye, the forces that are
resisting the dictator, that move in the opposite direction. It is the
impossibility of that illusion coming to life that we are going to
witness. If the novel's space is divided between the enclosed existence of the Parisian residence and the symbolic vastness of a Latin
American territory, it is due to an inevitable schism in the picaresque tyrant's own vacillating mind.[2] This pendular movement
in the life of someone who wants to be far from Latin America
ends up allowing us to discover that which is irreducibly and gen-
uinely Latin American. The two poles are revealed through the
attempt to deny one of them, clarifying what properly belongs to
each one. Beyond the uncertain middle ground where influences
are shared, where one imitates or covers the other, where mirrors
are erected, beyond the myths and the masks, a series of hard, in-
flexible, unrelenting traits of each sphere will gradually appear—
even for that tyrant attempting to escape from his origins. Because while the Head of State presumes to be advancing toward
the brilliant tomorrow of European culture, his real trip is to the
earth, the earth of death which will be his, the earth of life that
he will be unable to make into anything fruitful, the memory of
that earth which he was willing to betray and that will finally be
the only tangible and enduring reality in the midst of so many
mirages and simulacra. Submerged under the eyes of a man who
was so dominated that he would pay any price to attain a dominant
position, the "he" who desires above all to pronounce that short
word "I," we are incited towards a double reading of that process
whereby the desires of this Cinderella Dictator, as bloody as he
is "cultured," will be thwarted. We can see how Europe, distant
and powerful, is unable to quiet the Latin American experience;
and how Latin America, nearby and passive, can nevertheless fracture and resist the efforts of extermination and oblivion. Here
and there, there and here, without once leaving the consciousness
of someone nested in the unyielding intersection between these
worlds, we participate in a tentative aesthetic dialogue between
Europe and Latin America. If such a dialogue is to go beyond narrative, and is to formulate any possibility in real history, the necessary precondition should be that the inhabitants of our degraded
continent project their existences in the exact opposite direction

of the Head of State, finding in their everyday lives and actions the same liberating critical creative movement that the narrator has used to pulverize the colonized precepts of his tyrant. It is the very irony with which that biography has been constructed and demolished which proves and anticipates the persistence of an alternative to the illustrated ruffian's plans for his country and subjects.

III

From the start, it is remarkable how extraordinarily fragile the Head of State's grand designs are, how structurally inconsistent they are. His welcome into the "high class" social and intellectual communities of Europe depend on his skill in renewing, once in a while, the unruly and murky sources of his Latin American power. He is merely repeating the experience of all those emigrants who made good in the Indies as conquerors and who, ready later on to impress the Old World with their fortune, find out to their dismay that they have established such deep links with the new territories that they cannot that easily settle back into the ancestral continent and delight in it.

In the case of the Head of State, his problem is that the key to acceptance to the thresholds of culture resides in the violent exercise of the power which is the only category that he feels can make him worthy of that acceptance. Descartes's quotations are used in each chapter of the novel (called *El Recurso del Método* in Spanish, a pun on the *Discourse on Method*). If we were to use Descartes to explain the tyrant's dilemma, we would say that in order to enjoy the state of reason (*el discurso del método*) one must have recourse to reasons of state (*el recurso del método*). Or to put it rather more unpleasantly: to gain access to the salons over here, one must steal, kill, and lie over there. Which is, after all, no more than the same process of conquest and exploitation that has allowed Europe as we now know it to build its culture and its architecture. But our hero, poor refractory neo-colonial that he is, has arrived late: what the Europeans did with their colonies during centuries is now intolerable for the civilization of today's *savoir faire* (really *savoir taire*), whose well-mannered dandies are as horrified as they are hypocritical. The paradox could not be more self-evident: without that power, he is nothing; but with that power—and power has its own rules, then and now, always needing a certain dose of violence to be respected—he is treated as if he were nothing.

His dilemma is revealed to us twice in the novel, in two episodes which seem to refract and copy each other. On both occasions, he is acting out his daily ritual in his rue Tilsit mansion, collecting the rewards of his position as an educated man, showing off (and wasting) a knowledge of Western culture far more extensive than any European ever requires,[3] when he receives news of a military uprising in his own land. His whole point of view changes drastically, as does the narrative rhythm. In the first episode there is a dramatic, and in the second an imperceptible, dropping of the first person singular, emphasizing how his figure, which begins as the axis of everything, has become tangential and impotent. He must leave Europe and return to recuperate what is his; he must once again exercise the instinctual ferocity that has paved the way for his present prosperity. He must be more macho, ruthless, and clever than anyone else. To his secretary he repeats the words he heard an actor dressed up as Christ in a Holy Week procession pronounce when the public tried to help him with the cross: "And if they were to take that from me, what would I be, what would I have left?"

The Head of State's provincial passport to culture passes through barbarism.[4] His right to be a European will, as with any illegitimate bastard, as with any recently arrived immigrant, constantly be put to the test. There has not been enough time to erase or mythify the sources of his wealth, to ideologize and explain away what this power and cheating have accumulated: in the colonies, Marx once said, one can see capitalism in all its brute force. What the current empires have taken centuries to build, the Head of State must materialize in the brief, lightening-like span of a short existence. He's caught in a revolving door: no sooner is he in than he's on his way out. And his bitter complaints about the hypocrisy behind the attitude of the Europeans or Peralta's protests about their savagery, are to no avail. The massacres, the plagues, the persecutions—many of whose victims have been the ancestors of the Head of State's compatriots—do not matter, nor the fact that all too soon the First World War—not to mention the second one, with Auschwitz and Hirsohima—will outdo and far surpass the murderous dictator. The petty tyrant will be exiled from the European salons: his hosts cannot stand that image of themselves that he reflects back at them, the misshapen being that they have created, that they once were, that they will continue to secretly and hiddenly be. Without that violence, there is no way in which he can climb the ladder of success, no way to receive the praise and attention of the dominant class, the men and women who hold the key to the future. But with that violence, he distances himself from those "real persons" who neither wish to admit their origins nor are able to catch a glimpse of their own crisis which is looming on the horizon at that very time. This is a social class which, in the words of Walter Benjamin, "swears to camouflage its material base and for that very reason holds on to a feudalism which has no intrinsic economic significance, but which serves as a mask for the high middle class."[5] Monsters prefer not to live among mirrors.

Which brings us to the second reason why the Head of State's enterprise is so precarious. The culture to which he aspires is, within Europe itself, regressive, conservative, traditional, superficial. It is a form of culture put at the service of social life, the outer, status sign that is indulged in by the leisure class—thus denominated and analyzed by Veblen[6] in those very years. Art acts as a fashion or a conversation piece, but never as a challenge; as a form of interchange, never as a form of change. The ex-dictator, in fact, at the end of the book, in one of the funniest and most pathetic scenes, physically attacks the modern art which his daughter has adopted out of snobbery—though he has been perturbed all along by every object of art that comes out of the great experiment of the twentieth century aesthetic vanguard. Our dictator desires to assume the usages and polish of an epoch that is already agonizing, adoring an art of petrified and neoclassic forms that postulate an eternal and unalterable bourgeois order, an art that drowns in the bathos of mediocre nostalgia precisely at the moment when some of the most exciting quests for meaning are being attempted. He is a victim, according to Mejía Duque, of a "patriarcal anachronism."[7] Like every colonized human being, then, the Head of State wants to be accepted, monkey-like, by the established order and tenaciously opposes any renovation, dissidence, or experimentation. This will ultimately have political consequences for him: as we shall see, the fact that he looks backward to nineteenth-century

Europe will make him unable to accommodate the newer forms and needs of the United States, with its more technological and dynamic imperialism.

His project, born out of a fondness for the Europe that is already being substituted for by another empire, therefore moves counter to the currents of history. Worse still, the very myth to which he swears allegiance, the myth that culture (the act of fabulation, of conversation) can save him, elevate him, give him prestige, is being assaulted and fractured by the most advanced intellectual and artistic consciences of that so-desired continent, not to speak of its social and revolutionary movements. He longs to cross the thresholds of the salons in the same years when they are becoming more vacuous, empty, and insignificant. As usual, the colonized man is the last smothered refuge where one can hear the weak echoes of ideals already invalidated in their originating countries. Culture is not, for him, an instrument of humanization and contact, but rather the way in which he lets a presumably admiring public know that he belongs among the civilized and their rites, that he belongs here and not there. Because culture is for him merely a code, a badge, he cannot recognize how hopelessly residual his version of it is.[8]

The sign of his displacement can be noted by the fact that there are only two intellectuals who stay loyal to him, even after news of the massacre is known: the Distinguished Academician and D'Annunzio. Though both of them—just like the Head of State's tailor and his barber—do so because of the need for someone to bankroll them, there is an ideological reason as well. These "cultured" gentlemen who do not turn their backs on him are ultra right wing proto-fascists. Along with a series of old-fashioned, useless authors, the Distinguished Academician recommends reading his friend Barrès as well as Gobineau, that arch-racist, both of whom, in 1913, already formed part of the group, with Sorel and Drieu La Rochelle, which would eventually found *L'Action Française*.[9]

But this conservative strain in our main character is deeper than we might have supposed. His regressive efforts go far beyond his political methods or his rhetorical discourses: the organization of his everyday life is an attempt to cheat time, to find in a series of repeating and repeatable acts a familiarity that will cement in habits any disturbance or chance event. Behind his aspiring to perennial power and to sublime and immortal spirituality there lies a more irrevocable propensity to construct a world (a country, a consciousness) where time—and therefore history—cannot penetrate. The Head of State thus joins so many other Carpentier characters obsessed with the need to stop the clock and escape history. It is a yearning reiterated throughout the book, but it finds its major embodiment in a series of recurring identical episodes where the protagonist awakens to the same objects, always answering with the same words and gesticulations, an architecture of attitudes and postures which try to create the illusion that minutes and hours do not pass. Paradoxically, then, he participates in history with the secret inclination to abolish it. Nobody should accuse us of ruining the suspense of this essay if we inform the gentle reader that our hero is not quite going to be successful.

IV

Through the years the Head of State will carry out the gestures of typical dictators: quell rebellions, repress the opposition, stuff the air with used-up words, build jails and banks, recur to fraudulent elections and military garrisons when the people protest the fraud. On every occasion, he will present himself as the one who occupies the circus's center ring, the active subject and agent of history who can determine everything with a flick of a finger, a potency reinforced by the way in which the narrative focuses on his perspective, almost to the exclusion of all others.

He must, nevertheless, finally wake up to the fact that it is history which molds and moves him, that other human beings are in control of his destiny. Though the book contains one culminating moment of revelation when he realizes just how defenseless he has really been—the moment when he is overthrown with the smiling acquiescence of his erstwhile North American protectors—signs that he has all along been an instrument rather than the hand that wields it are strewn all over the novel. It is not merely that we constantly are reminded that he could not subsist without foreign support. If it were no more than this, *Reasons of State* would be merely pamphletary, denouncing a situation which does not need much literary adornment: it is the military, economic, and political force of the empire that has decided during most of our century the fortune (in all senses of the word) of the local oligarchies. What Carpentier manages is something less obvious and external: from the mind of a man who has conjectured that he is the owner of his own self and his land, in the very midst of that certainty, the author develops a counter-vision which belies and corrodes that certainty.

In spite of the Head of State's desire to stop time, history does pass, a passing that becomes manifest in totalizing variations of all walks and climates of life: customs, songs, urban growth, export-import cycles, infantile literature, colloquialisms, manners, popular festivities, everything suffers radical change. It is what Carpentier, in his book *Tientos y Diferencias*, has called a "context"— basically, the way in which a community experiences and expresses itself as a socio-cultural-economic entity. Confronted with this irresistible series of alterations imposed from abroad upon the country, the great willful macho feels defenseless and sad ("As he watched the metropolis grow and grow on him, the Head of State often felt anguish as he saw the scenery changing right in front of the windows of the Palace"). Like so many of his fellow countrymen, he's a spectator, almost seeing himself as a victim of events that happen in spite of his deepest desires. The country seems to be a gigantic piece of scenery where buildings are torn down almost before they are put up, where essential things are shipped abroad and useless trivia imported, where the whole economic process of development does not obey any profound need of the nation itself, lending an objective base to the feeling of the Head of State that life is a spectacle. This feeling is reinforced by the incessant recurrence of staged events that surround him, dramas, representations, facades, operas, carnivals, tragicomedy, masked balls. And, of course, he himself is constantly simulating, every gesture of his face calculated to create an impression on others. He may complain at the pace of change, but the theater of illusions and shadows that the nation has become, its conversion into a ruin before it can even be built up, are directly related to the way in which this pseudo-President erects his existence on cheating himself and others.

Again, he is reaping what he has sown. Before it was the fact that, in order to gain respect in the salons, he had to make enough money and accumulate sufficient power back home. Now we see that, in order to keep that power, he must offer up the entirety of the republic (not only its natural resources, but its cultural wealth as well, its social identity, the contextual materiality of everyday life) to the feverish rhythm of a foreign empire that transforms its satellites into ephemeral dramatic productions. What is ironic in this process is that what is being swept away are the traditional forms that he so adores. He is amazed at the historical changes he is witnessing, as if he were seeing them on a screen or on a stage and not as if he himself bore any responsibility for their existence. There is a good dose of hypocrisy and histrionics, no doubt, in his nostalgic protestations; and yet, we must also note that his pain has an authentic ring to it, that he glimpses the horrifying truth of who he is, the destroyer of what he loves, a minor ruffian in the immense universal farce of history.

This illusory, theatrical character of the country, this vision that all is unreal and fictitious, including the executive office, culminates precisely the day before the Head of State is overthrown. In order to squash a general strike, he exaggerates the buffoonish condition of reality, first by sending his soldiers out to stab and kill mannequins in the stores and second by proclaiming his own death as a way of coaxing the people to celebrate in the streets so he can savagely repress them. But it is too late. The operetta is over. The Head of State's blindness is going to finally catch up with him.

The next afternoon he will awaken to confusion and mutation, the distressing metamorphosis of everything, "a decor suddenly changed by the scene-shifters of tragedies hatched in secret, grown in shadow, born in my proximity, although, deafened as I was by other choirs, I would not have heard the sound of the real choirs." His defeat is, at the same time, a revelation. To escape, he must disguise himself as what he truly is, a sick man; to escape, he must pretend to be really dead, imitating his own make-believe death of only yesterday; and this very defenselessness makes him realize who have been all along the true protagonists, the chorus of Great Voices of the song he thought was his. The great Spanish baroque themes—life is a dream, all the world's a stage, illusion is all that exists, God is manipulating everything behind the curtain—take on in *Reasons of State* a bizarre Third Worldish twist. The Latin

American picaresque hero comprehends the true structure of the universe, his objective situation in the hierarchy of existence and of underdevelopment; if everything that came before was a dream or a play, it was because others were writing the words or painting the scenery. The Head of State is as vulnerable as the country he believed he was ruling. More vulnerable, in fact. Without power back there he could not successfully assault European society and culture. But without the support of the people of his country, without massive and vital forces of his own to channel into history, his power does not persist beyond what the authentic proprietors of the emporium deem convenient to their interests.

As in so many other works by Carpentier, the history of the country he inhabits has the main character trapped. What is peculiar about this history in *Reasons of State* is that it has two different ways of working. First of all, we are clearly in the presence of a relatively rigid chronological ordering in time. We see the country evolve synchronically from 1913 to 1927. Carpentier, drawing on his fabulous—and the word is well used in this case—readings, has re-created each minute detail of that era. But there is a second, underlying conception of history: the suggestion that an episode, no matter how objective and verifiable it may be, how documented its origin, at the same time represents something that happened before and may happen once again.[10] If the first version of history is chronological, structural seems to be the right word for the second.[11] During the Head of State's fourteen-year reign, we witness the repetition of incidents which seem to copy what has happened over and over again in Latin America: massacres and fraudulent elections and insurrections and *pronuniciamientos* and book burnings and on and on.

Both currents of history, that which is unique and happens but once, with name, geographic location, date; and that which is cyclical and points in the direction of a deeper truth, concur to create a fictitious country which, though it bears a considerable resemblance to Venezuela, is in fact composed out of the turbulent history of all the unfortunate Latin American nations. As in a gigantic mosaic or gothic vitraux,[12] the author condenses space and time in *Reasons of State*, synthesizing the different historical times that he had separated analytically in his previous novel *The Lost Steps*, allowing the reader (and the tyrant) to witness a panorama which surpasses the immediate undeniable facts which have captured them. This voyage between what is concrete and what is invisible, between the archetype and the everyday detail, which can be found in other Carpentier works, is more than just a fascinating stylistic device: it is essential to the central experience that *Reasons of State* imposes on us and on its main character.

The Head of State believes that he is residing in history as chronology, making it, screwing it, when in fact he is suffering— and making others suffer—that which is permanent and iterative: death, dependency, coups, empty stomachs, and empty rhethoric. History possesses him. He may, during a time, be its beneficiary, its paid prostitute, its hit man, but he will never really subject it to his will. Both a unique, unrepeatable, existential being and, at the same time, the incarnation of every Latin American dictator, he is condemned to swing between the two dimensions of his country and his being, because, as we have stated before, the real determining forces come from outside him.

He himself realizes the precarious and satanic circularity of a life which does not admit genuine change because, no matter how much he feels it to be unique, unrepeatable, and existential, it is simultaneously the iron incarnation of every Latin American dictator. When he has to return to fight Hoffmann who has now taken up arms against him, "the Head of State saw himself as someone who had been enclosed in a magic circle made by the sword of the Prince of Darkness. History, which was his, because he played a part in it, was something that repeated itself, that swallowed its own tail, and never moved forward—it made very little difference whether the pages of the calendar were printed with 185(?), 189(?), 190(?) or 190(6?): it was the same procession of uniforms and frock coats, high English top hats alternating with plumed Bolivian helmets, as one saw in second-rate theaters, where triumphal marches of thirty men passed and re-passed in front of the same drop curtain, running when they were behind it, so as to be in time to reenter the stage shouting for the fifth time: 'Victory! Victory! Long live the regime! Long live Liberty!' It was the classic example of the knife given a new handle when the old one wears out and a new blade when that wears out in its turn, so that after many years it is still the same knife—immobilized in time—although handle and blade have so often been changed that their mutations can't be counted. Time at a standstill, curfew, suspension of constitutional guarantees, restoration of normality, and words, words, words, . . . just as a watch returns to the time it indicated yesterday when yesterday it told today's time . . ."

All his efforts, therefore, will lead toward the extreme inertia to which he awakens on the day of his overthrow—a day which will end, symbolically enough, with his statues cast into the sea by an outraged populace. The North American Consular Agent anticipates the destiny of those works which the Head of State commissioned to glorify himself. They will be dragged out of the water thousands of years hence, suffering the fate of "those Roman sculptures of who knows what era that can be seen in so many museums," their names lost and only a generic denomination left behind: 'Bust, statue, of a Dictator. They were and will still be so many in this hemisphere that the real name won't matter at all.'"

That Rome has once again come up, so many years after Julius Caesar's commentaries put the mummy in its place, is not a coincidence. That ancient empire is everywhere in the novel. The Head of State loves to babble lines in Latin, looking for the right clichés to commemorate each occasion—even going so far as to mutter his (infamous and incomprehensible) last words, "Acta est Fabula," in that language. When he confronts the Student, his major adversary, the man who will lead the revolution which forces the United States to replace him, the Head of State makes it clear that "the gringos are the Romans of America. And you can't do anything against Rome." Having spoken the truth so bluntly, the Head of State is nevertheless surprised when a while later the Student tells him he is Caligula's horse instead of the Roman emperor himself. It is that same irreverent insolence which will, years later, find a popular outlet in the destruction of his statues, a fitting and representative end to his pretenses of hegemony.

He has done with those statues what he has done with the country itself: taken the earth and stamped upon it his effigy and his name, modeling the mud and the stone until they hardened into his semblance. One copy, like the mummy, may wind its way into a future museum to illustrate the only trait of his which will persist: in that (in this) sad time there existed (there exist) deaf, arrogant fossils of tyrants whose names have been obliterated and whose activities were and are and will be as ultimately interchangeable as the pieces of a puzzle.

Many years before, to that same Atlantic port where he now contemplates the devastation of his dreams, there had arrived another statue he had ordered from abroad—and which represented the republic. That gigantic image (Greco-Roman style, of course) had to be transported up to the capital piece by piece: its fragmentation eloquently comments both the nation it is supposed to personify and the final destiny of the man who saw it as a way to celebrate the centenary of a fictitious "independence."

But these statues, this use of stone to signify immobility and failure, are not the only figures of stone in the book.

It is time to commemorate, among others, Miguel Estatua.

V

Miguel Estatua was a worker who, in the city of New Córdoba, had one day discovered that the mountain was full of animals and that it was possible, and that it was good, to extract statues from the rocks. The legendary and mythical character of this black artist is accentuated by the narrator's use of biblical terms (starting in Genesis and ending in the Crucifixion) to tell his story and martyrdom. When the upstart military who have sworn to defend the city in its rebellion against the Head of State are bought off by the government, another fatiguing instance of that everlasting cycle of insurrection and betrayal which besmirches Latin America, Miguel decides to intervene. As his name indicates, he will fight in the place of the Lord, a prince in charge of God's army against Satan. This opposition to the dictator—which has the unforeseen consequence, through photographs of the massacre, of exiling the Head of State from the Parisian salons—is not, however, merely political. Miguel is the Head of State's alter ego as far as attitudes towards history, nature, and culture go. The President constantly justifies the violence of his strategy by alluding to the land where he must act: what supposedly prevails there is the law of the jungle and the survival of the fittest, instinct and ruthlessness emerging directly from surrounding nature. But this vision is belied by Miguel's earth, from which he extracts beautiful redemptive animals. His rebellion against the Antichrist (prefigured by his refusal, months before, to make a statue of the dictator) is the direct and logical result of his love for Latin America, his capacity to express in that love a unity between land and art and, finally, social struggle. Miguel Estatua's activity is described with the same verb, *sacar,* to extract or take out from, which have been used for the mummy and General Ataúlfo Galván. This is a taking out from, not in order to leave the mud behind and reach the pulchritude of superior culture, but rather so that the potentiality of the earth can be elaborated in such a way that its products do not stand in antagonism to the men who produce them, reconciling the worker with his work—a true aesthetic of production as a utopian enterprise.[13] If the Head of State's statues exhibit all the false passivity of the man who paid to have them made, Miguel's, more than a decade before, indicate another possible direction in history, the possibility of participating in a different way.

This liberating, alternative perspective will never be completely absent from the novel. At the beginning, of course, the Head of State hardly even notices its existence. The narrative point of view consists precisely in bringing the ferocious transcendence of the popular struggle against the dictatorship only insofar as it starts to perturb the protagonist's perception of what is going on around him. The novel gradually gravitates toward the forces that will manage to defeat the dictator. In fact, the subversive movement against him appears in direct correlation to the empire's gradual appropriation of the country's economy and everyday life. One example will do: the first Christmas in which the mercantile Santa Claus begins to substitute the native traditions is followed by the first Easter where workers invent the strike—a resurrection of Miguel Estatua's strife through other means. This collective struggle will be incarnated in the Student who will give an organization and a rational direction to the energies that in Miguel Estatua were instinctive and spontaneous.[14] The dictator, naturally, tries to buy the young agitator off, with a scholarship to Paris—in other words, offering that he should become "somebody," like the mummy or the opera-goers. The answer is eye-opening: "I've nothing to do in Paris." Both Miguel and the Student have chosen a way of persisting in history which gainsay the path of the Head of State: they refuse to be sufferers of reality and try to break out of the circuit of passive dictators who oppress a passive multitude. They try to make history by modifying the current inhumanity, attempting to transform the marginal continent into a center of rebellion and self-knowledge based on that rebellion. All the Head of State's power does not manage to open up one of the pages of the *Petit Larousse Dictionary* so his name can talk to the future. His two presumably powerless detractors, on the other hand, appear, from the start, surrounded by a halo of legend, myth, magic, words, already re-elaborated by the popular collective mind, projected into deeds which the people will keep in memory and reproduce in the way they live.[15]

The Student says in a conversation with Julio Antonio Mella (the real historical figure he is modeled on), while they travel to Brussels on a train in 1927, that for a hundred years the same spectacle of a dictator falling and another replacing him has been repeated. The other answers that the repetition will continue "until the public tires of seeing it over and over." Just as the self-glorifying statues of the Head of State are contrasted with the warm, talking, miraculous statues of the evangelical animals in Miguel Estatua's "Sixth Day of Creation," so the theatrical gestures with which the President as actor has obfuscated his audience will someday be answered by that audience standing up and taking over the stage. The only way to make sure that the chronological time in which we suffer will not eternally be subjected to the structural time which repeats and guarantees our oppression, is to fracture the relationship, to begin narrating our own lives, to invent a different system to organize our lives, a spiral in history instead of an endless circle.[16]

That this route is even remotely possible is brought out by one of the strangest characters in the book and probably in all Carpentier's production: the Consular Agent who protects the Head of State when he is overthrown.

The story of this man is the exact opposite of the dictator's: the Consular Agent had a brilliant diplomatic career until one day, coincidentally in Paris, his superiors realized that he was visiting too many black and Caribbean dance halls, and demoted him to ever minor posts in irrelevant backlands. The Consular Agent could pass for white but was discriminated against because he was unable to resist the call of his Afro-American origins.[17] As an agent of an empire, he could well have exercised in the world a more eloquent and lasting influence than that of the puppet-like President, but did not do so because it would have meant betraying his deepest roots. Underneath his false white skin is the substantial inner river of who he really is, provoked by the art and music of his ancestors. As a marginal in the system he serves, he has no illusions about the values in whose name the black, the indigenous, the Latino are suppressed. He has decided neither to dissimilate or assimilate, taking an antithetical trip to the one planned by our tyrant, abandoning the European inheritance that he could have embraced in the States to assume the subordinate and despised African heritage. Having the real possibility of sharing the power of the contemporary caesars, the Consular Agent prefers the jazz, the sun, and a prodigious collection of Latin American roots which he has picked up on multiple beaches of the continent. These roots contain the intersection of culture and land, because the sea and the trees of the continent have forged a hybrid, syncretic intercrossing of forms which are recognizable as mestizo art, nature anticipating what the men and women of these lands must do with their lives if they are to be authentic.

The irony could not be more salient: at the very moment when he departs from the country he ruled so brutally, the Head of State's trajectory crosses that of someone who was loyal to his own identity and whose only patrimony are fragments of Latin American nature. His life is no longer only criticized by the intellectual who denies the validity of Paris as a place where something can be done, or by the worker who, without even having heard of Paris, produced sculpture as magnificent and fantastic as those of Notre Dame (at least, according to the sagacious eyes of Elmira), but by a representative of the very North Americans who eject him and who warns him that no worldly success can compensate for the misery into which you fall if you betray your sources.

That dream-like day in which he must leave America to die in Europe is the turning point in the real trip the Head of State has been taking all these years and which he only now begins to faintly understand. We would be tempted to call it a trip toward the seed, because Carpentier has given this name to the leitmotiv of so many voyages back in time that he has written, if it were not that in this case behind the seed is death and not resurrection. So we prefer to say it is a trip toward . . . yes, our old friend, the mummy.

VI

When the Head of State awakens powerless, the day of his overthrow, his first memory is of having lived a similar scene, when he was an adolescent, "after an appendix full of *seeds* was taken out" (my emphasis). He is, therefore, returned, both symbolically and through memory, to the initial moment when he inaugurated the labyrinth which is now coming to its end: that youth when he was nobody and wanted to be "somebody." At the very moment when he can finally spend the rest of his life in the Europe he so desired, he has lost all the guises and gestures he accumulated throughout his life, the forms of power with which he presumed to defend himself against old age and loneliness. This opens up for him another sort of journey, of an internal sort, toward his origins, toward the only thing left to him, toward what he should never have abandoned, the earth which is neither theater nor mask nor statue.

In effect, once he is installed in the City of Light, ready to enjoy the delights of civilization, what the former President does is entirely different: he becomes obsessed with the land he left behind. He forsakes his palace to seek accommodations in the servants' quarters, cohabitating with the black mistress who is the sole person who has remained faithful to him. He no longer reads the European periodicals but lives waiting for the arrival of those published back home. His body begins to submit to the rhythm of life back there: the hours, the food, the flavors, all gradually force him to turn everything upside down, converting European day into Latin American night, living as if he were not in Paris at all.

It is a surprising paradox. When he was in Nueva Córdoba, he did everything within his means to mold the country into a simulacrum of Paris, offering it foreign interests and fashions. Now that he is definitely residing in Europe, he craves what has been hidden inside his own body since childhood, an emotional-sensual-intuitive Eden to which he can return. His whole life has been dedicated to denying the earth, just as Miguel Estatua and the Student have spent their existence trying to transform their love for Latin America in social rebellion, that is, a base of power which guarantees their enduring in history and not in mere sensorial memory. The *Petit Larousse Dictionary* ("Je sème à tout vent," goes its ironic epigraph) had nourished him with so many Latin phrases but now will not conserve him in its seedbed of words. All he has left after power has been taken from him is the uncertain dictionary of his tastes and his reminiscences, what was once his when he began his ascent towards the salons, that which the Consular Agent did not disavow, the inner, past land that the Head of State has carried around with him all his life and tried to erase. It is the secret source of his personality and his joy in life, what has even allowed him to be critical of the Distinguished Academic and formulate opinions of his own. But instead of searching for unity within that zone of himself, instead of attempting to integrate earth and society, roots and culture, origin and history, the Head of State did what he could to separate and confront them. And that is why his trip backward is toward death and not toward life. He goes from adulthood to adolescence to childhood, but the fetus that is awaiting him at the end of this journey is the mummy of death ("like some gigantic fleshless fetus that had gone through all the stages of growth, maturity, decrepitude and death"). He will finish shut up inside the circle which he built for himself, unable to project onto history his love of the earth or the body that harbored this love, unable to go beyond his own ego and find others who could recover what his existence meant. He was so obsessed with inscribing his image in European books that he missed out on the chance to persist in a less legible and "cultured" way, in the wonderful myths and legends of his continent.

The "land" he is returning to is not only the inner land of his infancy but the quite real and hard ground of the cemetery, where the last act of his farce will be consummated: the Earth of the Sacred Soil of the Fatherland which covers his tomb has, in point of fact, been stolen from the Jardin de Luxembourg. It is the last theatrical falsification for visitors who will not come to pay their respects. Contemplate this chaos—as Descartes's epigraph to the epilogue urges us to do, this world turned upside down. The Head of State finally obtains the (Parisian) earth for which he plundered, lied, and killed: he has fashioned his dirt into "somebody."

He has gone to join the mummy. The fact that the ancient monarch of America has found himself, after death, sealed in a French museum, is due to what the present sovereign of America, he who had some power in this century, has done with the land they both inhabited. By dispatching the mummy—its culture, its civilization, its American land, its ancestry—to Europe, the Head of State is dooming himself, in the future, to a similar fate: instead of being somebody, being nobody. That is why the voyage in time can bring no redemption to the old dictator. It is a return as regressive and hopeless as his life itself: beyond and before the seed which gave birth to him, beyond and before his childhood or his point of departure, there is only the empty mockery of a circle. There will be no resurrection in history or in the earth for those who did not fertilize them.[18]

The Head of State arrives at his Mecca of Harmony and Rationality only to anchor himself in the tunnels of memory, installing a small corner of America in the rue Tilsit, trying to find a way into the past through meat, perfume, songs, herbs, tastes, anything that is still left intact by time. This process, which organizes his whole last year of life, culminates in a banquet which is prepared for him by Black Elmira, who has managed to shop for the food without getting lost, simply by following the rays of the primitive sun, in the shadowy unknown Paris which has rejected "her" President. Her cooking will drag not only the Head of State back to his native land, but his daughter Ofelia as well, the snobbish monstrous prolongation of her father's longings for "high" culture. She also descends towards infancy, towards the forgotten intemporal America of her past, toward a love which she no longer feels for her doddering Polonius father "a maize tamale on the end of a fork approached her eyes and descended into her mouth. When it was opposite her nose, a sudden inner emotion, coming from a long way off, a fluttering in her entrails, weakened her knees . . . She bit into it and all at once her body grew younger by thirty years. . . . Her cheeks blazing from the cider mixed with tequila and pineapple juice, tasting this and that, plunging her spoon in the avocado salad and dipping a turkey joint into chili sauce . . . in a marvellous recovery of time past."

It is quite obvious that the preceding scene is clearly related to the famous opening of Proust's *A la recherche du temps perdu*, where young Marcel, transferred to his childhood through the bite in a madeleine, receives a first splendid and confusing intuition about how time and the world are constituted which will be confirmed, decades and volumes later (though written by Proust right after the madeleine episode), when the same protagonist stumbles in a courtyard and repeats a similar introspective operation. This allows him to comprehend the secret network of signs and ventures which can, if experienced, bring back time that was thought lost.

There are, of course, major differences between the two texts. Marcel's discovery impels him to bring back to life and explore the totality of his existence and that of the society where he lived it, while our Head of State's meal does not give any deeper order to his fragmented life and is not resolved in a creative or re-creative act. The former President has dilapidated his years denying that eternity of the senses which he can now glimpse weakly through his eyes and tongue and nose. The original source of the marvels that can stop time are not only separated from him by an enormous ocean, but by his own brutal life, which he dedicated to destroy the continent that is the basis for that experience. In order to reconquer time past, to make the past coherent with the present, to reconcile the ego that observes with those who act and fill the air with gestures, to transform the space of reality into the space of the imagination, Proust's protagonist must live history bit by bit (almost bite by bite). He must accumulate and analyze, one by one, the experiences which will finally offer up syntheses. What is discovered, therefore, in spite of the crisis which is shaking the foundations of Proust's world, is the continuity and cohesion of consciousness. This enterprise, perhaps open to a French intellectual who has transmuted his life into the book, is forbidden to the American dictator, whose books have all been written already by other men from industrialized nations, who longs to be the word in alien mouths. The only authentic book where the Head of State could find his truth as Marcel Proust did in *A la recherche* is, of course, *Reasons of State*.

The constant loss, however, of the first person, constantly interrupted by the third person singular, indicates that, for the dictator, there is no continuity between his point of departure and the events which followed it, that his consciousness is unable to build the bridges which his action in history blew up. What the Head of State recuperates in his exile is no more than what his body already possessed sixty years ago: his intervention in history has not modified at all—nor made grow—that emotional and sensorial substratum. To remount time, for our tyrant, is only a leap to a static retrogression, making believe that everything else—what we did, what was done to us—is entirely illusory. In *The Lost Steps*, Carpentier had verified that there is no lasting return to the origins—unless it is accompanied by the opening to the further fertility of history. The Head of State does not find in the restitution of his infantile paradise any key that opens the totality of his life to comprehension. Rather than explore the steps that led him here, that internal homecoming is one more evasive action. "I have forsaken my house, I have left mine heritage," the President reads in the Bible the day of his ouster. Even his memory cannot escape the circular destiny that has plagued every moment of his life so far, because the body that incorporated that memory was not defended by the mind that now remembers, because that body did not join with other bodies to liberate that mind.

If Carpentier's borrowing of one scene from *A la recherche* therefore substantiates, yet again, the same limitations we have seen so often in our dictator's life, this was not the primary purpose of bringing up the French author's masterpiece. In fact, our excursion into Proust has only just begun.

VII

Marcel Proust is not mentioned even once in the whole text of *Reasons of State*. It cannot be an accidental omission. The author must have prepared that absence carefully, because he has stuffed his tyrant's horizon with an overwhelming amount of indirect references to the French author, to his friends, his books, his characters, even to the titles to his volumes.

Though the following does not pretend to be exhaustive, it should be sufficient to prove the point.

The Head of State's Parisian social world is filled with Proustian figures, both real and fictitious. Reynaldo Hahn, the Venezuelan musician who was Proust's confidant and who corresponded with him over a lifetime, is the one who explains to the dictator why, after the Nueva Córdoba massacre, nobody wants to receive him any more. Louisa de Mornand, another of Proust's friends, refuses to answer the Head of State's telephone calls.[19] And Dr. Fournier—the doctor who attends the Head of State as he dies—was a colleague of Proust's father, intimate enough with the family to have gone to the funeral of Marcel's mother.[20]

The imaginary beings are more significant, however, than the real ones. Paintings by Elstir, the artist invented by Proust, hang in the mansions of the rue Tilsit and of Marbella on the Pacific coast. We are even informed that Elstir has tried and failed, after the First World War, to modernize his vision—which means that Carpentier is giving an autonomous development to a character created by someone else. Something similar happens in music (we hear several times about Vinteuil and his sonata—elaborated by Proust, as in the case of Elstir, from a variety of real sources) and topography (we hear about Balbec and a tavern in the rue des Acacias which only exist in *Du côté de chez Swann* and not in the reality of France). The Head of State brags at the beginning of the novel about having been invited three times to the soirées of Madame de Verdurin where more than half of Proust's book transpires. And at the end of *Reasons of State* he says he dare not call her again because, in the years since he visited her, she has become related to princes. In other words, Carpentier's book takes into account the parallel alterations in the world that Proust was narrating. Other minor personages make cameo appearances in *Reasons of State*: the violinist Morel will not answer the phone; Brichot is outraged at the Head of State; and the Forchevilles, those snobs in search of the Verdurin's limelight, are briefly mentioned. To this must be added a series of literary borrowings,[21] along with the ironic insertion of several of *A la recherche*'s volume titles in the text itself.

These are only the most obvious, but not the most essential, connections. The Head of State's Parisian circumstances are modeled on Proust's literary and social world. They read the same papers and books, go to the same places, breathe the same air, watch the same ballet and opera. Like any of Proust's characters, the Head of State lives in leisure, thriving on gossip, a practitioner of the art of conversation. They share a context, an inter-text, a pre-text and—as we shall see—even a sort of text. In effect, *Reasons of State* opens on the day of the Drags at the end of 1913—at about the time that the first volume of *A la recherche* was being published.[22] And the end date of Carpentier's book, the day of his protagonist's death, is the Day of the Drags in 1927, exactly fourteen years later, which happens to also coincide with the appearance of the seventh and last volume of Proust's work. We are focused, therefore, on the fourteen years in the dictator's life during which that specific French novel was being published: his appearance and disappearance as a character coincides with the evolution of a real book, a book which—as we have mentioned—depicts the society that he wanted, above all things, to belong to. And just so no one will accuse us of using exclusively bookish images, let us add that a racing metaphor will do just as well: his odyssey stretches, as if he were indeed Caligula's horse, between two openings of a French steeplechase in Auteuil (which, by the way, is Proust's birthplace), once again racing toward the same circular destiny that has always plagued him.

The Head of State's situation seems, then, to be more fragile and precarious than we had reason to suspect. Not only will he be refused admission to the desired salons of "civilization," he is so marginal that he cannot even enter the fictitious salons imagined by a French writer. He is so dead among the dead, to quote Baudelaire, a character of such inferior ontological existence, that he is excluded, not only from the European world, but from the world of European literature. When Proust exhausted all the corners of that vast social world in decadence, he did not see any minor dictator floating there, worthy of the attention he spreads to lackeys, servants, cooks, chauffeurs. The Head of State's three visits to Madame Verudrin were not remembered (how could they be?) by the one narrator in the universe who proposed as his central task in life to forget absolutely nothing, not one person. The only one he forgot was the tinhorn tyrant.

The Head of State's blindness—already remarked as an incapacity to see that the real protagonists of his saga and his century are the empire and the resistant people—is therefore deepened. During his fourteen brief years of (literary) existence, he must have been incited constantly to plunge into the French novel which contains his life. Residing in those circles, knowing Reynaldo Hahn and Lousia de Mornand and Calmette (the *Figaro* editor who was responsible for Proust's journalistic pieces), reading the newspapers that the French novelist wrote in, he should have encountered him many times over. What a sweet vengeance exacted by Carpentier: the world of snobs that Proust subjected to an implacable critical eye,[23] whose values are adored by the Latin American dictator, will treat him like an object, with the same lack of commiseration that he used with his own country. This cruelty and lack of loyalty is certainly something that Marcel discovers over and over, but it reaches its culmination when Swann announces to the Princes of Guermantes that he is dying and has but a year of life, and they, instead of staying with him that night, run off to a party. They do have time, though, for the Princess to hurriedly return to change a piece of apparel that her husband has noted does not blend well with the other colors she is wearing.[24] This scene, which initiates the process of disillusionment with that world (which shall be, in Proust's case, emphasized by the Dreyfus case and French anti-Semitism) has its equivalent at the end of *Reasons of State* when Ofelia closes her father's eyes and declares that his death is not to be announced so as not to perturb her day at the races.[25] The daughter is doing nothing more than carrying out to its last consequences the dream that the dictator has proclaimed: in those supreme and cultivated social circles there is no place for the old, for the weak, for the dying, for the poor, for those who are worthless. (Let's not speak, heaven forbid, about workers, blacks, or Indians). The Head of State will be treated by his own progeny in the same way he treated the mummy: something dead to be used to one's own benefit.

Like a good laggard, our President has once again arrived late: the world he wishes to access is not only aesthetically backward, but morally corrupted—whose decadence and destruction Proust witnessed and narrated. The Head of State is missing both the analytic and synthetic consciousness[26] which is, finally, the real protagonist of *A la recherche*, the need to plunge into an emotion or an experience until its essential marrow can be extracted and understood. No wonder he cannot recognize the contemporary works of art that are struggling to express precisely those emotions, those experiences.

This allows us to comprehend the abundant use of Descartes in the book. We have already remarked on the title, but the

French philosopher is also quoted in each chapter heading as "an ironic counterpoint to Latin America's unpredictable, unstable and asymmetric social being,"[27] mocking the Head of State's grotesque attempts at imitation. He has taken as his model a world that pretends to be rational, illuminated, harmonious, measured, which proclaims the Cartesian preeminence of the intelligence and the spirit while at the same time imposing as his sole reason the need to conserve the state (and the state of disorder) at his service.

The dictator's literary existence opens, of course, at the very moment when, just before the First World War, the moral and social universe of Descartes is foundering. It is precisely those norms and preconceptions that Descartes has established as the a priori basis for a normal functioning of the world that are being assaulted by Proust as he establishs other relations between consciousness, time, and space. The Head of State takes pride in his Cartesian judgments when Europe is already exploring a different scientific, artistic, and philosophical dimension of the world. While the Europeans are discovering the validity and danger of instinct, emotion, involuntary memory, and intuition, in Latin America one need not search for these traits in dark closets. They can be found in the everyday light of days and bodies. And politically, Descartes's unlineal idealism is being disputed by Marxism's dialectic materialism which, in that same period, is finding its first historical triumph in the Bolshevik revolution. The Head of State is living in the most profound and aberrant chaos, a world of the upside down and the inside out. He applies to the exercise of power the irrational egocentricity of his instincts and attempts simultaneously to model his everyday behavior on the civilized refinements born of reason. He does this instead of impressing reason on his politics and searching in his private life for that adventure of emotion and love which could break down the solitude of stationary, repetitive time and official lies.

Perhaps the divorce between Proust and the Head of State is best symbolized by the latter's incapacity to understand the Debussy opera, *Pelléas and Mélisande*, that had fascinated the French author in 1902. Carpentier, in one of the few liberties with history that he takes in the novel,[28] moves back the opening of that opera from 1921 to 1914 so that the retrograde character of the Head of State can be made categorically manifest. His surface culture cannot possibly understand the depths that are already rebutting, as Adorno has shown, the positivist facades of reality.[29]

Less apparent than Carpentier's debt to Proust in reference to characters and social world is the importance of *A la recherche* for the ways in *Reasons of State* is composed and narrated.

The most evident of these influences is that Proust's magical number seven (his seven volumes) spreads all over the Carpentier novel. It is a number, as Roberto González-Echevarría has shown,[30] which is constantly repeated: the action lasts fourteen years, there are twenty-one sub-chapters (plus the previously mentioned epilogue, of which more later), and the central historic upheavals all occur in chapters 7, 14, and 21. Let me add—all of us have rights, I suppose, to our own personal obsession—that there are seven mummies in the cave and that Karl Marx's *Capital* sells for twenty-two pesos ("Let them sell it, let them sell it; let them keep on selling it," the Head of State chortles when he hears the price. "There aren't twenty-two persons in the country who would pay twenty-two pesos for that book.") Of course, enough people, twenty-two plus twenty-two plus twenty-two will read the book, or be inspired by it, to help oust the Head of State, to break the round numerology of twenty-one, to force an epilogue that destroys the European framework that tries to contain his life. The number which is not included, which falls outside the text prepared for the dictator, marks the distance that Carpentier and Latin America have established with Proust and Europe.

That *A la recherche* serves as a correlative for the Carpentier novel should not surprise us. This is a literary procedure which the Cuban novelist uses frequently in his other works. Beethoven's Eroica Symphony, along with commenting on the escape of the anti-heroic gangster of *The Chase*, indicates the last forty-six minutes of life left to the hunted protagonist, weaving in and out of his mind with the leitmotivs of the musical work. *Baroque Concert* experiments with baroque musical techniques to tell the long years that pass between the opening of a Vivaldi opera and its rediscovery in the 1930s. Carpentier's last novel, *The Rites of Spring*, develops a counterpoint between Stravinsky's subversive music and the political struggle of the twentieth century, the way in which the marginal millions enter the earth both of music and the revolution. Though music is Carpentier's preferred artistic form for this sort of experiment, he has also used painting, as in the invented picture, "Explosion in a Cathedral" which concentrates and reflects all the reverberations and cataclysms of the late eighteenth century. In all these cases, it is someone else's artistic creation which helps to frame and submit to order an abundant literary material threatening to break loose. So it is, I believe, with *A la recherche* (with its recurring musical structure[31]): it sets firm limits to the dispersed and disorderly existence of an American dictator, measuring his efforts from the simultaneous set of signs that Proust disseminates in the Paris where both of them are to die. The heartbeats of the tyrant will last only the time it takes for Proust's book to be published. Foreign culture will act then, as in so many of Carpentier's contemporaries, as an organizer of a fragmented world that the instability of underdevelopment has made doubly unsteady and inexplicable. There is, therefore, in *Reasons of State* and in the way the dictator's life is shaped, that "ordonnance cachée" which André Gide considered the key to Proust's work.[32]

When Carpentier synthesizes a country, its history, its dictator in such a way that they represent all the countries and dictators of the continent as well as a unique story told only once, he is using Proust's technique of "régroupement," used for his own characters, places, and scenes.[33] The invented novelist Bergotte is very similar to Anatole France, but also recalls other intellectuals of the time. The nonexistent Balbec is born of the confluence of Cabourg, Evian, and Trouville. Many of the characteristics of the fictional figures can be traced back to real components, but their sum total goes beyond their documented source to function as a full human being—not a mere metaphor.[34] This allows Proust to join what is intimate with what is historical, what is biographical with what is imaginary, what is witnessed with what is elaborated through memory, what is observed with what is re-created: this is the way in which he desired to have his life endure as a work of art, the aesthetic experience sustaining what something means in the very instant of its apprehension, in what came before and came afterward. Proust himself, defending his work in 1914, suggested that in it the telescope and the microscope were joined, the vastest laws finding themselves incorporated in the minutest details—and that critics were only noticing the second aspects and not the first.[35]

Mario Benedetti has studied the way in which Carpentier uses humor in *Reasons of State* to obtain the exact equilibrium between complicity and distancing that his subject requires.[36] This is the sort of literary strategy that Carpentier adds to the Proustian models in order to solve dilemmas that neither the French authors nor his European followers ever had to face:

How to present, simultaneously, history as a repeated circle of oppression and history as a liberating spiral? How to show from inside an abominable and dominant character without withdrawing from him a certain sympathy, a certain sense of pity? How to insert the dictator in a rigid network of historical contingencies and also allow him to point in the direction of his deeper and more permanent structure? How to take up residence in the date by date calendar and in the system which surpasses it? How is it possible to write a work which is totally Latin American dealing with a period, a man, a continent which have been forged from external models and pressures?

Epilogue

Alejo Carpentier arrives in Paris in the year 1928. It is the year after his fictitious character is bound to die, the year which follows the publication of *Le temps retrouvé*. The difference with the Head of State could not be more considerable: he is escaping from the Machado dictatorship that had jailed him for seven (yes, seven, though I doubt there is any connection) months and knew Proust's work thoroughly.[37] Indeed, "the discovery of Marcel Proust, whose works were beginning to arrive in Havana, absolutely devastated me," he said in an interview,[38] disclosing to him the possibility of overcoming the narrative traditions of realism which copies and reproduces only the surface of things.

Carpentier, therefore, will be neither Proust nor the Head of State's contemporary, but he will take up residence in the world that they made, that each of them, in rather opposite ways, left him as a legacy. Decades later he will return to Paris as a member of revolutionary Cuba's diplomatic mission. And one hundred years after the birth of Marcel Proust, one hundred years after the Commune which was to shake the foundations of the world that the illustrated dictator was seeking to enter, in 1971, Carpentier will begin to transmit and transpose the faithful and sarcastic chronicle of those fourteen years which preceded his first Parisian visit.

The Cuban novelist is able, therefore, to know and recover—
through reading, art, documents, journals, meditations, in other
words through memoirs and memories, through research and *la
recherche*—those years which he did not live with his immediate
body and who anybody with a lesser imagination would have
thought completely lost. His Head of State inhabited that city during the whole period and did not accumulate sufficient culture or
power to draw near to the era in which he was presumably acting out his story, to enter into a legitimate relationship with the
Proust book in whose index his name does not appear.

So *Reasons of State* would seem to demonstrate an intellectual
maturing of Latin America, betokening in its aesthetics the exactly
opposite itinerary to the one the dictator attempts. What better
homage to Proust than to use him fully, making him pass through
the mirror (and the mud) of Latin America? Is there a less dependent, a less subjected, way of exploring and recognizing an influence, a learning process, a distance? What is political, therefore, in
this novel is not so much the Student's theses, on the struggle of
the somewhat anonymous masses, or Miguel Estatua's dynamite,
or the insurrection which will reveal the *carnavalesque* reality of
authoritarian institutions, as the discovery of an intellectual act
which seeks and puts into practice the lost independence of a supposedly lost continent, the discovery of the time we have wasted
in a continent which is both miserable and marvelous.

Carpentier's vision is the result of two historical events: one, the
Cuban revolution which, with all its imperfections and problems,
became the first Latin American society that rejected the path and
destiny of the mummies; and two, the language and literature of
Latin America which has been creating a tradition secure enough
in its identity to allow us to claim that we own those ways of seeing
with which the world—including Europe—has been determining
our lives.

Alejo Carpentier establishes with the French novel of Marcel
Proust a relationship among equals, almost fraternal one might
say, murmuring to him in low tones that the deaf and dead dictator
cannot overhear, that dictator who still threatens to continue mur-
dering and deceiving in Latin America today and tomorrow, that
the precondition for any dialogue, and for any permanent place in
history that we must all build as we suffer it, is our own dignity.

1980

■ Political Code and Literary Code: The Testimonial Genre in Chile Today

The abundance of material written about Chile since the coup in 1973 should surprise no one. The interpretations, exegeses, and informative books flow both out of the sympathy that the popular government of Salvador Allende awoke in the world and the feeling that there was something universally ominous about the brutality with which the military, decades after it was supposed that Hitler and Mussolini had been defeated and buried, punished the Chilean people for having dared to pursue their liberation.

Within this immense variety it is interesting that a vast quantity of literature has been published that could be gathered under the common rubric of "testimonial literature," refering to the repression Chilean men and women have suffered under the dictatorship and the time that they have spent in concentration camps. In many cases, these are newspaper reports in which an author attempts to recover and make explicit the experience of dozens of victims, centralizing the various points of view, realizing a typical job of *editing* a text: he investigates and researches, collects and selects, tapes and cuts, adds, eliminates and polishes. Most of these efforts were born at the end of 1973[1] and were shaped in 1974 and 1975, made urgent by the need for political denunciation and possible because it catered to a large public that constituted an attractive commercial market for publishing houses. Diverse, creative methods were used in these investigations: from the sophisticated and panoramic collage of *Dossier Noir* to the skillful, sober, and vibrant work of Sergio Villegas in *El Estadio*, to the narrow and Dantesque spiral of horror in *Evidence on the Terror in Chile*,[2] strategies were elaborated to mold the voices into a unity, diverse in tone but unfortunately similar in experience, of people who had been through a form of hell. It is not, however, the purpose of the present essay to examine those articles. It does matter, nevertheless, to remark that, since such reports originated in a stimulus that does not come from the witnesses themselves, but rather from an investigator who takes their oral language and, after some modifications, transfers it to paper, a type of discourse is established for each speaker that is quite natural and fluid, and free of that uncomfortable self-consciousness of having to directly confront a reader. That is, when the witness reveals his experience, he does not feel at the same time the responsibility to give literary expression to it; he does not review it critically; there is an organizer of what is said, who without having witnessed himself what he will transcribe, resolves, eliminates, orients, and annuls, making decisions about what should be the points of conflict and of plot, as well as the order of events.[3]

Many of those voices, anonymous or not, remained at that first step, what we could call the oral stage, having a precise and spontaneous plasticity, vibrating like conversations, bubbling with action and life. But they did not confront the necessity of enlarging the nucleus of their experience beyond the oral. Others saw themselves, more significantly, pressed to take a second step, to express in writing the horror of which they had been a part, to fix it in time, for once and for all. If, as we shall see, the oral idiom, its temptation and origin, continues to haunt them like a ghost, by taking that step, they admitted that they had something more to do than to pronounce words into a tape recorder; they were something more than eyes watching a pencil move across a page perhaps with the autonomy with which other hands they had seen were capable of inflicting pain. They felt that they had to be the translators and organizers of their own materials: moving forward, they took the risk of sitting down and searching for the written words that would give expression to what they had to articulate, and later they circulated it in the form of a manuscript or a mimeograph copy or even as a book—the transposition of that enclosed episode in their lives.

Here we are going to study exclusively a representative sample of those many texts which achieved, for one reason or another, the culmination of appearing in print, going beyond the private sphere. But even more remain unpublished, being passed from hand to hand within political parties, within the circles of solidarity, among friends or acquaintances, soliciting the opinion of writers, critics, and journalists. The books that we will examine, therefore, are part of a vaster and more meaningful phenomenon: hundreds, and eventually thousands, of Chileans who earlier had never considered expressing themselves through what we could call literary means, give priority after the coup to their obligation to do so, to leave their observations to the future.

I have already discussed elsewhere the general causes of this displacement of time and energies toward the field of culture.[4] Periods which follow defeat after years of activism and service to society usually demand the exteriorization of thoughts and emotions that had been germinating earlier. But the ebb not only produces the immediate need of a self-examination of the past and of our responsibility as we confront it, but in addition offers sufficient time to carry out those reflections or balances, since many enthusiasms that were channeled into politics now, under the protection of new rhythms, attempt some other, perhaps more solitary, outlet. Just as important is the fact that people tend to realize in defeat, and in the struggle against a dictatorship, that culture is essential, more than an adornment or a propagandistic aid. The repressive tactics of authoritarianism play a paradoxical role, by revealing to those muzzled the value of their expressive inventory. In the case of the exiles—and it is in exile that most of the testimonials were generated—one can note that language begins to present itself as a territory to continuously retain and reclaim, subject as it is to the deterioration and the augury of distance, and that the presence of foreigners pushes many to communicate with those who have not shared those specific experiences. While solidarity offers means and windows for expression, the dispersion of the diaspora lays bare the need for culture as a network of unity and integration for the wasted country left behind and lost. All these characteristics, which apply equally to poetry, theater, music, and the plastic arts, assume their true meaning within the context of the disorganization of the national culture being attempted by the tyranny back home and the reorganization upon other foundations to which the democratic forces are compelled.[5] These similarities should not blind us, however, to the fact that certain, specific characteristics are the result of the person's experience in particular.

The need for the written word is rooted in several causes: indig-

nation at the treatment received and the desire and duty to proclaim the infamy of their captors; the silence enforced during their
captivity; the linguistic counterproposal that was quietly being
formulated during the events; service to a cause, making comprehensible—and bearable—past afflictions; and emphasizing the
heroism (at least in the majority of cases) of those who did not
succumb in the face of this catastrophe. Neither should we ignore
the cathartic, almost therapeutic and confessional, direction taken
by certain testimonies.[6] But if all this is true, what one senses more
than anything else in each one of the accounts, whether published
or not, whether formulated by professionals of the word or by
amateurs, is the dignity of the prisoners.

   This dignity of so many human beings is not abstract and metaphysical: it can be considered a victory of the Chilean people, a
product of their entire history, the result of decades of struggle
whose most significant incarnation was the three years of Popular
Unity. To be able to write these visions, to dare emerge, they must
have been seduced by a fundamental certainty: they are capable
of becoming the narrative voices of their own destiny, believers
in the permanency and durability granted by the dynasty of the
written word, people who are (or were) equal to history.

   There can be no doubt that this process of dignification had one
of its clearest manifestations in the very testimonials that arose
during the Popular Unity movement, giving expression to different experiments in universities, communities, industries, towns,
etc., and whose most fascinating materialization was the collection published by Editorial Quimantú, "Nosotros los Chilenos"
("We the Chileans"), which delved into various facets and activities of the people's invisible life, mixing such bizarre characters as
the organ-grinders with faces as unquestionably typical as the coal
miners.

   Nevertheless, what really stands out is that not one of those
who have written post-coup testimony had devoted himself to that
genre at the time of Popular Unity, nor other forms of literature.
I will discuss the exceptional case of Hernán Valdés in a separate
subchapter, precisely because he is the only writer of a testimonial
who had earlier made literary production his vocation, although
he had never directly narrated an episode of his autobiography.

   This means that, to the decency and the integrity they already possessed, these chroniclers of themselves add the feeling of having inhabited an exceptional experience, something that only happens from time to time, something that has led them to see themselves as representatives of a collective destiny that transcends them, but representatives of something, in any case, out of the ordinary. If the revolutionary process in Chile and the decades of previous democratic struggle gave these men a sense of their own humanity, what Pinochet has offered them—a harsh and savage gift—is the consciousness of having passed the test victoriously, of having defended and developed that right to call themselves human. Each testimony—and above all, all of them together, their extraordinary abundance—extends a certain concept of man and of woman opposite to the one exercised and cultivated by the torturers. Having fulfilled their duty, having given a sense and a reason to the rage and to the humiliation they have suffered, becomes in the secret source of all the accounts, a very concrete form to reiterate their ethical superiority in the face of totalitarianism. If we accentuate this trait, it is because we believe that the hundreds, and perhaps thousands, of testimonies would not have been possible if during so many dawns of waiting the people had not persisted in the multiple task of dignifying the everyday man, if that man who would be tortured in dark cellars had not tasted the forbidden fruit of history, the joy of dreaming he was in the very center of the light and not at its outer edge.

At the same time, these accounts are the product of another phenomenon: in the concentration camps, the prisoners discovered the importance of art and of culture as a means of drawing a line between the oppressors and themselves. Many of those who wrote these testimonies attained some new and original form of culture (generally written) within these enclosures. Poetry, theater, short stories, and cantatas flourished, and there were contests, rehearsals, and classes. Two of the witnesses whose works we are going to analyze in detail became so enthused with their integration into the cultural struggle that not only is it possible to see their testimonies as a continuation of that experience in captivity, but also since then they have dedicated themselves to go on writing other works.[7]

The new writers, therefore, have no previous professional, literary knowledge with which to carry out their task. Some have worked in journalism, others have written essays or analytic works, many may have written in the loneliness of their own rooms; but no one, at least publicly, had attempted to organize the material of his own experience into words, and to unfold an account—even in first person—that had a beginning, a middle and an end, trying to produce specific effects on the readers. The eruption of these hundreds of new cultivators of the written word—an essential tendency of current Spanish American, and specifically Chilean, culture—is an unparalleled opportunity, then, to analyze the relationship between ordinary people and literary language, between militants and cultural models, between tradition and innovation in a period of change, between political expression and social contact, and also to see close-up the forms—their perspectives and their limitations—which the democratic cultural alternative will take as it confronts the dominant imperial pressures in Chile.

II

The works I have chosen to analyze (*Prisión en Chile* [*Prison in Chile*] by Alejandro Witker; *Jamás de rodillas: Acusación de un prisionero de la junta fascista de Chile* [*Never on My Knees: A Prisoner's Accusation against the Chilean Fascist Junta*] by Rodrigo Rojas; *Prigué* [*Prisoner of War*] by Rolando Carrasco; *El alcaide preso* [*The Imprisoned Warden*] by Carlos Lira; *Cerco de púas* [*Barbed-wire Fence*] by Aníbal Quijada Cerda; *Chile: 11807 horas en campos de concentración* [*Chile: 11807 Hours in Concentration Camps*] by Manuel Cabieses; *Testimonio* [*Testimony*] by Jorge Montealegre)[8] offer us, among other things, an ample and representative panorama of the repression as well as of the resistance of the Chilean people. The participants cover a wide gamut:[9] of diverse ages, social and professional origins, coming from different branches of the Chilean left and occupying hierarchies of a varied nature within the parties, even from geographic locations scattered throughout the country, the witnesses invite us to cross the borders of the tormented land that was born in September of 1973. Reading how the vanguard that brought about the triumph of 1970, and that could not prevent its defeat three years later, survived that defeat can also help us to understand the strengths and weaknesses of the struggle in present-day Chile.

■ Almost twenty years before the Chilean testimonies were published, a former prisoner summarized in a precise manner the basic
dilemma that underlies any account which tries to reveal in the
first person the effects of torture and captivity.

"In this enormous, overpopulated prison in which each cell
shelters a suffering, to speak of oneself, seems to be indecent."

The voice is that of Henri Alleg in Algiers in 1957, opening *La
Question* (*The Question*), a wrenching and dispassionate account
of his own martyrdom at the hands of the French army,[10] whose
methods would be passed on to the training courses for Latin
American officers.[11] He narrates the interminable tortures, his
equally interminable refusal to denounce his companions in the
resistance, his stubborn heroism, and the "forbidden songs, the
magnificent songs,"[12] which filtered in from the barracks' underground. Where, then, is the indecency? Why this feeling that to
exhibit one's own torture is, curiously, to come close to quasi-
obscenity?

A revolutionary, of course, prefers to belittle himself and call
attention to the other, silent members of the struggle, particularly
when he has survived a horrible experience. As evidenced by several analyses of those who managed to escape cold death in the
Nazi extermination camps,[13] whoever emerges from a disaster has
difficulty communicating his experiences, bearing, as he does, the
weight of thousands who succumbed and who could have been
himself, feeling a dark shame for the wonderful fact of being alive.
Nor does the witness of degradation wish to confront again in
brutal detail what was done to his body. All victims of an overwhelming humiliation, however bravely they have borne it, prefer
to cover certain naked facts, forget the limits of the bearable. It is
not strange, then, that these heroes would rather keep their own
face in the shadows and their name in anonymity, without "running the risk of self praise."[14] Their fearlessness and bravery were
not exercised with the object of boasting about it later. The epic
should be a third-person genre, distant and removed, a rhythm
entoned by others and not by oneself.

Although the witnesses do decide, in spite of these inner qualms,
to unchain their voices, this dilemma will have consequences
throughout their accounts: in the methods of depersonalization;
in the negligence with which they treat the language, riding rough-

shod over their vehicle of communication as if there were no doubt that there is no room for an "aesthetic" and calculated elaboration of so much sadness and inhumanity; and in the very structure of the narrative.

Perhaps for that reason, also, almost all the testimonies are preceded by a prologuist who underscores the value for the readers of the deed that they are about to witness, many of them indicating that those responsible for exteriorizing those experiences are not the authors themselves but rather the ones who stimulated them to publish, thus legitimizing that action. There is even the case of a prologuist, Galo Gómez, who himself opens his introduction pointing out the difficulties of writing it: "It is hard for me, in fact it pains me, to write this prologue. . . It is not easy to do it; it is like writing about oneself, remembering so many things, but it is good to do it."[15]

The usefulness of testimony, then, overrides the pain of having had to transmit it. The account, with all its unpleasantness and even repugnance, fulfills practical functions in the war against an occupying army, in the war to democratize the country, answering not only the brutal and repressive policies of an irrational government, but also the ideological arguments and the cultural strategies that accompany, reinforce, and justify that violence. Terror, to be effective, has *to be known*. The greater the fear, the easier it is to manipulate, to "normalize," and to exploit.

Terror, then, has a public character. As such, it leads to a great ideological operation,[16] which authorizes, in the name of Western, Christian values, a purifying crusade against the forces of the Devil and of the anti-nation. This demonic image erected and publicized by the military is essential to exercise their fury and to do so in an immaculate manner. Thus, for each arbitrary act that becomes public, for each act of cruelty, a legislation is created, often after the fact, which serves as both excuse and apology.[17] Combining— as corresponds to a dependent and underdeveloped country—the threads of Catholic and Hispanic traditionalism with the powerful modernizing technocracy of the multinational corporations,[18] the principal obsession of authoritarian politics is to suppress history and those who could modify it, postulating an unchangeable and superior reality (God, fatherland, family) to which one owes loyalty.

What is paradoxical about this ideological framework is that it excuses a repression that, in fact, is never admitted by official channels. Memory of the suffering must survive in gossip, in rumor, in the whispering of what they did to Juana, or to Carlos's neighbor, and where is Pedrito, did you know that . . . ?, and even in official threats, but at the same time, in each concrete case, in each undeniable and documented case, with damaged teeth, and genitals and ribs, in spite of each relative's identification, in spite of the cries of pain, the truth of that violence is denied and attributed to international communist conspiracies. On the one hand, therefore, the repression is justified, and on the other, those who have suffered at its hands are accused of being liars. The excesses and the consequences of torture are abstracted, while all its admonitory advantages and its brutal threat are maintained. The people are punished, but in the long run the relationship is made benevolently and paternally innocent, translating it into terms that are almost "familial" and intimate: expulsion and exclusion of the wayward, the recalcitrant, the disturbers of public order; reintegration of the misguided and the repentant. Neo-colonial fascism takes the bourgeois dream to its totalitarian culmination: eliminating the materiality of the body while at the same time benefiting from its production and consumption. An eternal present of fear is created, meant to purge the past that has led the person to rebellion and to eliminate the future toward which it led. It is not enough to suppress the adversary if you do not erase her memory and her ability to organize an alternative project.

In the face of this strategy, we can understand that the three primary functions of the testimonies are *to accuse* the executioners, *to record* the sufferings and the epics, *to inspire* the other combatants in the middle of retreat. A fourth function, which we see less in these texts than in others, is to carry out a rational analysis of the problems and the reversals that are being suffered today (for example, we find this capacity in Witker).

Above all, *to accuse*.

Although the emotional tone varies and blends, going from Carrasco's fervent passion to Quijada's serene, always controlled vision, it is clear that all these authors believe that, in the first place, their words constitute a denunciation. In the case of Rodrigo Rojas, that fact is incorporated into the subtitle of his book, while

Cabieses's book is, in fact, the transcription of his deposition before the War Crimes Court held in Mexico City in February of 1975, in which case his immediate interlocutors are the judges who would weigh and evaluate the evidence and pronounce a verdict that, for now, can have only a moral impact. But although the others are not offering testimony directly, they all act as if they were doing so, presenting their authentic observations as part of a worldwide trial of the insanity of the Chilean government, with the peoples of the world, history or posterity, indistinctly, acting in the role of judges. The bases of the retribution, "the moment of judgment and of punishment" (Carrasco, p. 250), therefore, are founded upon the allegations and imputations of those who were implacably repressed. "The assassins elevated to power," Cabieses prophesies, ". . . know that they are condemned, even if they manage to escape the country. Wherever they go, the people's justice will follow them and will make them pay for their crimes" (p. 64). This confidence in the equanimity and probity of the verdict of history leads them to abolish the present of defeat and to conceive their work itself as a minimal and vicarious revenge for the torments they have received. The one who carries this imprecatory judgment forward with the most stubborn scrupulousness is Rolando Carrasco, who on many occasions interrupts the march of his own account to directly rebuke the torturers, the heads of the concentration camps, the members of the junta, as if in the text itself he could confirm aloud all the words that he had been mulling over in his mind throughout the years of his captivity but had been forced to keep silent. In the face of "Príncipe," the sadistic master of the Chile Stadium, who asked them not to forget what they were suffering, Carrasco replies: "We will not forget it. Several thousand Chileans saw you, Príncipe, and we will remember every one of your features. Even if you take off the uniform and let your hair and your beard grow we will recognize you. And if you hide we'll recognize you and find you. You, and the others like you, will pay for every blow, every insult. Traitorous murderer of your own country, your flag and your uniform. You will have no peace to your dying day! You remember it, too!" (pp. 53–54). Carrasco repeats this procedure at several opportunities, rebuking Pinochet or Merino ("The poor do have honor, Merino . . . Did you take note of that, Merino?", p. 209). Promising that "every one of the violations of the most basic norms of respect for women is recorded for the public trial that we will institute" (p. 285), with his words punishing the criminals who, years later, go on, comfortably like anti-Macbeths, installed in power. "Just like this son of a bitch," says Lira in his typically colloquial language, "there are many that history should know,"[19] and he devotes many pages to reconstructing the antecedents, names, participation, and guilt of his jailers, with determined, implacable, and fierce devotion. At times, this reduces each account to a boring series of names, only some of which manage to attach themselves to a real face. All the former prisoners are sustained by the certainty that if now they must be satisfied with ethical condemnations, tomorrow these detailed dossiers will render a concrete and real service. Language assumes meaning because history also has meaning.

The second function, that of *recording*, is intimately tied to the first. For the future to be different (for the merely moral judgment to follow and execute its desired course), the past must be retained. If the object of the concentration-camp mentality—also in that vaster and more subtle concentration camp that is the country itself—is to leave "the people naked, innerly denuded," in the words of a survivor of Buchenwald,[20] the prisoners must be filled, sown, fertilized with history from within, transforming the impossible present moment into memory. Through their consciousness they escape the limits which the guards impose on their visions, preparing in the middle of that swampland of humiliation a version that will transcend it. In the face of the official positions, in the face of the censors' monopoly, the witnesses offer their counter-interpretation. This has always been, in fact, one of the deepest roots of testimony in Latin America: to gather up the vision of the conquered and the marginal, to transmit the lives and hopes and frustrations of those who have no place in history books or newspapers. This distance between the public version and the private observations has stimulated many chronicles on our continent since Bernal Díaz del Castillo's narrative of the conquest of Mexico.

To forget, then, even if it's just an incident or a name, is to allow the jailors to control the conscious minds just as they control the bodies, as if a storm were allowed to go on exercising its tidal wave of power over the wreckage after it had sunk the ship.

The military project their insurrection as definitive, a quick and eternal cut in the development of the country so that from there on an unbridgeable chasm will be opened between the inhabitants of the new territory and the place that for centuries they called their own. Memory, then, serves as a bridge in the face of the surgeon's attempt. Witker presents it, speaking for the others, when he establishes that the challenge of a raised fist in the National Stadium is a symbol of forty years of socialist history: "To gather up the legacy of that history is basic to realizing our unfinished project; a task which we humbly hope will be served in part by this book . . ." (p. 25). To remember, to report, is to guarantee the continuity of a struggle, of a cause and, basically, of a country.

This leads us to the third function of testimony: *to inspire*. Memory inscribes its elaboration within a project of hope and will only retain those manifestations that contribute to strengthening that "mad faith" (a phrase used by Carrasco) of the people in the midst of defeat. What the neo-fascists have constructed as a monument to terror and to destruction, in order to bend the popular will, the witnesses transform into an homage to the future, proof of a faraway victory, lessons in courage, perserverance, elevation, which verify that verbs conjugated in the future tense do not lack a present foundation. The junta has attempted to isolate Chileans to cynical, spiritless atoms with no other destiny than to produce cheaply and consume expensively. All the testimonies react against this enterprise with indignation, attempting to convince the readers that satanic power is not infinite, proven by the epic of those small, bound titans, their cycle of sacrifice, abnegation, and solidarity. The emotive tone, often heightened to the point of the melodramatic, has as a backdrop the miserable, gray litany that the military would like their captives to chant day and night.

The testimonies end up by being an exploration of what Chile really is, what it might become. Behind the two major themes (testing the courage of the people; unmasking the insane twists and turns of repression) two countries join in combat, that of the junta and that of the rebels or, if you prefer, two concepts of the same country face off, two possible directions for Chile and for the world. Which means that we are invited on a voyage of discovery, an introduction to the new Chile: the armed forces demon-

strating their renewed (and old) savage face; the patriots exhibiting their recent (and deeply rooted) signs of courage. All the witnesses live, therefore, a process of confrontation with reality and
revelations concerning the nature of the country: in this "extreme"
situation they can come close to both the people in solidarity and
the mechanisms of defense adopted by dependent capitalism when
it is threatened by forces seeking radical change. They can find—
beyond all the myths, the prejudices and the theories—the profound Chile, the worst and the best beneath the appearances.[21]

Although any of the testimonies could exemplify this crossing of
a wasteland to truth, this descent into an inferno in order to be reborn with greater confidence, the one by Jorge Montealegre is the
one that demonstrates these characteristics with the most trans-
parency, perhaps due to the narrator's youth, perhaps because of
his Christianity; the faith in humanity, the attempt to share in the
suffering of the dispossessed and the injured, the anger aroused by
injustice and hypocrisy, are all heightened here. Far from breaking the protagonist, what the torturers have done is to confirm
him in his pathway, not a road to Damascus, therefore, of conversion, but a road to Golgotha. The history of a captive people
blends with the evolution and apprenticeship of the speaker, who
has grown and become politicized in jail. To the official, dominant Christianity of the chaplains, he opposes revolutionary Christianity, liberation theology, the multiplying of the loaves. It is
clear—as will become apparent later—that such pathos and sustained exaltation cannot but affect the structure of the communication. The narrator constantly intervenes, expressing opinions,
becoming lyrical, adding abundant adjectives, flooding each word
with his youthful subjectivity and his preaching (the cement is
cold and imprisoned, the wait is great, dark, and tedious). His testimony vacillates, then, between narrative and almost mystical en-
thusiasm, between anecdotal description and invention, between
the recounting of what happened and the moralizing and didactic
intervention of the protagonist.

By not questioning the process of his own suffering, Montealegre, in his own way, solves one of the basic problems that plague
these testimonies: that of heroism. Perhaps unconsciously, he has
followed the arguments of his companion in captivity, Manuel

Cabieses, who explains that "the hardships of prison are lessened when one thinks that he is not, in any way, the center of the problem."

Though all these accounts are structured by the struggle of good against evil, shining with examples of revolutionary firmness, for reasons mentioned earlier, it is impossible for the hero to exhibit his own greatness, to place his own person above that of the others, to pass his own legend along to the coming generations.

The witnesses resolve this dilemma of all resistance literature, by Cabieses's methods of depersonalization: "Depersonalizing our situation, to the extent possible, not only alleviates it, but also enables us to better understand it" (p. 67). It is the answer that each and every one of them gives to the words of one of the torturers, a captain, as recorded by Quijada: "There's no place for the word 'we' here. Each one should think of himself, of his own family. Just *his own* personal situation" (p. 25, *his own* underlined in the text).

Perhaps the best example of this technique for reconstructing and presenting the "we"—which should not be confused with a conscious and rational literary strategy, but seems rather a spontaneous translation of each narrator's ethic—is that which underlies the entire account of Rodrigo Rojas.[22] The mistreatment that he received (three simulated firing squads, weeks submitted to the infamous velodrome in the National Stadium), in keeping with his high political position, is not conceived by him as "an individual drama," in the words of Volodia Teitelboim in the prologue, "but rather as an enormous, collective tragedy." When he explains to his lawyer, at the end of the work, that he does not want to use any kind of trickery to achieve his own liberation ("I understand that individually I have no importance or value. The process is not directed against me, but rather against my party," p. 85), he is making explicit something we already find in the way in which he has drawn us close to his own tortures during the previous narrative. Here, for example, is how he describes his first beating:

"Sergeant, form the guard to honor the prisoner."
I imagined what those "honors" would be. I thought I would be killed immediately. But that wasn't the case.
Two lines of between 20 and 30 soldiers formed in square at the barracks entrance.

The prisoner had to walk down the street formed by the soldiers, receiving "honors" which consisted of blows and kicks. I woke up bleeding and in pain in a cell. (p. 10)

The third person is used here (the prisoner) in order to objectify, to remove any sense of the heroic, to distance the individual "I." He returns immediately to the first person (I woke up), when the ceremony is over. The same intention results in the constant use of the infinitive: "Form a line, be numbered and wait" (p. 23), or "Returning to the Stadium in the afternoons, in pain and bloody, weak and firm, hopeful and certain like all the others who were beaten by Pinochet's minions" (p. 50).

A similar attitude is observed in Carrasco's lack of interest in his own person during the following interrogation:

"What's your name?
I give my name.
"What party do you belong to?
To the Communist Party.
(pp. 28–29)

But it is not just a question of specific scenes or linguistic formulas, but rather of a general strategy, as demonstrated, for example, by a meticulous analysis of *Prisión en Chile* (*Prison in Chile*). There Witker sees himself more as an eye and an ear at the scene than as a body that suffers privations. He reduces his personal experience to the minimum, communicating the circumstances of his arrest and its first hours in an introduction that comes before the first chapter, as if in that way he were placing it outside the text itself. Whenever he can, he moves to a general point of view, to the impersonal or suprapersonal passive, to retelling the experiences of others. Witker emphasizes "nuestro testimonio" ("our testimony"), underscoring the "our" in the plural and not in the proprietary sense. It is a collective chronicle, in which concrete occurrences serve to demonstrate their archetypical function (our people are like that, the left is like that, the party, in this case the socialist party, is like that). Although Lira puts more emphasis on his own perception, and in the picaresque quality of his own unusual experience (after all, being a prisoner in the jail which one has presided over oneself only a few hours earlier doesn't happen to everyone, does it?), he also adopts this technique, telling us anecdotes or stories that he could not have witnessed but which he relates as if he had seen them. Carrasco also breaks the barriers of isolation in that way, at times lifting himself above the events. For all of them, the "we" is the true protagonist. Witker and Montealegre reach such extremes of modesty that at times we forget that the accounts are being narrated in the first person singular.

It is Quijada who uses the most sophisticated procedures of greatest literary craftsmanship. During the first four chapters our tension builds as, simply and soberly, he prepares us for the tortures; the atmosphere is condensed and what is to come is insinuated. And, in effect, in the fifth chapter, he shows us the mistreatment in all its explicit, uncompromising violence. But the victim is not the narrator himself, but rather an unknown youth, without name or face. It is related in the third person, totally lacking in any "I" or "we": the subject is the impersonal and warm "they" of the collectivity. The "I" retires, strips away everything (personality, name, perspective), to be left only with the closeness of what it sees or of what it would have seen if it had been present. The torture victim is also depersonalized: we learn of his heroism indirectly through the comments of the sergeant and the soldiers. The case that is presented, thus, tends to be typical (representative of every prisoner) yet at the same time very individual. And it is interpolated within an account which already makes use of all the typical techniques of depersonalization, a narrative that is almost a short story, experienced by one and by none of the prisoners. Other chapters of *Cerco de púas* (*Barbed-wire Fence*) also maintain the same relative autonomy: one of them was even published independently in a Mexican magazine before the author received the Casa de las Américas Prize.[23]

That we are dealing with a systematic and deliberate distancing of the "I" is proven by the fact that the next chapter, "Doctor de cambios" ("Doctor of Changes") is presented from the point of view of a "we" that does not individualize the narrator. It is only in the seventh chapter, then, that he returns to the first person singular, and that is done suddenly, as if he were awakening from a nightmare: "A strange dream awakened me, in a state of fright" (p. 55).

Quijada shows the same subtlety in his treatment of the other fundamental theme of these testimonies: the military.

For all of them, the surprise of the coup, the suddenness of the inversion of the relationship between the uniformed and the civilian populations (who only the day before had apparently belonged to the same species), the inconsolable demonstration that none of them expected that kind of conduct from "the Englishmen of South America," dramatize and accentuate the brutality and stupidity of those soldiers. To approach the subject of their guards, the witnesses adopt two opposite, but complementary, methods: ridiculing the adversary; and the over-adjectivized and somewhat monotonous description of power (sadism has little variety or imagination), subsuming each torturing entity in a kind of fog of indistinguishable, almost undifferentiated, fear. There is also a constant mention of those soldiers who attempted to lessen the effects of their captivity. This division, within the military sector, responds as much to political requirements (the need to find allies in the armed forces in order to return to democracy) as it does to the veracity with which these witnesses would portray what happened. Nevertheless, Quijada is the only one who goes further than the others, understanding that those who carry out such dirty work are also victims of degradation.

This perception of differences among those who hold the power of life and death is necessary if the prisoners are to survive. Courage is not enough. They must resort to astuteness, manipulating the guards, playing one off against the other, uncovering the slightest, most subtle cracks. What is original in the Chilean situation is that both captives and captors were born in the same country; that the interaction between them goes on for a prolonged period; and that the distance between the moralistic preaching of the military and their actual cruel conduct is immense. It is in this context that it becomes essential to build bridges toward the guards, to achieve some improvements in treatment without losing one's pride: "Nevertheless, we," explains Quijada, "understood the importance and the urgency of creating points of contact with those armed beings who seemed to have come from other worlds. It was necessary to find a human language that would permit some point of understanding capable of changing the conditions of life" (p. 30). It is precisely in that language of details that Quijada's book is transcribed, as if it were distilling in its own testimony the soft, firm, ironic perspective that allowed him to gauge the openings in a tentative dialogue with the jailers. In the end, if our attention is drawn to the fact that to be a prisoner is to become a number, a shadow with a number, mist in someone else's nightmare, the guards are just as imprisoned, perhaps more trapped, than the prisoners. This allows Quijada's calm, sad, somewhat tender and distant eye to give itself over to the moderate stance of distinguishing levels, shades, tones of humanity, vacillations, movements in one direction or another, which makes the violence even more unbridled and incomprehensible when it does occur. The line that separates the good and the bad, patriots and traitors, seems ethically clear, but to distinguish it becomes difficult in the midst of the everyday conditions of degradation. When Quijada, for instance, refers to people who wanted to pass over to the enemy (in the chapter "Menos uno, más uno"—"One More, One Less") such an eventuality increases the heroism of the majority that stood firm, precisely because betrayal and weakness are not discarded a priori but rather must be continuously rejected in the fray of each day's living.

But this dispassionate, grandfatherly tone, this ability to visualize the plural backsliding to which the guards are more subject than the prisoners themselves, is not the one that predominates in the other testimonies, though moments of pity and understanding, especially in reference to the young conscripts who do not know what they are doing, are not absent.

Another way of softening the virulent, grotesque, denunciatory descriptions of the jailers is through humor. Elsewhere[24] we have pointed out that the use of such a resource is discovered the day after the coup, as a way of beginning popular, cultural resistance: besides vilifying the adversary with arrows of ridicule, besides giving vent to an energy that otherwise would have no outlet, this is a massive attempt to explore a new, dangerous territory in search of the complicity of laughter, reconstituting an intimate brotherhood from which the censors would be excluded.

All these characteristics, of course, are found in the testimonies. Irony, for example, is not lacking in some descriptions, and in that way the prisoner, through language, reclaims his calm superiority. "It's easier to hand him over dead than alive," says a soldier, referring to Rodrigo Rojas, who comments to the reader, as if in one of those asides typical in the theater of the Spanish Golden Age, that it is "a comforting recommendation" (p. 11). Orders are "genteel" and "kind," "the exercise of kicking me in the testicles is edifying," and "the wonders of military therapy" are emphasized. In addition, such observations help the reader to bear the inventory of horrors.

Carlos Lira is the one who carries this humoristic procedure furthest, making it the real core of his account. Although insult and invective and the reliving of the torments are not lacking in his narrative, as in the others, what is central and permanent in his vision is the corrosive criticism to which he subjects his guards, equivalent to the ironic and vengeful point of view that sustained him and the others during such terrible trials. There is something profoundly Chilean in this ability to joke at the very edge of death, to wink your eye at the reader in the middle of a paragraph about electric shock torture, of flitting about, poking at and playing with the incidents until you find something in them that is redeemable, something joyful, something that permits you to confront the powerful and to unsettle them. The humorous scenes and observations, in fact, are the ones most deeply rooted in the collective mind of the prisoners, the ones that come closest to the language used by the exploited classes who have perennially had to express their situation in the world by being oblique rather than using a frontal attack.[25] Although there may also be a self-disparaging attitude in all this, the tendency to take nothing seriously, to destabilize everything, to put on a mask and to hide your true eyes behind the perpetual joking, I am more inclined to see the embers of an unbending spirit in this invocation of laughter. If satire can be a symbol of impotence, it is also a proof that human beings cannot be mutilated nor left in silence. In Chile, humor has always functioned as a way of unifying and even informally educating vast sectors of the population, creating an inimitable and unique idiom, a consensus of the sardonic.[26] Such a hypothesis could perhaps be confirmed by examining some of the most important cultural production in Chile since the coup, especially in the theater, which, even in the concentration camps or among amateurs in festivals,[27] was fundamentally based on humor as an instrument both to criticize and to inspire.

But it is possible to analyze humor as more than an offensive or a defensive instrument. It is not exclusively a matter of looking at the military through that lens, submitting the rigidity of power to the rigor of laughter, but rather that the prisoners also admit that there is something of the comic, or the tragicomic, in their own situation. Observers of the Jewish holocaust had already called attention to the Ubuesque inspiration of the concentration camps, their relationship with the absurd: "Buchenwald lives under the sign of an enormous humor, a tragic sense of jest."[28] In this way, the victim often denies the importance of what is happening, allows himself to be surprised that such horrors can be raining down upon his own body. The Chilean accounts are full of really comic incidents, which often constitute the most memorable parts of the book, situations which have as a common denominator the fact that the prisoner retains sufficient humanity to be astonished—and with the astonishment comes the distance which provokes a smile at what is happening. Several examples from Lira will serve as an illustration. One of the narrative weaknesses of almost all the accounts is their repetitive character, a reiteration of outrages within the text which reflects their reiteration in reality. This means, of course, a certain aesthetic monotony, a tendency to desensitize the reader with recurrent details and techniques. Lira abuses this narrative weakness as much as, and perhaps more than, the others.[29] But from time to time his sense of humor manages to moderate that cyclical redundancy. He returns to the same place after having been taken to some other corner of the jail, and he says: "Perhaps the lice, the bedbugs and the fleas had missed me." Or the following paragraph: "'Let's move it, asshole' . . . and I knew what was coming better than I knew my own name. A couple of 'fuck yous,' kicks in the ass, being knocked around a little, then I'd pick up my poncho again, since I wouldn't abandon it for anything, it was not only my mattress, but also my pillow, my towel and once its fringe stood in for toilet paper." Or when he describes a meal consisting of weevils (beans with worms): "Doctor Rebolledo, director of the Sewell Hospital, a member of the Socialist Party, got the prize for his plate. He had more worms than beans and noodles." We have the same kind of humor when the telephone rang, in an unlikely fashion, in the middle of a torture session: "The Lieutenant answered. It was his mother, calling to wish him a happy birthday. I knew about it because they turned down the volume of the electronic apparatus and we had to be keep quiet for a moment." We note a similar tendency in Carrasco from time to time. A model chapter is "Con compás" ("With Beat"), which tells how a band of musicians, in Chacabuco, suddenly feeling the earth beneath their feet, and completely self-absorbed and moved by the music they themselves were producing, started marching beyond the barbed-wire barriers, before the astonished eyes of their guards. The presence of humor can, therefore, be found scattered throughout the texts, or even as in the next to the last chapter of Witker's book, "Locuras en tiempo de guerra" ("Craziness in Time of War"), all grouped together (fourteen brief humorous anecdotes separated from the rest of the text). This rather unusual procedure is symptomatic of a problem found in all the accounts: how to organize the narrative structure.

In effect, there is an almost inevitable tendency to narrative fragmentation implicit in all the functions examined up to now. Memory, accusation, the panoramic sense, the hidden variations of the "we" to whom the tragedy is happening, the multiplicity of the "they" who inflict it, all contain an unavoidable germ of dispersion. We have already mentioned the repetition of situations, the views of victims and of torturers, the leaps from one perspective to another, the anecdotal interpolation as a necessity. The urgency with which the prisoners write determines a horizon in which everything tends to fit almost indiscriminately, something like those attics where we keep everything we think we might need someday, piling up as many different levels of discourse and as many characters as there are social sectors juxtaposed in the cellars of repression. They insert letters, harangues, replies to accusations, historical flashbacks, stories heard from others. In addition, there are moments in which the author suspends the narrative in order to present an opinion, much like the omniscient speaker of the nineteenth century novel: they analyze the present or past situation there, they judge conduct or justify attitudes, trying to emphasize the justice or the correctness of their own party's line. The thread that unites these incidents and fragments is appallingly weak. There is, as a matter of fact, little suspense, since the depersonalization also merges the individual protagonist into a higher, heroic, blandly collective personality. If you were to extract the best episodes from each book, those moments when we are invited to cohabit an individual point of view, the final result would be a splendid, albeit slender, anthology (as is the case of the aforementioned *El estadio* [*The Stadium*]). But these episodes tend to be scarce, and the monotony and the disorder end up boring the reader. We suddenly have the impression that the authors who are writing their memoirs are interchangeable. There may be excellent reasons for these limitations of individuality, but the net result is to deprive the accounts of one of those narrative axes from which it would have been possible to organize the material, and make it vibrate unforgettably.

Interestingly, such tedium does not usually appear when the narrators are recounting the first day of their arrest: there they bond themselves to their experience, they intensely observe all the confusion, chaos, and danger. But afterward they frequently get lost in the tangle of passing time and the terror it contains and we enter a realm of confused panoramic flights.

This is, after all, a literature born of urgency. Is not this sort of communication produced by casting aside beforehand any idea of a sustained, intellectual elaboration? If such a necessity stems, as we have seen, as much from the nonprofessional character of the writers as it does from their desire to avoid, to the extent possible, any stylizing of their own voice as a means of camouflaging their individuality, are we not committing an act of methodological folly, applying traditional literary criteria to texts that do not pretend to be anything more than immediate memory and emotion, texts that present themselves as instruments to drastically influence the social flow of events? Latin American critics have confronted of late the problem, that when we apply elite criteria to some works all too often we are attempting to make them fit canons and categories of dominant Western models, which, inevitably, do not apply wholly to products of underdeveloped countries. In this case, additionally, these accounts are drawn from sectors of the working class or of those who have identified with them. It is possible, therefore, that the very concept of "unity," as Antonio Cornejo Polar suggests, can be a comfortable albeit useless disguise to judge a work that does not intend to unify but rather to pour out a multifaceted, unwieldy, and ultimately uncontrollable reality. Although we will return to these questions when we examine *Tejas verdes* by Hernán Valdés, a cautious preliminary answer might be helpful.

It is true that, on the one hand, such a dispersed and fragmentary structure springs from the conditions that make possible and justify the very production of the text. In accordance with this perspective, we would not be dealing with a fault or a defect, but rather with an almost inevitable form of communicating the events of life in captivity. Many of the best Latin American works, as Roberto Fernández Retamar has pointed out, have arisen out of the heat and the richness of the immediate, that which is hardly mediated at all.[30]

A second perspective, however, could point out that several of the authors themselves feel that such a fragmented structure is insufficient to communicate the true experience of the concentration camps, that there is a vacuum which needs filing. Such is the case, notably so, with Witker and Quijada, who have produced works which aspire to a permanence greater than that of a merely journalistic account or a chronicle of protest. In both cases, the authors have juxtaposed within their accounts chapters of a completely different nature, elaborated in a kind of language that falls under a different sign. In my view, Witker's attempt is successful, and enhances and improves his book, while that of Quijada weakens his text and adds an element of distraction to a vision that until that moment had achieved considerable synthesis.

Witker, as we indicated earlier, approaches the insanity of the coup by bringing together in a single chapter diverse anecdotes written with narrative spark. Jaime Concha, in a review of the book, goes so far as to describe those moments in the book "which, by their popular charm and by the use of regional language, can be compared to the discoveries of García Márquez."[31] Witker did not himself witness most of the incidents that he will recount, a fact that perhaps helped him to give free rein to his pen, to show off his capacity for verbal conciseness and playful interaction with the reader. This distance through orality, the ability not to weigh the events down under the weight of a true "eyewitness," might explain a change of tone compared to the other chapters. In general, he deals with absurd situations, in which the armed forces arrest "innocents," people who are relatively speaking at the fringes of the fierce politization that Chile experienced in 1973: two thieves who think they can escape a beating by pretending to be militants of the MIR, a couple of peasants who have been arrested by mistake but who, asked to "cantar" ("squeal") really start to "sing," etc. The point of interest here for Witker is not really the denunciation itself but rather curiosity about the fates of ordinary but memorable human beings, the brutality transcending its everyday reality. Some of the anecdotes had even reached me earlier in the form of jokes, that is, with no attributable author. The protagonists of these little stories, therefore, are not important for their archetypal nature, as models of conduct who stand up to adversity, but rather as examples of absurd life experiences. One hypothesis that could explain this difference refers to the form taken by military excess. When what dominates the soldier is rage and cruelty, it would seem that Witker (along with all the other witnesses) automatically confronts it with the solemn, although often ironic, dignity of the heroic. On the other hand, when it is a matter of general stupidity and confusion, when the military commit mistakes, the protagonists can be portrayed as bewildered sufferers who do not understand what is happening to them. Thus, when the focus of the confrontation is not so much on the conflict between torturers and heroes as it is upon that between the idiotic and the innocent, room is left to work with greater freedom, with procedures that more closely resemble those of comedic fiction, an attempt at another kind of communicative discourse, different from that which predominates in the rest of the book. There is, therefore, a break with the formal structure which the narrator has established, approaching the tradition of the joke, the legend, the prophesy. Walter Benjamin[32] has derived—of course without taking the existence of the Third World into account—the erosion of the dexterity of relating, of telling a story, to the rise of the bourgeois world and of the novel as a genre. He traces this ability to transmit a collective experience to the strata of peasants, sailors (travelers), and artisans, and the way in which those sectors make a deed memorable, a sort of authentic and secret history of daily events. This need to recur to the oral tradition, to the collective experience, and to myth that is being born in its first, most recent and effervescent step of creation, has much about it that is Latin American and popular, contrasting with the other style, the confession, accusation, or reportage. It could be said that this eruption of *popular* elements not only breaks and desanctifies the generic and traditional testimonial approaches, but makes them more Latin American. If we observe

the works of the Europeans Fucik, Alleg, Victor Serge, Solzhenit-
syn, just to take a few, we will see the almost total absence of those
discontinuities, the tight cohesiveness of the text. We have also
pointed out that what Witker brings together in one chapter the
other authors evoke throughout their narratives, although they
don't all have a form that is as light and even comic as *Prisión en
Chile* (*Prison in Chile*). For example, both Carrasco and Montealegre relate the suicide of a political prisoner in Chacabuco: he
hangs himself from a beam of the same house where, forty years
earlier, he had lived as a saltpeter miner. In both cases, the authors
allow themselves to become involved in that tragedy and make it
intensely vibrant. Carrasco repeats this quality when he juxtaposes
the present and the past in Chacabuco from the perspective of the
diary of a nightwatchman employed in the past, having the two
time periods, one of an imprisoned and defeated Chile, the other
of an expectant and combatant Chile, comment upon each other.
In reality, what happens is that from time to time the witnesses
faintly brush upon the possibility of giving free reign to their
imaginations, of "fictionalizing" a little, of abandoning the role of
an eyewitness who was present. These elaborations work because
they are not illustrations of a thesis, prior to and superior to the
events, but permit the reader to participate, to tie up loose ends,
to complete ideas. Almost symbolic of this interweaving of genre
is the name "cuentimonio" ("storimony") which was given as the
title of an anonymous account about Quiriquina Island which,
adopting the narrative formulas of fiction, referred to strictly real
events.

In general, however, the level of concern with regard to the narrative structure or of questions of genre is minimal, which is not
surprising, given that the accounts themselves are written with
considerable carelessness. The authors have little interest in the
how of writing, in form and language, almost as if to show consciousness about the aesthetic elaboration of their account were a
matter of shame. Spontaneous indignation, epic modesty, naked
and unadorned truth, all lead them to write without caring for a
linguistic strategy which would control and orient the material.
We have already mentioned the repetitions, the monotony, certain excessive verbalization. To these must be added the frequent
use of clichés and of worn out language that, at times, almost becomes a caricature of itself. This is especially true when they write

about the military, as if the impossibility of judging them in flesh and blood and of achieving a quick victory, leads the authors to transfer to their own formulations and style the retribution that reality has postponed. We do not find a careful and attentive process of filtering words from emotions, an attempt to moderate their passion in such a way that it finds a workable and appropriate expression. If we were to use a metaphor taken from the political sphere, we would say that when he uses a cliché or a commonplace expression, what the speaker does is *to isolate himself,* demonstrating an inability to transcend already consecrated formulas, which are comfortable, perhaps, for the members of a group to understand each other, but which set up obstacles to the integration of the uninitiated. When, for example, they say, "Pinochet's alienated minions and their cronies," each word may be rigorously exact when looked up in the dictionary, but the whole is not describing reality but rather has as its actual point of reference the passion of the one emitting the judgment. In this context, nonetheless, such linguistic exaggerations are understandable, however aesthetically unjustifiable. They represent a mechanical, automatic attempt to reproduce their own rage and nausea. The incredible nature of their predicament literally leaves them wordless, causing them to resort to the most worn and hackneyed phrases. Revenge is carried out in the language of verbal aggression, however much they have promised to exercise it in the court of reality.

But there are other reasons. In great measure, some of those formulae (clichés, unnecessary circumlocutions, abuse of adjectives, obvious metaphors, redundancies, poorly assimilated canons of taste) can originate in a situation which we mentioned at the beginning: when someone sits down *to write* about an experience that, transmitted orally or in conversation, is immediate, lively and flexible, he tends to adopt a posture which is almost sacred and, in any case, solemn. He begins to imitate past literary models which enjoy a certain prestige, falling back upon an arsenal of the easy and the evident, stiffening the material. It is interesting to note that such defects disappear as soon as the author forgets that he is making "literature" (that is, he forgets the invisible vigilance of a public that will judge him) and begins to narrate his immediate experience with dramatism and simplicity. By writing, he feels that he is *elevating* his experiences or conferring a special *status* upon them. That step, to civilization or to memory, makes his own life solemn, exceptional, almost beatific. That is why the best fragments tend to be those with humor or the ones in which the authors lose their sense of discomfort and self-consciousness.

We must add to this panorama certain other defects that have already been mentioned: disintegration of form, absence of suspense, and the abstraction of some experiences. Humor and irony, popular stories and anecdotes, the narrative flow of many episodes, the sense of the collectivity which grows strong and speaks through a thousand cracks, all these virtues which we have been discussing, may supplement and support the accounts, but they do not eliminate the problems of language and form that we have just drawn attention to. One could argue that, by verifying this stylistic critique, what we are doing is judging these efforts from an illegitimate, elitist, and professional point of view, when, in fact, the value of these testimonies stems precisely from their justified, amateurish, and mass character.[33] The reason, however, why I mention this first great defect of these accounts is that I believe that their carelessness with language, the fact that they consider it a mere vehicle for a truth that is already pre-established, that is, as an instrument that is almost extraneous to what is really important, is one of the most pronounced weaknesses of the left in Chile and, beyond them, of those who want to change the world in a revolutionary way.[34]

Behind this mode of understanding the communicative act, what is really stirring is a second limitation of these accounts: the public to which they are directed. Although supposedly the witness is appealing to the entire world (with explanations and footnotes for foreign readers) so that their opprobrium will fall upon the "minions," the fact is that their real public is more circumscribed and precise: it consists of those who are already convinced beforehand, in other words, a "sect." Many of these texts have an almost religious tone, very much like a sermon for the faithful pointing to a promised land. For those who do not share the political or party positions they are expounding upon, there will be a sense of admiration of their courage . . . if they read the whole book or at least get beyond the first few chapters. In fact, for the unconvinced, even for those who admit their veracity, the accounts will seem like exercises in propaganda. Although the origins of this attitude toward the readers is found, therefore, in an ironclad and tenacious practice of the left, and one which has its deeper roots in a rigid and self-glorifying dogmatism, we must recognize that there are particular reasons, in the concrete case of testimonial literature, which explain such a mode of operation with language. Not only because they write to maintain ideological cohesiveness within a brutal retreat of the historical tide, but also because we are confronting a means of communication that prolongs and reproduces the codes with which prisoners of any kind, but especially those in a concentration camp, circumscribe their linguistic horizon. The Jewish survivors of the Nazi extermination point out that, after being liberated, "those who were suffering continued directing words to one another."[35]

In the concentration camp morale must be maintained at all costs. Rodrigo Rojas points out that "if they became taciturn, silent and tried to isolate themselves from others, lost in their own thoughts, in the memory of their loved ones, the others tried to lift their spirits" (p. 75). Under those conditions, any fragility, any doubt, any intimate dissection is equivalent to suicide, can lead to betrayal. Among the prisoners, then, there arises a certain mode of communication, a means to hold the group together, to maintain their primary identity. Without that esprit de corps there is no way to survive. Those codes of conduct, which are like the ones that freedom fighters constructed in the long struggle against fascism, restrict the degree of doubt, of acceptable error, of problems to elaborate. Heroism and shared nobility in language end up being proof of the correctness of the unquestioned and unquestionable political line. Furthermore, to doubt victory or to delve into causes and effects could lead to questioning their own imprisonment and suffering, their possible senselessness. Only a fierce and unlimited determination can continue to justify the life, and suffering, of these dedicated to such sacrifices for liberation.

These prisoners' retrospection is a continuation of how they organized their lives to survive that captivity. After being freed, they narrate things as if they were still prisoners: with the same will to struggle and the same social cohesiveness, as if the public were still a small group that must be self-exhorted in order not to succumb. The fact that they are now free to tell what happened does not change their narrative strategy, which is fed by the moral posture they adopted in the camps. Psychologists and psychiatrists have studied this phenomenon among ex-prisoners (whether political or not) who refer everything, for years afterward, to the group of which they formed a part in jail.

The act of writing, then, is a continuation of the act of resistance and of survival; it is the culmination of the challenge on another level. It is still resistance, but now in words: what they lived through together, shared, and were able to construct, serves them forever afterward to go on communicating with the world. And how else could we understand the fact that, in reality, they have survived, that they have walked out of that place where they were sent to die. The disproportionate effort needed to achieve that moral victory in the midst of catastrophe makes their lack of care with the language they use to tell their epic story understandable.

We could suggest, then, that the situation of having been prisoners leads these revolutionaries to exacerbate a tendency toward sectarianism which is, of itself, part of the tradition of revolutionary, political struggle, especially in those countries in which there have been no conditions for democratic mobilization in the past.[36]

Although the fact that the prisoners speak to those "inside" is, therefore, entirely explainable, its consequences are many and serious. The works we have here are, to a great extent, closed, with little participation by the reader. From the moment we know that the author-protagonist has successfully come through his period of testing and temptation, there is no longer any suspense. If evil reigns in the world, its power is not sufficient to bring to a crisis point the view which orders and purifies experience. Those minimal islands of freedom and of pride which are won here and now in these degrading circumstances are supposed to foreshadow the continent that tomorrow we will presumably create together. Without this conviction, without this certainty, who would be willing to die or even mobilize for a cause?

With this, we touch upon a third limitation of these accounts. By placing the accent upon exemplary conduct, upon the ought-to-be, they help to create a magnificent myth: we are invincible. Indeed, it would be very hard for me, personally, to go on with my political work, if I thought that my *compañeros* could be broken and could betray the cause, if (in the words of Carrasco) I did not believe that my *compañeros* "have come out or will come out of the prisons more than ever convinced of the just cause of our people, more combative, more determined fighters."

The problem, of course, is that this marvellous version being presented is not entirely true. As far as I have been able to determine, and objective data are lacking, the great majority of those who were taken prisoner reacted in an heroic manner. But there were those who talked, those who betrayed, those who gave information. These cases have simply been ignored, erased from the map, by the witnesses. Even the most burning dilemmas related to torture (whether to talk, how much to talk, what kind of cover to use, dilemmas which the oral accounts and conversations of the prisoners are compulsively full of), are nowhere present in these books. To inspire those involved in the struggle, an enormous, offensive and unsettling part of the truth is therefore kept silent: those who did not withstand the pressure are more than could be counted on the finger of one hand (to use Luis Corvalán's phrase, in his prologue to Carrasco's book). But it is not just a matter of wanting in this way to give the impression that betrayal and weakness are so secondary that they are not even worth referring to, that they are just distant and accidental shores of the great river that flows toward freedom. At the same time that they remember the martyrs and praise the rebels of the future, the witnesses are placing the vast, nonheroic (although potentially revolutionary) majority at the margins of the process of struggle. They are affirming their own strength, but are unable to discern degrees, shades, levels of heroism; instead it almost appears to be a matter of the apocalyptic or nothing. There is more: we have said that it seems understandable that such exemplary conduct should rule over the revolutionary struggle and militant life. The most substantial problem is a certain static conception of Chile: if one does not confront the demoralization signified by prison, if one does not emphasize those who no longer participate because of that failure, if you do not look clearly at those who are determined never again to go through such an experience,[37] what you are doing is supposing that Pinochet is simply a transitory crossroads for Chile, that he will not have profound effects on the economic, social, and cultural panorama of the country. In fact, these testimonies seem to deny the permanent effect which a regime like the present one can have upon its citizens. It is as though the hero-ism of these witnesses, or of their comrades whose bravery and patience they observed, were enough to give a new birth to the captive people.

It is not easy for me to call attention to these difficulties. In the first place, because I have not personally gone through the experi-ence of prison or torture myself, and I feel a certain shame (there is Alleg's key word) in criticizing those who survived, fighting faithfully for my right to my country. But also because I under-stand this as a form of self-criticism, directed at my own practice, at that of my brothers and sisters, at the people with whom I have struggled and searched for a better world.

In order to better understand these limitations, to place them, along with the virtues of these works, in the proper perspective, it may be time to approach another account, *Tejas verdes, Diario de un campo de concentración* (*Tejas Verdes, Diary of a Concentration Camp*) by Hernán Valdés. The testimony of an artist. And con-temporary art incessantly concerns itself with three areas of reality which the political and amateur accounts confront with greatest weakness: the possibility of a language lived as an adventure, the desire of reaching a broad public, and a concept of humanity that is subtle, anti-Manichaean and open to contradictions.

III

Reading the preliminary note which Valdés wrote for his book, one might presume, even if he introduces his own self and eschews a godfather to do the introduction, that the distance separating him from his compatriots who decided to discuss concentration-camp life is not that sizeable. He makes explicit the "deep repug-nance" he feels on having to exhibit that world, and the nakedness to which they reduced him, but he justifies it in that he is not communicating "an unfortunate, personal experience, but rather showing the *present-day* experience of the Chilean people." Thus he recognizes his experience as emblematic, his own suffering as something that is being repeated right now in the Chile of the generals.

This attempt to remove any sense of exceptionality allows him to present himself, rather than as a professional writer, as anybody to whom this could have happened, so much so that he points out changes from his previous work, since here there is "no literary elaboration. The language is basically functional and this signifies a new experience for me." Supposedly, then, this work, just like the others we have analyzed, would have been shaped by no particular strategy. We will see, nonetheless, that such is not the case. It is true that one does not find in *Tejas Verdes* a voyage of linguistic experimentation or a modernist odyssey of invention such as one could find in his earlier trajectory, or most contemporary novels. Without denying a cardinal break with his own tradition, at the same time, he has used vast literary resources, structures, and techniques to create a work extremely differnt from our other witnesses, none of whom would define themselves as professional literati. Nevertheless, the writer takes special pains to present his experience as typical and ordinary, as though he were trying to erase a priori any eventual doubts that might invalidate the weight of his experience as expressing "subjectivity" or an ultra-sensitive vision.

Valdés's protestations may indicate that he suspects that, if the military excesses and the barbarity he describes are identical to those portrayed in other accounts, the profound meaning of his work is divergent. *Tejas Verdes* is, above all, the story of how a dictatorship succeeds, and not—like the other works—that of triumph in the midst of death. What we are going to live through is a victorious process of "depolitization" of the prisoners and, through them, the implied long range neutralization of an entire nation. One does not unfold such an unpleasant vision in order to proclaim again one's confidence in the glorious march of the working class into the future, but rather as a means of preserving a minimal sense of worth and consciousness, a last ember of innocence in an atmosphere of complicity that reaches out and stains each terrorized inhabitant of the country. Steiner has pointed out that Nazi fascism automatically generates this need among writers, changing the way in which they understand their own function: let no one be able to say he did not know what was happening, let no one declare himself immaculate or ignorant.[38] Valdés himself will explore this theme in his own work: reality is divided into two time planes, that of those who do not know or do not want to know, and that of those who have already suffered under the shadow of the tree of evil. This division is revealed to him when he suddenly recognizes the place where he is presently detained, remembering that just a few weeks ago he looked at it from the outside, as an innocent tourist.

Thus, although in many aspects Valdés's work is like that of other witnesses (he denounces the cruelty; establishes the experience as representative, presumably to eradicate subjectivity from the text; declares the commemorative nature of what is written); he separates himself from the others in fundamental ways. To begin with, he starts out from a different situation with respect to the horror he endures: since he has not been a militant in any political party and does not belong to any specific, self-reference group, nor was he carrying on any subversive activity at the time of his arrest, he does not consider his punishment to have a collective meaning. His experience itself, physical, temporal, and ethical, was also different. His imprisonment was short, concentrating in one month all the brutality that the others suffered spread over years. And he ends up confessing to crimes he has not committed and betraying innocent friends, doing whatever his jailers desire, to end the torture. It also matters that we are dealing with an intellectual, one of those who "in Chile did not know what to do with our inapprehensible and contradictory reality." However much the author himself denies it, however much he points out the "functional" character of this book's language, we are indisputably in the presence of someone who sees his existence as an attempt at understanding and transmitting, someone who has dedicated his days and nights (both before and after his arrest) to the search for communication. This means that he has an acute sense of how special an instrument culture is. The political effect of what he is writing resides, for Valdés, more in terms of the changes that he can bring about in the way human beings look at reality than in terms of certain immediate, measurable contributions of a mere propagandistic nature.

It is this conscious use of language, this overwhelming presence of a particular strategy with regard to the material of his own life, that determines the entire structure of *Tejas Verdes*, from the first to the last word.

The book itself has its origin in a convention that could not be more literary. We are face to face with what the author calls a *diary*, in which each day he presumably writes what happens and what is happening. The time of captivity, then, is offered to us in the present tense and under severe, chronological rigor, enclosing the reader (like the character himself) in the suffocating, restricted point of view of the first person singular. But it is evident that this work was not really written during the imprisonment, but rather after the author's release, reproducing what was with aftersight lived through. It is enough to compare this book with a real diary, like the one scratched out on scraps of paper by the painter Guillermo Núñez. The anguished and clandestine conditions under which Núñez's work is put together provoke a rhythm of urgency, a slow delirium of self-searching, a dialogue with the window that does not exist and the labyrinth that leads to it, orbiting madness so as not to give in to it. Núñez had not intended it for publication or even to produce an effect upon listeners, but as a way to elucidate for *himself* what is happening to him.[39] When the painter gives public testimony in Paris before UNESCO he employs a cautious, precise vocabulary of ironic denunciation similar to the best accounts of the other witnesses.[40]

Tejas Verdes, on the other hand, is not a document but rather a reconstituted diary, written after the events as if it had been recorded at the time, as if at that moment he had been given the opportunity to take down what he was feeling. Valdés has resorted to a narrative point of view that, basing itself upon a real experience, and in order to transmit it more effectively, invents an eminently fictional situation. The distance that separates Valdés from his fellow witnesses can already be observed here. They, like he, write after their imprisonment, already knowing the outcome. But while they offer us a retrospective panorama, in which the real writer and the fictional narrator coincide in the same perspective, Hernán Valdés restricts himself to the same limited point of view from which he suffers the threat of death day after day. His strategy of trimming, summarizing, and communicating in such an elaborate fashion would have been absolutely impossible in those circumstances. There is here a cross between the fictive and the real, between literature and testimony, between an elaborated treatment of great inventiveness and a crude and realistic recording of events. Once the reader accepts the literary convention that what we are reading, as in so many novels, is the retrieved simultaneous version of events, he is effectively hooked.

Valdés's narrative tactic, far from being a rhetorical game, is indispensable. If the author rejects the relative (and easy) omniscience that allows him to tell a story after it is closed, if he rejects the natural and spontaneous past of memory, it is in order to impress the reader more cruelly with the claustrophobic reclusion of prison, to create the sense of a reality whose uncertainty, fear, and limitations we share, living the narrative with the same rhythms with which the author lived his arrest and degradation. Valdés sweats over his material, he labors at it, he converts it into a watchful consciousness, precisely so that nothing, or as little as possible, will mediate between the narrator and ourselves, so that the identification will be complete. The diary and the confession are precisely literary genres that are used to subordinate and to control the flow of events, to impose an order upon the oral multiplicity of experience.[41] This simultaneity, which is, furthermore, a generic characteristic of theater, influences the dramatic construction of the account, since we live the same suspense as the victim, who, like us, does not know what awaits him, what awaits us. The sordid and deaf reality is discovered only insofar as the body of that prisoner painfully manages to transfer it to our attention.[42]

The closure of time and perspective is accompanied by yet another sort of literary strategy: the narrator is operating on himself, in effect, as if he were a character in a novel, implacably, dispassionately, with the critical distance we often reserve for fictional beings. Those layers of the mind do not open up to us so that we can admire its nobility, or the intimations of a myth in the making, but in order to lay it before us in all its vulnerability. Readers tend to be fascinated by imaginary creatures being treated in this manner, mercilessly, with nothing hidden, and even relish the cruelty of that sort of attack, glad that they are not the ones exposed to such naked scrutiny. But Latin American tradition, which combines an exaggerated, Hispanic sense of honor with the wariness and secrecy learned and nurtured by a loss of power that comes with underdevelopment, tends to reject this procedure when applied to flesh-and-blood beings—even though in recent years a younger generation of writers have used this unwillingness ironically. It is not strange, therefore, that *Tejas Verdes*'s brutally frank approach to the author's experience, its destruction of what is conventionally acceptable and expected in a Latin American auto-biographical text, has lead to its being called a "novel" by most of the people (students, colleagues, critics, book dealers) with whom I have discussed it.[43]

The reader is submitted, therefore, to a double procedure of horror: on the one hand, we are going to travel with the narrator, inside him, beside him, toward his total possession by the infernal forces that have begun to preside over that universe; while, at the same time, being forced to watch how the narrator distances himself, focusing on his own body and consciousness almost as if they were objects to be registered and described. The conflicting development reinforces the central alienation of the protagonist, who is both subject and object, sufferer and observer, immediate pain and point of view which records, present view and retrospective view, narrative domination and lack of control over life itself. What Valdés has ultimately constructed is a communicative structure that allows us to experience his alienation and, at the same time, to believe in its verisimilitude, carrying out a process of simultaneous identification and distancing. And isn't this what torture does to a human being? Isn't it a matter of turning him into a strange object, making him touch the horrifying dead end of his own material being, ending up as a stranger to himself, mirrored but unrecognizable?

This is how horror challenges literature. For Valdés what is fundamental are not the techniques, the electric prod, the screams at midnight. The essence of dictatorship is not there, but in the psychic wound, the devastation of a man or a woman's identity, the twisting of the inner being in order to consolidate external economic and political power: the transformation of the subject into object, of consciousness into thing, of body into a laboratory specimen, the appropriation of our personal point of view by the torturers. The narrative technique attempts to account for an experience that is strange, impossible, distant, abnormal, and that has, nonetheless, become habitual, external, possible, almost obvious. If the "I" can be treated as "he" by the narrator, can be perceived in all its desolation, it is because that subject has previously been treated as if he were a bag of muscles without a soul by other men.

The effectiveness of *Tejas Verdes* resides, then, in the fact that it makes us suffer, by means of its language, something that is akin to the overwhelming and dense immediacy endured by the author, or, at least, it imitates that immediacy. We move toward an act of total rapedness, toward that moment when the subject must face himself alone, with an ego that has been neutralized; we suffer all the steps through which he is gradually reduced to the ever narrower walls of his own body, a body which becomes ever larger as it suffers in the midst of indifference, while the consciousness or the imagination which would enable him to escape, the memory which would allow him to compare and to reject what is happening, become ever smaller. Prison and humiliation and torture are processes of emptying, of becoming empty, of destroying normality and remembrance, until consciousness is no more than a transmitting echo and the body is only a wasteland of nerves which obey and twitch, until the "I" is nothing more than a core that is exposed to commands from the outside world. It fights a losing battle, trying to maintain nooks and crannies that will grant it the momentary boon of still being what it thought it once was. What we witness, what we must breathe and execrate is an inverted, mystical journey, in which instead of the soul that frees itself from the material world to unite with God, it is the body which sheds all illusions and spiritual attributes to remain alone with the Devil. Because what is discovered at the end of the journey is pure evil. The descent into Hell, which is symbolized by the fact that he is taken down into a cellar for the torture sessions, is alluded to and prepared with subconscious subtlety throughout the narrative. "Up there, on the earth," he suddenly says to us, refering to his previous life, or he describes the implacable sensation of seeing himself invaded "by the infernal noise of the scream."

Repression leads him, therefore, from a moment in which he inhabits a universe dressed and adorned (with clothing, myths, objects, protectors, screens, answers, habits) to the moment in which he is inhabited only by the demonic, floating voices of his interrogators.

Valdés's originality, his fierce pact with the "cinematographic fidelity"[44] of what happened, is that along with that journey toward physical nudity, he constrains the reader to another kind of journey: toward the stripping and self-revelation of the character who is narrating, all the layers with which he ordered and controlled his life laid bare. The physical journey and the narrative journey accompany and comment upon each other.

Those men torture him in order to "read his thoughts," to make his body transparent, his ideas explicit and public. But they are incapable of accepting the truth that the protagonist offers them: that he has nothing to do with resistance, that he has no confession to make. That intimate voice, the one that speaks precisely to us in the middle of a painful and outrageous act, is the very one that the torturers can neither perceive nor understand.

His truth, the truth of what he discovered about himself, was his infinitely vulnerable and fragile body that his consciousness could not save. The mocking and all-powerful voices revealed his own inner self to him, while at the same time pressing him to falsify everything, betraying his ideals and his friends. So Valdés's account tries to fill the gap between the truth he discovered and the one they rejected. That inability on their part to accept his authentic version of things probably fueled his need to tell it all later. Thus, not only does he wish to establish the Truth (in the face of official lies), as do the authors of the other reports, but also the small, flickering, hidden truths that he was able to discern within himself, the ones that surfaced gradually and uselessly, that did not convince his tormentors.

If truth, then, could not prevent pain, at least now it may be able to transmit that which the lords of pain forced him to uncover. If, as a man, he betrayed certain loyalties, he must now, as a writer, be faithful to what he lived through. That's why Valdés's narrative is so radical, so electrifying, so free of disguises or artificial consolations. He refuses to falsify what happened; he refuses to enlarge upon it or exaggerate it; he refuses to hide the antiheroic. He does not want to repeat what the dictatorship did to him: to subordinate the complex fabric of truth to convenience.

The faithfulness to sensory detail, to the grating earthiness of a consciousness submitted to an escalating degradation, seems to be a reply, therefore, to the process of dehumanization. If those men stripped him bare in a cold cellar, forcing him to explore the limits of his consciousness, the myths he had constructed, his class situation, his relationships with others, his profession, he voluntarily strips himself for a second time for the reader. Nothing of what he endured should be turned into myth, linguistic masquerades that could hide the meanness, the fear, the shame. The re-telling, without a shred of self-pity, tries to be as brutal as the torture itself. The present-tense narration contributes to this feeling of intensity: it would seem there is no time to reconstruct, interpret, or cover up the raw material of experience. From the difficulties of defecation to certain women prisoners who slept with soldiers in order to get food, from those who became disheartened to the one who talked and falsely accused his comrades, everything is recorded, nothing is excused. He will not cast a veil of silence over the worm-like functions of the organism nor the abysses of the spirit. In the end, the only thing heroic, for Valdés, lies in a linguistic act: telling the truth now.

But, what is this unmasked truth that is so painful? In the final analysis, what is it that Valdés discovered? In no sense is it what Witker, Rojas, Cabieses, and Montealegre confirmed, more than discovered, the resistance of a people to their oppressors. Although Valdés's vision includes some acts of solidarity among the prisoners and a few heroes (for example, a communist professor, p. 98), the central nucleus of his experience is, of course, quite different. The militant witnesses manifest the boundary beyond which barbarism and insanity cannot cross. For Valdés, on the other hand, the horror of fascism in the Third World is that it does not find any final, inner barriers that successfully resist its dehumanization. The defenses against this satanic power that invades everything are, though complex and multiform, insufficient in the end to protect the personality's precarious autonomy, insufficient to go on trusting what up until now has been accepted as reality, insufficient to reconstruct a collectivity which could give some meaning to one's acts or provide a destiny for the heroic. It becomes painfully clear to the protagonist that he does not have, has not prepared, any weapons for this kind of combat which is, if we come to think about it, the most important one, the only important one, in his life. As it was for the militants, astonishment in the face of such unheard of savagery forms the basis for the detailed minute by minute account of the prisoner Valdés. Not one of them had anticipated, beyond some theoretical discussions about the state, the armed forces, imperialism, this sort of behavior by those who, only yesterday, played according to the rules of democracy. But Valdés's real surprise is himself, what he discovers about his own body and his conscience. When the culminating moment of the torture arrives, he will have no boundary to oppose to the occupation of his bones and his kidneys and his genitals. On discovering solitude, instead of solidarity, as the irreducible dimension of what is human, he has no allies for his own salvation. Perhaps this solitude can be symbolized by the fact that when Valdés mentions to the others what has happened to him (stories or anecdotes), he never abandons his own central point or concern. He has turned into a country infinitely and incessantly invaded.

This process of alienation is not something abstract for the reader. Valdés does not talk about the degradation; he immerses us in it, trying to make those who were not present understand such a monstrous, amazing experience.

Communicating one's progressive degradation, the devouring loss of one's conscience and one's dignity, how one becomes alien to oneself, is not an easy task, aesthetically or ethically. The horror of this process can only operate on the reader's mind if he is constantly reminded, through the narrator's struggle, that there is a normal universe that is prior, parallel, and still somehow belongs to that narrator. The torturers have created a world in which the prisoner is deluded and pressed to internalize the domination.[45] For the protagonist, then, it is essential to his survival to distinguish at every moment between the threatening world that is outside and the inner world that he would preserve with the final wall of his own lucidity. His words, his conduct, everything that the hands of his captors can take over, everything external, must be adapted to the superior, authoritarian demands, while what he thinks—an ever more uncontrollable redoubt, a distant and retractable room—holds on to another, invented rhythm and time. The dramatic quality of the account depends upon this agonizing exertion to maintain, through memory, through habits that do not disappear, through certain language mechanisms, zones of normalcy within the nightmare. A minimal victory is seeing oneself as a stranger, representing the presence of what he once was and may aspire to become again in some future. He spies on himself, turns himself into an entity as rare, unexpected, and remote as those who are interrogating him. It is this aloof tone applied to such intimate zones that forms one of the book's most interesting contrasts.

The intent of dictatorship, in fact, is to control the last fiber of that being, to destroy that interior, narrative point of view, any reminiscence or hope for another world. Completely internalizing torture, then, means the disappearance of any sense of amazement, that the interludes of horror become normal and permanent. Valdés will be less and less surprised by himself; his aching and unimaginable conduct and body will be the only norm by which to judge and to appraise, until in one dramatic instant, having surrendered absolutely to his captors, he will be inhabited and possessed totally by evil. That culminating moment is minutely prepared and conditioned throughout the account.

From the very beginning, the world outside the narrator errupts violently into his existence without prior warning ("There was not a lapse of time between my opening and the situation of finding myself with the barrel of a machine gun against my throat," p. 11), and this is shown through two channels: actions or words. The control that the enemy forces have acquired over reality is not shown exclusively by blows and mistreatment but also in the coercive language that comes naturally to them, the crude and vulgar vernacular which the writer, in a measured fashion, soberly and elegantly, must transmit. In the distance that lies between those words pronounced in the air outside and the words he reserves to himself inside, one senses and learns, along with the narrator, what is controlled and what has already disappeared, what is still a subject and what has definitively become an object at the mercy of others. When that distance disappears, the demonic will have taken over not only the mouth and language but also the brain that orders the muscles that control speech.

The care that Valdés exercises in his use of language is therefore not surprising.

There is, for instance, the absence of *dicendi* words. In general, the narrator tends not to identify who is mocking him.[46] The reader is submerged inside Valdés's perspective. And then—like a whiplash or a nail being driven in—comes the voice with no owner, no name, no face, not a trace of identity, a voice from without. It is similar to what is happening to Chile: again and again we must bear intervention in our most intimate and secret places, the endless repetition of a vast tragedy reproduced in every structure of the system. This shocking immediacy makes that voice more threatening and abrupt for us, but also more unreal and floating, all of which, once again, combines violence and dematerialization, the nearness of the brutal and the distance of the concrete. While this technique forces us to assume the point of view of someone who is blindfolded and defenseless, immersing us in his uncertainty and hesitation, at the same time it expresses a more general, underlying perception, existential in nature. One is no more than a mere sounding board for other voices, an "all-of-a-sudden" that is there only to be invaded, a being without origins and without children, without tenderness or history. The dehumanizing morass to which the narrator is submitted is reinforced by the distance of the voices which are outside, but have the power to make the subject scream and which are going to end up being the only, interminable wall of reality for that tortured body.

Occasionally, the narrator further degrades himself by answering directly with a "sir" to the "assholes and motherfuckers" and other jewels that are heaped upon him. When an obsequious "usted" replies to an insultingly familiar "tú" or "vos," it is clear that the victim is caught in the "semantics of power," the lack of intimacy or reciprocity with those who control his environment.[47]

Nevertheless, most of the time the narrator refers indirectly to what he is responding or saying, that is, he avoids admitting the language of domination—at least in front of us. In this way he attenuates his own loss of control, and in passing, accentuates and emphasizes those moments when we witness his discourse directly, those moments in which he himself is amazed by his own words. It would seem that this will to narrate indirectly what he surrendered publicly and out loud is one more attempt, in his own private and personal sphere, to hold on to the world that is slipping out of his reach. When he portrays himself speaking directly, when he renounces any intervention as a narrative mediator, he has come to depend entirely on the world and words of the torturer, and thus loses even that small margin of operation that remained to his abbreviated point of view. The power of a dictatorship resides in its capacity to erase the narrator's own words from his innermost being, so that what he henceforth says publicly and thinks privately will be synchronic.

An example will help to better understand the matter:

"You, asshole, let's see," he said, when we were in front of him. "Tell me your I.D. number. Make it fast."
I recited it, as fast as possible.
"Show it to me."
Of course, we had all left our documents in the shack.
"Bend over, asshole. Going around without your I.D. is like going around with no balls. You'll remember." (p. 88)

This dichotomy in his own perspective, a rivalry expressed and incorporated into the dialogue itself, is symptomatic of a deeper schizophrenia to which he is submitted. Something similar happens, for instance, in his descriptions. He starts off with a vague perception, then moves to a more precise individualization, and only at the end is able to conceptualize and give meaning to that experience. This primitivism, to adopt the term applied by Jaime Concha to Valdés,[48] gives priority to what the body senses, postponing what his consciousness explores. This method accentuates our exposed, helpless character. The feverish, anchorless mind gradually exhausts all arguments, reasoning, doubts, and explanations, trying to search out an escape or a crack through which to save itself, making presumptions and demolishing them immediately, discovering over and over that our sole resource is our poor body, that garbage dump. This anguishing procedure reproduces, on a narrative level, the sensorial loss of the world, when the survival of civilization is tied to the delirium of an abandoned body, to a "pure vigilance of the present." It is an ironic journey back to one's origins, but there is only pain at the origin: the body itself begins to forget its own functions, a body that does not sleep, cannot defecate, scarcely eats or covers itself, and has no company.

We are prepared, then, we have been made ready by the narrator, as he was prepared by his guards, for the unavoidable moment of the torture session. By mutilating his mouth and his genitals, the organs of generation, by leaving him naked, the torturers merely carry out the final step in the invasion of that integrity that he has tried to keep hidden, innocent, and free. The pain transcends memory, according to the narrator, which means that it becomes eternal; it is so intense that there is no memory of it, only a pure, endless presence. There is nothing that he can place nor impose nor superimpose between himself and death. He is a conquered wasteland, again and again repeating the blank, empty words, nothing. Cold, which has evolved from the beginning of the book as a white and terrifying leitmotiv, reaches the final ice of "I feel a tremendous pity for myself, a tremendous coldness for myself." The electrical discharges have been successful. They make his body become "everything they shout." And he will say everything they want him to say. There is no inner self at that moment and therefore all notions that there may be any kind of external world also disappear. The before and the after disappear. Repression is like an endless wave; the demons have become integrated into the innermost self. Torture has been the final stage in a more prolonged, bestial possession, an all-powerful disposition of the body, of time, of oxygen, so that a divorce of ways may occur, so that his consciousness ("my head drops") will be absolutely cornered and undone, incapable of interceding between his body and the bodies that are torturing him. If consciousness is blank and the voices ultimately close him off, then he cannot avoid being violated by them and must inevitably give birth to monsters. It is the sexual relationship with the Devil of which tradition speaks. We see a man who did not have the strength to resist evil, who did not find within himself, within his past, within the slow dominions of his own conscience or of community with others, that courage or identity to keep himself whole. But who does have the strength to admit it, not to cover up his weakness or what they did to him. Through literature, he will attempt to recover and win the battle he lost as a human being.

The truth which he corroborates, then, in his endless, dawnless night, is that he has failed. It is a failure that he understands as being collective as well as personal, the failure of an entire country, of an entire generation, the failure of a way of living and of writing humanity. In the middle of the despair, there is, of course, no collective solution to respond to that failure and to make sense of it. There is no future nor commitment down the road, "obsurely occupying ourselves by holding on to our lives. Melancholy for what we did not manage to do with history" (p. 72). The demonic resides precisely in the omnipotence and the invulnerability of evil, the fact that the victim is sure that his torturers will never be held accountable for their actions. And if there were retribution, even that would not annul his suffering.

Valdés, then, is going to pluralize his own case and condition; he will propose them as general parameters by which what is real and what is false can be measured in Chile.

This projection from his own life is carried out in spite of the fact that he has been careful, with his sad and dispassionate objectivity, to inform us that he is living this process from a special viewpoint. In fact, the day before his interrogation, he realizes that he has never been alone during those weeks and that he has had no time to think about himself. He understands then that, in the face of what he was, he does not feel the slightest nostalgia for the past, nothing ties him to the outside world. His previous life was a wasteland.

This anchorless condition was, in fact, the point at which the character started at the beginning of the book: "Exactly what am I doing here, at home, at 6:30 in the afternoon?"—a question that will be repeated, mockingly, with the echo of another urgency, many pages later ("What am I doing here, in this cellar where they are going to hurt me?"). As the account opens, he does not feel like the subject of his own life, but instead like a disconnected, solitary phantom, who, in the middle of his rootlessness and his depression, tries to go on living through a love relationship that is foundering. On the point of leaving the country, he is already someone who is surprised at his own destiny, the inhabitant of a "dead time" in which nothing can happen. The first three pages of the book evoke, almost like an anthology, so many other novels, European or otherwise, which focus on a character in the midst of an existential crisis. But Latin American violence is going to erupt into that disconnected existence. To the backdrop of listless alienation and angst which tends to fill so much contemporary literature will be added another kind of suffering, *another kind of alienation.* Instead of the torture of incommunication between a man and a woman, we have the less metaphorical physical and mental torture imposed by some men upon others. Instead of quests and misunderstandings on the faded wallpaper of a failing love affair, another, more identifiable evil appears. Instead of dead time where you do not know what to do, there is the all too fast time, the amazing rhythm that is incessantly ordained by the captors. It is as if he were introducing us to one typical form of solitude in order that he might project from it another, different, more radical, definitive loneliness. The character who is to become an object, who will eventually lose all normality, already felt like a stranger, a man apart, before his captivity. Perhaps his obsessive capacity for observation of his own consciousness-under-siege is the extension of his general condition, the fact that he starts out by being an observer of himself, cut off from everything. The irony is that this extremely sensitive man should be the one to learn that there are more frightening ways to feel pain than those to which he was accustomed.

In fact, the problems which beset the character in the first pages of the book appear to be a continuation of the sort that the characters in Valdés's prior literary work, and especially in *Zoom*, are beset with.[49] In that novel, everything centers on the concept of being a foreigner—as foreign in a remote city like Prague as in Santiago de Chile—the fundamental burden of being a body that is just as foreign and derails us along absurd routes. Alienated, paralyzed, incapable of formulating any desire that will not lead to its opposite, both protagonists of *Zoom* seek "to travel, which means to be no place in particular," in the words of Antonio Skármeta in his reference to that book,[50] preparing or dreaming "a revealing encounter," "an adventure of the imagination, of the senses, of ideas which, if they were accessible to him, could transform and break into his entire life" (*Zoom*, p. 149), a redeeming paradise which might abolish the previous absurdity, overcoming the current, senseless succession of events. But then comes the surprising awakening, some disaster into which the protagonists fall and from which the only escape is an even greater catastrophe. "Sometimes it occurs to you that some special intelligence in life could uncover your desires, offering you some fortuitous situation that could suddenly commit you to another destiny. Little by little, you become convinced that sometime, by dint of insisting on that belief you will experience a revealing encounter" (p. 66). But it will not happen. Unlike the child-narrator of Valdés's *Cuerpo creciente* (one of the best Chilean novels of the sixties), those characters do not even have that fierce, sensual spark of childhood, the loyalty of a grandfather, or a mythical country (the Spain of the Second Republic) in which to save themselves. They are left without illusions, almost mute.

The two entities which so frustrate the characters in *Zoom* are called body and country. It is the separation from those two fundamental landscapes, the places where we should and need to carry out the practice of what we want to be and of what we are, which makes it impossible "to link yourself to some enduring structure, you would like to recognize, in its (the country's) progress your own growth, your own reality" (*Zoom*, p. 65). Over and over, the narrator asks himself if he is not inhabiting a postcard, a temporary, fleeting piece of scenery, rather than a country: "By some stupefying force, the country seemed to have the power of destroying memory and, with it, any continuity of ideas and purposes, and in the long run, with no opposition, the energies of any passion" (*Zoom*, p. 88). This vision of Chile (and of Latin America) as a layer of ash and extinguished fire, with deteriorated, irrelevant cities, with a precarious and drunken history, "a place without references, a phantom of civilization" (*Zoom*, p. 119), is what leads him to deny any permanence to his own actions, to forge a future that lacks any meaning: "Why rebel? Why look for a remedy? Why do anything any more enduring than what is demanded by its immediate utility? Why save anything, if everything, sooner or later, will be destroyed? . . . Who, before a considerable amount of time has passed, could conceive of any enduring creation on that soil?" (*Zoom*, p. 65).[51]

This amazement in regard to his own land, this distance from the community, is accompanied by amazement toward his own body. He is bewildered and surprised, again and again, by the obligatory, vindictive bonds between the sphere of consciousness and that of materiality, the way in which individual freedom is extenuated in a struggle without quarter between these two adversaries: "To depend on that body, to be subordinated to its weight, to its will, to its fatigue. Just as his body acted as if his thought had been an alien tumor that must be extracted and expelled, he, in his turn, lived in his body as in an alien milieu, which during almost his entire existence he had tried to ignore and to vilify, adulterating its taste, disguising its needs, denying its pleasure and its health. But, perhaps with even more powerful resources than his thoughts, his body was taking revenge, producing phenomena that made it more and more ostensible: eruptions, ulcers, unhealthy oils, gray pigments, . . ." (*Zoom*, p. 59).

He who enters the torture chamber, therefore, is someone who has meditated extensively upon the vast, ambiguous frontiers that separate his organism from the world. That body, "an almost fictional support," different and distant from his thoughts, a mere "mount and depository" in *Zoom*, is the one that will connect him with pain in *Tejas Verdes*. The protagonist of *Tejas Verdes*, from the beginning, will feel more bitter and defeated than his fictional alter egos in *Zoom*, Héctor and Teófilo, since the military coup has allowed him to confirm that his own disastrous personal history is now equivalent to that of his broken people. It is in those depressing circumstances that he accedes to the bewildering encounter that will violate and transform him. But the apprenticeship that awaits him is infernal, not Edenic. It will not be life in general that plays a dirty trick on him, it's not a matter, as in *Zoom*, of wanting to win over a young Czech beauty and finding oneself slurping tea with a miserable, toothless old woman, or of opening a mysterious package that could be the long-expected messianic revelation but turns out to be his laundry. What in *Zoom* was a metaphysical structure, a mocking smile on the lips of the life that is writing him, in *Tejas Verdes* becomes tangible, concrete, throbbing, a threat to his physical life and not just to a soul lost among time and dusty objects.

The experience of *Tejas Verdes*, therefore, leads Valdés to doubt the entire civilized construction upon which he had in the past secretly based his salvation. What his imprisonment is denying and placing in jeopardy is, in reality, nothing more nor less than the structure or literary system that intellectuals, living in underdevelopment, have taken refuge in, the vision that has allowed them a certain autonomy in the face of the market. Consciousness (that is, the interconnected elaboration of that social practice which we accumulate and call consciousness) is conceived as alien to the body that must suffer, and just as alien to the country which is now the scenario for a struggle between the military and the people, in which that body, to its sorrow, has become involved.

This is the reason that the author can conceive of *Tejas Verdes* as a break. Although in his previous books (and I include his poems) he explores the limitations, constraints, and traps that besiege the liberal conception of the person, of one's ultimate sovereignty, there always remained, in the final analysis, between the narrow framework of the consciousness and the defiant sensuality of art, a timid margin which left an illusion of freedom.[52] *Tejas Verdes* makes him discover that man is, in reality, a prisoner, that capitalism and underdevelopment not only oppress and alienate, but on occasions also repress and destroy physically. In his essays and in his fiction Valdés had already confronted that possibility in theory, but his own life had not been touched by it. It is one thing to tolerate the absurd in the trifles of everyday life (the tedious and infinite cartography of alienation), but it is quite another to endure it in the material necessities of a spirit reduced to the manifestations of the body, trying to survive, "proposing mental categories that are aprioristic or originate in a distant divinity."[53]

Thus, the man who at the beginning of *Tejas Verdes* had so much time at his disposal that he ended up being suspended between parentheses, with no one to give him a sense of permanence, with no reason to stay in the country, disposing of unconditional freedom that led no where, will suddenly be forced into another time frame, one regulated by others, in which he will never be able to hurry enough, his physical well-being and his very existence constantly on the line.

Therefore, from the start the protagonist will be a victim who does not control the forces that dominate him, like so many contemporary human beings, like so many characters in literature from Dostoyevski on. But he is a double victim, because another kind of persecution will be imposed upon him: the weight of hitherto invisible, uncontrollable forces are about to press upon a body with nails and fists and guns. Unlike the case of those prisoners who were militants, at the heart of that rootless being there are no dimensions that enable him to successfully confront the process of animalization. He sits with a blanket, in the sun, uselessly trying to warm himself, trembling beneath the sun's rays ("I'm incapable of thinking of myself in terms of possibility, as a project"), devoted to the impossible task of his own body.

The only thing that keeps him going is that other time frame of habit, normality, and supposed innocence. That time frame that is torn from him like a ferocious tidal wave, minute by minute, layer by layer, useless object after useless object. That time of normality which he attempts to preserve and remember in the midst of the inhuman time of torture. But that time of normality is false, precarious and fragile, because it does not contain a true project within it. A dictatorship, in its gradual and systematic assault, can erase that existence and put its own voices in its place, because Valdés already began his journey dead, without identity, gnawed by paralyzing doubts and problems.

The last images we have of him confirm this prognosis. They release him, along with other prisoners, with the warning, "Get lost, fast." And he begins to obey, like an automaton, "as quickly as possible, holding myself back to keep from running," possessed by that absurd and forced time frame of the torturers, running without running, free but still a prisoner. "Without looking to see where the Spaniard has gone, without looking back at the truck . . . without looking back, without seeing anybody . . . at the same time, forcing myself not to turn my head and look" (p. 174). On the unknown street where they release him, there is nothing to hold him, nothing he loves or is looking for, that can shelter him. He will have to cross "the space ahead of him" with no saving reference point.

In these circumstances, returned to his point of origin, but now without the slightest possibility of creating an illusion for himself or of constructing even a mirage to head for, nauseated by what he has come to know about himself and humanity, the only possibility remaining to him is to overcome that commandment not to look back, a look that has as much real as symbolic value. It is the only unconscious myth that he allows himself in a process that breaks all mythology or hope: like Eurydice or Lot's wife, he must be capable of escaping Hell and also of looking back without being turned to stone or dying yet again. What his now-internalized guards want is for him to hurry away forever, forgetting what had happened, but not its effects, like someone who has had amnesia but whose head still aches from the beatings. The book is that retrospective view, and the only victory Valdés can permit himself against his enemy.

It is a paradoxical conclusion, one not lacking in splendor. Precisely during his ordeal, literature had shown itself to be useless, both as a preparation for that experience or as a means of protection through the social position it supposedly gave him ("because what I knew about evil, before, was pure caricature, pure literature," p. 147). He is a creator, a demiurge, an imaginer of realities, a worker of the intellect, handed over to the rigors of his own body and to the outrages of those who give no relevance whatsoever to that kind of spiritual elevation, trapped in an experience that is not "literary" but rather fiercely real. Not only does being a man of culture not prevent the pain, but, to the contrary, his exaggerated sensibility turns into an obstacle to his own survival. This becomes clear when Valdés briefly analyzes the characteristics of an account given to him by a peasant, which is in fact another, divergent literary system, almost a counter-definition of his own work (which imitates orality but depends so much upon refined and subtle writing): "I quickly imagine the verbal impotence of those peasants, their inability to skillfully express their adventure, their tendency to attribute those evils to their fate and to quickly forget the manifestations of that fate." Valdés's verbal power, his skill, his ability to overanalyze that tangle of causes and super-causes, his almost sickly memory, will be factors that will weaken him during his imprisonment, even though they strengthen him in retrospect. Throughout his trajectory, he devalues cultural expression, only to fall back on it as the only route that can return him to even a small island of dignity.

In any case it is not a question, as in the other accounts, of remembering in order to judge the murderers or to make the torturers pay for their crimes. Rather it is a matter of integrating that memory into the national culture, fulfilling a political function on another level: to store up conscience, to permit no lies or false constructions, to reach no accords or complicity with the authorities and, in that way, to purify the nation's demon-possessed soul. That is the function Valdés assigns to the intellectual, to serve as watchtower and warning shout, to corjure up and even to exorcize the evil. Thus, if Carrasco, for example, named the devil so he would appear, Valdés stammers his name with the hope that someday he will disappear.

But before continuing with these comparisons between the two types of accounts, first we should resolve a previous doubt: Does it make any sense? Is there any legitimate reason to carry out such a comparison?

IV

The differences between Valdés's view and that of his militant comrades have been shown to be truly significant. They are members of political parties; he sees himself as a nonaffiliated observer, independent of any collectivity, feeling no responsibility to movement, group, or party, his words compromising no one but himself.[54] The experiences of all the militants begin on September 11 and end, in many cases, years, and in all cases, several places of enclosure later; Valdés's experience is brief, savage, and starts many months after the camp, when a different phase of the cycle of repression has commenced.[55] They are amateurs, who would never proclaim themselves as writers at the moment of their capture, although several of them have gone on producing literature since then; he already had a considerable body of poetry and fiction. We must not confuse this with the fact that Valdés may be an intellectual and the others are not. On the contrary, they all would consider themselves organic intellectuals of the working class in the Gramscian sense, at the service of a cause, with their thought and their mental and emotional labor dedicated to social change, accentuating the validity of creating *propaganda* in the best sense of the word, while the definition of Valdés would be that of the progressive intellectual, with leftist sympathies, but with no desire to tie himself to any organization. He is one who imagines himself to be sovereign in the creative field and who does not see himself as a servant of a superior cause, but rather as an artist observing it.

On the other hand, if both Valdés and the others understand their works as a form of achieving self-knowledge (in such extreme circumstances, I reveal myself as I am, I have the opportunity to measure my own humanity), the different conclusion that they reach in the face of such phenomena could be explained merely by differences in personality without projecting it socially: Valdés just happens to be weak or cowardly or non-radicalized, while they are heroes, conscientious, firm unto death. "The ones who suffer most today," explains Cabieses in a letter to his wife, "are those who live for themselves, who only understand their own pain and for whom any escape or personal solution appears as the only goal for which to struggle. It is a grave error that is translated into attitudes which undermine the dignity and the respect of our ideals" (Cabieses, p. 69). He might be referring to Valdés himself. From Cabieses's perspective, then, the fact that Valdés manages to uncover the unreal, nightmarish character of the process of torture should not cause dismay, but is the consequence of a discontinuity and fracture in his existence. The militants could stand as firm as oaks because, in fact, what happened to them was never unreal, but rather impressively real; they were never pulled out of their own identity. They tortured Rodrigo Rojas for days and days and he never lost his condition of patriot, communist, and revolutionary: the nightmare never completely overcame him; his conscience never stopped functioning. He does not, of course, communicate to us any aspects of the inner struggle.

The two versions of what happens in a concentration camp— identical in their indignation, in their desire for decency and fraternity [56]—almost evade each other mutually, almost exclude each other, placing the other experience in the realm of the accidental or the merely transitory.[57] While for Valdés his captivity ratifies the general absurdity of the anti-idyll that is life, the abysmal precariousness of everything, the revolutionaries seem completely clear as to what is happening and why and for what reason and in what direction.

In spite of these and other differences, I believe that drawing a comparison makes sense, and that such a juxtaposition will shed light upon the two opposing worlds.

Because what is interesting and unites both visions beyond their repudiation of repression, is that in both cases what they desire is *to communicate,* that is, to write in order to have a concrete political effect. It is true that the militants and Valdés would not understand the strategic function of their texts in exactly the same way. This may be due to the fact that the former are narrating the failure of the torturers, while Valdés presents their success. If the first is transcendent for our nation's history, opens the path to resistance, the second is important for the history of our conscience, a way of analyzing the obstacles to that victory. But despite this divergence, all of them wish to denounce their monstrous treatment, to help insure that such acts are neither forgotten nor repeated, to isolate the regime within the international community, and, finally, to punish the guilty within the pages of a book, since they cannot yet demand retribution on the elusive pages of historical reality.

Who best achieves all this is, undoubtedly, Hernán Valdés. Proof is not limited to the fact that his is the only book that does not enter the production-distribution circuit of solidarity, but competes on the commercial market, with several editions in

Spanish and translations into many languages. More significant is the fact that Valdés, perhaps because he belongs to that vast sector of humanity that does not live for revolution and was unable to weather the storm of repression, is able to carry out a decisive mission: to reach out to a larger audience than any of his fellow writers. The others, who participated in the accomplishments of the Allende government, who represent the backbone of the resistance, the builders and the heroes, nevertheless, throw themselves headlong into an approach to writing that is so restrictive and sectorial (not to say sectarian), that it is limited to the small coterie of the already convinced.

A paradoxical phenomenon: it is the solitary, somewhat skeptical intellectual (if he believes in anything, it is in a certain fragmented tenderness, as he demonstrates in *Cuerpo creciente*), isolated from the majority of the people by so many structural motives (his situation in society; the tradition of rebellion, rupture, and self-destruction of contemporary art; the search for literary autonomy; the fear of all control, whether by the state or the market), disconnected from the public, who becomes, nonetheless, the one who, by descending into the inferno of that historical juncture, can best express what happens to the ordinary man. The hero in the Greek tradition was the son of gods and men, a mixture of both, a being who is both mythic and, at the same time, real. His imperfection did not compromise his heroism, his capacity to hold up under fire, and to carry out his deeds. But he was always distant from ordinary men, however much he may be presented as an almost superhuman model who brings redemption in difficult times. The existence of the hero can revive, generate confidence in the future and in the possibility of changing the world, but rarely is he able to orient us in subtle and complex situations. "How can I tell you," asks Guillermo Núñez in his travel journal, "that I was afraid?" An essential question that demands an answer. It may be true, then, that the hero (in this case, the proletarian hero, the hero of the revolutionary scene) is invincible, although that depends on the reader's convictions, whether he does or does not believe in the principles of that heroism; but what is just as undeniable is that the majority of the readers have many weaknesses and their problem is what to do with them, how to portray them, how to look them in the face? One of the most basic questions of any literature that refers to revolutionary struggle is how to lay reality bare, nerve by nerve, to reveal it as it is, and nevertheless to keep the faith, that is, how to designate the contradictory present, while preserving some hope of a different future. In any case, when Rojas, for example, before being shot, describes his feelings ("a bitter feeling of impotence to be dying without having succeeded in doing the greatest damage possible . . . to our people's enemies. But, at the same time, I felt joy because I had confidence in the definitive victory of the Chilean people"), at the same time that he elicits our respect, he distances himself from us. In that sense, Rojas is faithful to the word "testimony," which comes from "testes," testicles in Latin, since one could not give testimony in Rome if the latter were not healthy and in their place. To testify, to tell the truth, was originally related to virility, to speak with the capacity to father children. It is worth mentioning here, as a kind of parenthesis, a sad appendix, that there are no women among those who have written of their experience in captivity, and that this absence, from the texts although not from the concentration camps, could be one of the keys to explore more deeply the dichotomies that we are examining and the concept of "manliness" that magnifies at the same time that it distances the combatants.

The fact that Valdés is not a "man" may in part explain why he communicates well, in his work, the true nature of the national experience of repression. Because what happens in Chile is not just a war against the vanguard, against the most selfless and solemn representatives of a future that has not yet materialized, but rather a process of alienation, of making alien, distant, exiled, everything the country was. Paradoxically, though, Valdés does not believe in this country that was lost, suggesting, in fact, in his next novel[58] that it is another invention of a left which has succumbed to illusions of the dominant oligarchy; he represents Chile, or at least, the desolation felt by vast, democratic sectors of the Chilean population. In this sense, his *marginality* is, in the end, a valuable position from which to judge and examine the epidemic which has befallen us.

It is not that the other accounts remain unsurprised at what is happening. In both cases, the official country, that debased territory into which we sank, seems unrecognizable. But the militants are not shocked that this is happening to them: their works stubbornly allude to previous repressions, especially those of González Videla.[59] What disturbs them is that they do not recognize the country in which they believed they were living only a short time ago, which it took them decades to build and which has been lost because of their mistakes (for the most part, unconfessed and evaded). For Valdés, on the other hand, what is strange is that this can happen to him. The experience is not, as in the case of the militants, something that in the final analysis is assumed to be part of the rules of the game, a risk that somewhere in the back of our heads is calculated even as we try to persuade ourselves that it does not exist. Thus, for the working class, repression is terrible, but it constitutes a historical factor with which one must always take into account; it is part of the struggle, of the memory of the poor. An intellectual, on the other hand, presumes that, existing on the margin of that violence, he is safe from its most barbaric vicissitudes. So, the passage from one state (observer) to another (victim) is revealed with all the exaggerated sensibility and eroticism of the trauma, a transit which lets him contact all those unpoliticized groups of society that do not have a prior conception from which to understand, assume, and transcend that phenomenon. It is something that can touch anyone, the arbitrary elevated to norm. And Valdés refuses to project a future that will cleanse and comfort, a heaven that will compensate for all the pain, a promised land that will erase the ghetto and the gas chamber. Nor is there a past that is sufficiently intense and positive to offer him anything solid to grasp during the passage. The present of the prison, the wild archetype of the concentration camp universe, pollutes all other times. While Valdés's vision translates an experience of impotence, alienation, lack of control over one's own life, which symbolizes contemporary life in the twentieth century under capitalism (in Lukács's interpretation of Kafka), and as such, is rooted in an entire, current cultural and literary tradition, the truth is that at the same time he brings his experience closer to men who do not understand what is happening to them. This antiheroism is, thus, at the base of the reader's identification with the protagonist: if earlier we saw how the narrator's degradation, his limited and rigid perspective, made the suspense flow, not knowing whether the victim would or would not betray his companions, now this same procedure appears to us as a means of including the reader in an experience that is not previously interpreted, in which the fate of the one suffering has not yet been decided. At this point, a distinction made by Noé Jitrik might be useful. Jitrik distinguishes testimony and denunciation, pointing out that the first is full of vibrations, allowing the experience to shake and to bother the communication project, while the second mediates the virginal experience through a political, conceptual, and ideological filter.[60]

Valdés is not content with merely condemning the violation of human rights, but adds another dimension, incorporating the degradation of the witness himself, the moral invalidity and the sensory hierarchy of the eye that sees. This double direction of Valdés's book means that, at the same time that it has the characteristics of Latin American testimony (what we could call the journalism of the dominated), it also attempts to rebel against the false and immaculate tranquility of the official versions, exhibiting the quests of vanguard literature, which, in an underdeveloped country even more than elsewhere, is inevitably isolated and limited to a minority. Because, like it or not, Valdés, in this book at least, places himself in what Octavio Paz has called "the tradition of rupture," wherein literature is emphasized as a means of exploring and questioning, literature as a journey of discovery which is the linguistic act. It was, of course, a theoretical concern of Valdés, as demonstrated in certain ideological texts of his published during the Popular Unity period, to solve the basic problem of every honest and decent intellectual in countries that are dominated and poor: how to create a culture that "would reach people."[61] But, during the Popular Unity period, he never found a situation that forced him to carry out that project, that would have put him in touch with reality and its limits as deeply as happened after the coup.[62] Now the experience has come to him and has led Valdés to distance himself from the (more hermetical) language of the initiated elite, abandoning the code with which he has always written and which, in order to be part of literary tradition, poses intellectual requirements most people do not meet. The writer thus now rejects experiments and techniques of the vanguard in order to reach a mass audience with immediately comprehensible material. In that way he connects to a public which is not the same as the one that read his earlier works, without abandoning, as we have noted, a series of interests and themes that were previously present.

The concentration camp, then, jolts the internees: it makes some, who had never written before, take up the pen; it grinds at another, who had worked for a restricted audience, until he writes a book that goes beyond the elite. But the attitude toward truth has not varied because of that crossing in either case: if the truth is revealed beforehand, then it is necessary to preach, to bring about a conversion; if the truth is something that is only perceived along the way, then language is an intermittent battle to draw it out, to convince it to come out of hiding. If literature is a way of exemplifying, of signaling an "ought to be," what is shameful and detracts from one's dignity ends up being contingent and accidental. If, on the other hand, literature does not set out to persuade anyone but rather—though it is not guaranteed—to make others participate in a revelation that some day could be common, what matters is to remain faithful to certain basic human tensions, not to hide the contradictions. In the one case it is a matter of erecting and brandishing a titanic legend; in the other, of eroding myths and profaning dogmas. For the militant few, the struggle is already won; the battle is considered to be over in the perfect and triumphant present example, however small it may be, and when there are cases of those who did not hold up, they are passed over, almost abstractly, and imputed to a minority, denied by the courage and bravery of the resistors, whose texts become defiant replies, solutions, and absolutions. For Valdés, on the other hand, the dimension of the turncoat and of the weak lies within each one of us, like a crossroads or a temptation, and what matters is the ability to dig deeply into a crisis that will admit of no delay. Beyond the fact, then, that we can admire the conduct of the revolutionary and criticize Hernán Valdés as an "uncommitted" petit bourgeois (the exact words militants use to dismiss him and that I have heard on diverse occasions), the problem is that the revolutionary, because of his very will to overcome, usually does not analyze himself or lay bare the entire situation, even though he appears—and this does not refute but rather confirms our thesis—as very rich and overflowing in his private, oral language in conversations that do not transcend to the public domain. The militant would even say, holding out Valdés's case as proof, that excessive introspection weakens and that there is no place for those who feel self-pity and introduce the enemy within their own fortress.[63]

Thus, we return by another route to the problem of *indecency,* to which we referred earlier. If displaying one's own heroism made almost no sense, if it is justified only by making it representative of a greater, collective cause, how much more obscene is it to display the victim's cowardice, the resultant despair, the mea culpa of expiation of one who ought to be silent after having betrayed his friends.

But what if that "indecency" ends up being an aesthetic strategy to limit the communication of that experience, a form of censoring inconvenient truths? The "political" testimonies all give the impression of having been transcribed without great effort (Quijada is the exception). They no doubt had to overcome the nausea, the sweat and the trauma, but at no time do we feel that they have labored, as a kind of prior and simultaneous question, the *how* of what they are to. accomplish. At times, as in the Realist (or regional or social) novels of Latin America, one senses that the authors seem to believe that it is enough to refer to a "real" world for the transmission automatically to be authentic, as if there were something mistaken and guilty in being concerned with the form in which the communication should be carried out. That is, in none of them do we note a struggle with the language or the organization of the material to respond to the vital question about the perception of the phenomenon itself, because the language is already *there,* a merely auxilliary vehicle. We should not be surprised by such a lack of problematization of the world or of the way in which it is elaborated, since, if it is indecent to speak of oneself, to be concerned about the dilemmas of the presentation should be even more indecent. Heroism lies in conduct, not language, and there is nothing individual about it. For Valdés, on the other hand, the only thing heroic is happening later, in the act of telling the unconfessable truth.

Though the militant accounts are open, loose, and disorderly, while Valdés's account is a finished, highly worked product with the constant intervention of an artist's techniques and resources, we hardly realize that this is so, precisely because Valdés, instead of surrendering himself to the spontaneous, ingenuous and oral, narrates events as if everything were happening at that very moment, taking us back to the original instant, maintaining total control over his ordeal. He shortens the distance between the reader and the experience because he himself draws back from the material sufficiently to adopt a strategy, while the militant accounts allow the reader to identify with the narrative only to the degree to which they commune a priori with the author's political and moral point of view. In the case of the militants, it is precisely a question of not writing "literature," distrusting, as they do, whatever might alter the brutal evidence: events speak for themselves; it is truth itself that is presented here, as the writers of the inevitable prologues do not tire of warning us. The experience has been too serious, too grave, and tremendous, to admit of any stylistic ventilation. It must be presented without any order other than that of the naked experience in its raw form, trying to erase to the extent possible the eye that perceives it, pushing the individual personality of the one who suffered and resisted far into the background. When Quijada quotes Neruda, "I speak of what exists. God forbid I should invent anything!" he is speaking for all of them.

The real problem, of course, is that left-wing political cadres attempt, in theory and in practice, to deny domination and alienation, but such attempts do not find an expression in language. Instead, they assume formulas, structuring a sensibility which freezes reality instead of showing its contradictory dynamics, thus tending to hide the crisis rather than revealing it. In a word, they insufficiently democratize the primary instrument that will contact, analyze, expose, and convince. Such a failure could well be traced to a paradoxical dissymmetry which Umberto Eco notes:[64] the language, demands, and claims of the contemporary working class coexist with the consumption of middle-class mass cultural models. The frequently dispersed, disconnected, and fragmentary character of these political testimonies might be interpreted, therefore, as the stammerings of a counterculture that is searching for its own coherent shape, its own "internal hegemony." In that sense, they might be the result of the growth of democratic expression among millions of citizens during the Popular Unity period, growing immensely in coherence and organization. Or are those real deficiencies, attributable to a cultural incapacity of the Chilean left? Self-stereotyping from within, accentuating the note of urgency or of exaltation, ignoring stylistic and technical re-

sources, eluding subtlety or shading, appealing to a public searching for short-term effects, these are some of the less promising
tendencies of that culture which sees itself as alternative but often
only succeeds in being marginal. When, in addition, history forces
it to become a culture of retreat, closed in on itself, this thesis that
a good, ethically praiseworthy content automatically includes its
own perfect form and expression, can lead to blindness and stasis.
The presentation of a static world in which the Manichaean an-
tagonists are previously defined and the triumphant result of the
struggle is assumed beforehand is symptomatic of a certain fear of
the contamination that exploring the truth supposes, a rigid conception of ideological struggle, understood mainly as propaganda,
the practice of truth as something that has already been discovered
and is then dictated and fixed once and for all, immobilizing and
petrifying thought. The predictions of victory, which I gropingly
share, can, by being so often repeated, blind us to the depth of the
national catastrophe, and turn language into a place of enclosed
communion with the past rather than of struggle and understanding. The happy ending, constructed by the vision of the left,[65] like
a fairy tale full of witches and ogres that will be defeated in the
end, is too much like the subliterary products of the mass media
and end up by turning us into a caricature for our enemies. It is as
if Pinochet were a parenthesis or a passing phase and not a defeat
that makes evident an even deeper and earlier crisis of an entire
country, one which, of course, permeates and divides the left as
well, and which, if we are to be rid of the dictator, must be faced
in all its unavoidable multiplicity.

Some will observe that in advancing these criticisms through
the work of Hernán Valdés, I end up invalidating them, or at least
introducing an element of unnecessary confusion into the debate.
To ask the militants to write like Valdés would be as impossible
a task as to require the author of *Tejas Verdes* not to talk in the
torture chamber. When those involved in the struggle sit down to
write of their experiences they cannot allow themselves to have
any doubts about their words nor about the public image they are
going to project. It is the condition of all literature that would be
ethical or didactic, not only in that it portrays the final triumph
of good over evil, but also in that it proposes that the reading of
the *work itself* be inscribed within the struggle, that it should serve

to change the injustice which it denounces. Valdés, on the other hand, must encounter the meaning of that world as it unfolds; it is something that is not given from the beginning. Perhaps, therefore, I am asking each one of these prisoners for something that he cannot give and, moreover, does not want to give, attempting to reconcile divergent social, and therefore literary, projects. Perhaps it would have been simpler to present both messages as complementary, two steps or panoramas in the same process (one that is centered in debasement, the other in the overcoming of that infamy), instead of as mutually exclusive siren calls.

And, nonetheless, I still believe that the juxtaposition of both visions can serve at least to begin to formulate important questions concerning the intellectual task confronting Chile, its elite and masses, during the coming decades. The limitations that each one of these worlds exhibits, the way in which they somehow lead to different literary systems, to diverse conceptions of their function and of their public, can help us to find solutions to the crisis we are living. Do we need an epic literature or a literature that holds up no models of conduct? In the midst of defeat, must we hide all imperfection? Or is it precisely in the midst of defeat that we must shout out the imperfections as the only way to heal the finger and the wound, to change men as they are and not as we dream them to be? Is the degradation we are living an accident? Or does it become more central with each month that passes without our seeing a way out of the critical situation? Is the present-day reality of Chile, at the start of the eighties, compatible with an image of triumphalism? And yet without that triumphalism, how can simple and concrete human beings be mobilized? And how do we rescue the fierce capacity for rebellion of the working class and at the same time contemplate its sordid defeat today? How do we strengthen faith in victory without opening the doors to doubt? And what if we open them so much that we no longer have either doors or thresholds? How do we mobilize titanically and at the same time search out the traitor within? How do we convince if we ourselves are in the process of exploring the everyday adventure of certainty? How do we advance, stripping away the myths? How do we strip away the myths without bringing despair? Do the people, then, not have the right to be complex? Is it possible to survive, to raise spirits, to record the collective memory, without hiding a reality that is difficult, twisted and suffocating?

Deciding the degree of truth in the experience recounted by Valdés will depend, in the final analysis, on the intellectual framework which we make of the fundamental human problems of this century. If one thinks, and this is my deepest sentiment, that the central tendency today is the conquest of liberation by the great, oppressed majorities, it is clear that Valdés's book will appear as a moving account—but nothing more—of the torment that one man can suffer at the hands of a faraway, dependent, transitory dictatorship. In those circumstances we could only lament the fact that the author was not born with the privilege of finding the seeds of hope in other human beings, a transfusion that can be neither artificial nor authoritarian but must be born out of one's own experience and history. But if what happens in this last part of the twentieth century, and suddenly in my nightmares and in the fragile crucible of my own exile I hardly find the strength to completely belie those visions, is a deeper crisis within the reigning contemporary civilization, then Valdés's book is not merely an account of the excesses of an underdeveloped tyranny but represents a more basic, utter marginalization of many of the human beings who today live and survive on this planet.

The question is: which of the two myths is stronger? Prometheus or Orpheus? He who defies the eagles who are eating his entrails because he tried to save humanity, or he who descends into hell and looks back; he who rebels against authority and gives fire to the dispossessed, or he who loses his beloved, sinks into degradation with his music and will in the end be torn to pieces on the shores of a drunken river?

For now, let us say that the Chilean resistance produced these two ways, Siamese twins at least as regards the torture, of confronting the per-version of the dictatorship with their own sub-version, and that we hope that a dialogue between the two is possible and not entirely irreconcilable.

The day we are willing to admit that revolutionary change cannot be brought about, dictators overthrown, without persons like those who appear in the pages of *Tejas Verdes*, perhaps on that day we will be nearer to victory, which is also always and above all a victory over our own inner selves, over the demons that keep us from being truthful. It is a victory we must achieve by ourselves. There is, after all, no one else who can do it.

1982

■ The Rivers of Roa Bastos

It was in 1961, during one long night to be exact, that I first read a book by Augusto Roa Bastos. I was not yet twenty and spent as much time as I could avidly pursuing every Latin American novel I could lay my hands on, exploring through fiction a continent that seemed—at least to my ardent eyes—on the verge of an impending revolution. Though my readings came from almost every country in the hemisphere, I had not included even one author from Paraguay on my list. I was vaguely aware of its somber fate, landlocked and impoverished and under a dictator, Stroessner, who even then had been around much too long; but to my limited knowledge, its misfortune had not yet produced any interesting literature.

A Paraguayan lawyer, exiled in Chile, who had, on a previous visit to my parents' house, noticed my ignorance, stopped briefly by one evening and thrust a recently published book into my hands. "Read this," he said, "and then you'll understand my country."

It was *Son of Man*.

I opened the novel and did not put it down until the next day was dawning. When I finished it—around the time other, presumably more responsible, Chileans were rising to go to work—I had begun, not only to dimly understand, but to enthusiastically fall in love with the brutal and tender land of Paraguay. A love affair which has, as so often is the case, been primarily carried out through literature, that of Roa Bastos and many others (unpub-

Originally published as a foreword to the second English-language translation of *Son of Man* (New York: Monthly Review Press, 1988).

lished in English), political circumstances forbidding any personal visits there.

But I did not read the book at the time, and it should not be read now, merely as an introduction to an unknown landscape. Roa Bastos also dazzled me because he had managed to discover adequate narrative solutions to a number of moral and aesthetic dilemmas that were rushing through my head and the heads of so many young Latin Americans at the time. I was obsessed then, as I still am now, with finding the voice with which one could tell the truth about the miseries and betrayals that prevail in our republics, the cyclical repetition of sorrow and frustration, and yet not give in to hopelessness. Nor to its facile opposite, propaganda. Roa Bastos brilliantly pointed a way, one of several possible paths.

Reading the novel again so many years later, I am convinced that the importance of its message has not diminished. It is filled with the difficult certainty of redemption, but that redemption cannot be abstracted from the implacable portrayal of the horrors that have befallen Paraguay during most of its history. (Though *Son of Man* concentrates on the twenty-five years from 1910 to 1935, it reaches back to the beginning of the nineteenth century and anticipates some later developments as well.)

If in this novel there is, therefore, a persistent rumor of possible salvation, it is not uttered without having passed through the inferno. The images are terrifying. Paraguay is like the eroded crater left by a bomb, where the living are hardly more alive than the dead. Paraguay is an infinite plantation guarded by savage overseers and hallucinatory sicknesses. Paraguay is a besieged garrison fighting a senseless war without water in the middle of a desert. And, for those who manage to escape these geographic zones of the country, the nation itself is conceived as a vast prison from which escape is impossible.

Because the author does not lie about his ravaged land, because the violence is relentless and death apparently unending, the slow creation of hope is all the more powerful. "Man has two births," Macario Francia says to the children who listen to his tales, the children who, during the rest of the novel, are gradually going to witness their destinies fractured by forces they cannot control. "One when he is born, the other when he dies. . . . He dies, but he remains alive in others, if he has dealt kindly with his brothers. If he has helped others during his lifetime, when he dies, the earth may devour his body, but his memory will live on . . ." If the multiple protagonists of this novel cannot liberate themselves, or find ways of effecting social change and ending injustice, they can however transform their lives, and often their very extinction, into a message for those who will come.

That message, however, is not easily harvested. Rather than developing along the typically chronological and unitary pattern which is found in so many epic and social narratives, *Son of Man* is built out of fragments and meanderings, as irregular and dissevered as the lives it is recounting, which rarely touch one another directly. Due to the novel's discontinuous structure, the reader is forced to participate in the search for a way to transmit and link the whirlwind of dispersed existences. Not unlike the characters themselves, those who plunge into the dense delta of this novel must articulate the secretly connected lives, must work out the symbols, must establish the web of past memory and present action which allows the dead to continue speaking years after they have been buried.

For Roa Bastos, men's lives are like rivers: they can flow into other lives or they can end up in a swamp. The main narrator of the novel, the embittered, isolated Miguel Vera, ends up in a swamp. Most of the others, though not endowed as Miguel is with the gift of literary language, find more significant ways of depositing their lives in the flow that others have almost invisibly created. Cristóbal Jara crosses the enemy lines to bring water to comrades-in-arms he does not know, just as his father moved an abandoned railroad car across the country so that people would never forget that once upon a time he had planned to use it to free his land of tyranny, so that the remembrance would be of struggle rather than failure. Both father and son, as so many other men and women in this novel, are reborn in the form of myth in the minds of the survivors, nurturing in oblique ways a popular version of Paraguay which belies the official historical lies. The leper who carves a sick Christ does not tell those who come after him what to do with it or how to interpret his work. He gives them the basic freedom to work out comprehension for themselves, to carve out a message from his life just as he carved it from the wood, from the deepest nature, of Paraguay. He allows us, if we are human enough, to imagine the oppressed in the center of history and not forever on its shores.

Twenty-five years after that Paraguayan lawyer gave me *Son of Man*, I find that I need that flickering denial of despair more than ever. Augusto Roa Bastos is still in exile and I have joined him, along with countless others. Stroessner is still the ruler of that country and my own Chile has a dictator who has now been in power more years than Stroessner had been in power when I first read the book. We all need *Son of Man* more than ever.

May it flow into the lives of many readers.

1988

■ Someone Writes to the Future: Meditations on Hope and Violence in García Márquez

History is full of telling coincidences. So it is with the year 1928. José Eustacio Rivera, until then Colombia's greatest novelist, was dying that year—and across the country, in Aracataca, a woman was giving birth to a man-child who would surpass Rivera's literary achievements—Gabriel García Márquez. Rivera's major novel, *The Vortex*, had ended with the famous words: "Y se los devoró la selva"—"and the jungle devoured them," referring to protagonists engulfed by the ferocious, never-forgiving alien land of Latin America. Though nature would certainly be a brooding presence in the future works of García Márquez, his fundamental obsession was extremely different from Rivera's: to find out why history had devoured his people, history, that entity which men and women supposedly make and which should, at least in principle, be the territory where they exercise some command over their lives—hammer out some recognizable image of themselves.

But in that same year, 1928, remotely, perhaps ironically, echoing the cries of labor of little Gabriel's mother, an act was being committed that would express, if not radically symbolize, how far Colombians were from deciding their own destiny. Hundreds, some estimates say thousands, of workers were being massacred by government troops in the town of Ciénaga—an incident which would serve García Márquez as the basis for one of the most dramatic incidents of his fictitious village of Macondo, an incident which leads to Macondo's irrevocable decline and decadence, as if from that moment onward it would be impossible for its inhabitants to even dream of controlling their own existence. In fact, in the novel, it is only after the massacre that nature begins, Rivera-like, to encroach upon them. What had been a paradisiacal climate turns to horror—almost half a decade of rain followed by ten years more of absolute drought.

That rain, however, is not an objective, neutral force that develops independently of peoples' lives or wills, outside humanity. Not only is the downpour in *One Hundred Years of Solitude* the result of the United Fruit Company's desire to create some phenomenon that covers up the tracks of its villainy, but the author himself has used it, exaggerated its boundaries, in order to press upon his characters some proxy for history, experienced as if it were a deluge or an earthquake or a hurricane, something felt to be beyond the efforts of everyday men and women, somewhat like Rivera's jungle.

The flexible, malleable character of this rain, its openness to the tactics of a literary strategy, can be proven by examining how its author deals with its evolution in his own work. The storm of *One Hundred Years of Solitude* (written in 1967), and which lasts "four years, eleven months and two days," had already appeared in a work by García Márquez twelve years earlier in 1955. In a fragment which was going to be part of *Leafstorm* (*La Hojarasca*), but was then published as a separate story called "Isabel watching the rain fall in Macondo," García Márquez had invented a never-ending shower which swept away rails, opened graves, destroyed the foundations of the town, a tunnel of water in the mind of a woman and her feelings of desolation. Time: one week.

Twelve years later, when the writer transforms that almost commonplace, almost interior, event into an epic and prodigious phenomenon, he is signaling his desire to break out of normal time, to discover ways in which to transcend the limitations of what is conventionally called reality. That ordinary, albeit exceedingly wet, week has not only been metamorphosed into five years, it has become a myth, something unforgettable, that will remain with the generations to come—and as such, it provides a clue to what García Márquez is trying to accomplish in his masterpiece, how far he has come from the world of José Eustacio Rivera into which he was born. And that is precisely what he is attempting: García Márquez will try and tell the story of his country, of his continent, of his century, before his birth, before 1928—in other words, he is going to explore what has transpired without his presence, that which he only knows by hearsay, without having been a real witness. He will recount the one hundred years that preceded him, that led to his conception, the hundred years which have receded from him enough so they are in danger of being forgotten, the hundred years which are still near enough to be grasped and remembered.

The story has been told before, of course. Once by the droning, lying voice of official history which most definitely does not offer any indication of why things have gone wrong, why the people of Colombia have produced so much abundant wealth and are so copiously poor. And it has also been told once, and often, by the mouths, ears, and hands of collective memory. It is time to look back now, before it is too late, and tell the story in such a way that the errors of the past will not be repeated, but also told in such a way that it can be transmitted and understood, the literary act as the form in which readers (and writers) can supposedly break out of the brutal cycle of misery and violence.

In order to do this, García Márquez must be true to two different traditions which have, in general, opposed one another throughout history and particularly Latin American history: one is the literature of an illustrated minority, elaborated with all the forms that belong to so-called "high culture," basically centered in the cities; while the other, nurtured in a popular, oral, folk tradition, finds its roots in the countryside. García Márquez's justly famous "style" is not something artificial imposed upon a distant subject matter, but emerges—with its perfect blend of the colloquial and the cultivated, its ability to address both the most demanding jargon-weary academics as well as men and women who do not care much for literature, its success at home and abroad—from a need to communicate in a new way, attempting to bring together the antagonistic, mutually mistrustful, forms of elite and popular culture that have fractured Latin America so far. *One Hundred Years of Solitude* tries to work out in the space and language of a novel what the people of Latin America themselves have been unable to do thus far in history—combine the separate ways in which they know, in which they understand, in which they inscribe and read (or speak) their reality.

It is a task which has been prepared for by many generations of Latin American writers. This is not the place to examine how, since the beginning of our literature, the challenge from the discourse of excluded majorities in the hinterlands has determined an arduous search for a new language by writers. García Márquez's efforts would not be possible, or even conceivable, without those attempts, particularly in lyrical poetry from the end of the nineteenth century and narrative experiments after the Second World War. But just as important is that those excluded millions, having suffered silence and incessant marginalization, found ways of ferosciously keeping their version alive, murmuring it onward to their communities and, beyond them, to children and grandchildren and the unborn. It is only recently that their stubborn dynamic creativity can be recognized by intellectuals and artists as the basis for an alternative cultural (and political) vision. This is as much due to a newfound irrepressible protagonism of those hitherto outcast classes and groups as to parallel developments in twentieth-century vanguard and modernist culture in Europe and the United States. These developments reject the rationalist perspective both in subject matter and in form, coming to see in mythic thinking, in the "primitive mentality" or its equivalent in the unconscious of each of us, the suppressed substratum from which a different story can be told.

When García Márquez narrates the story of the Buendía family from a mythical perspective he is situating his voice at the precise confluence of the popular and the cultivated traditions, satisfying both the cosmopolitan and the local, bringing together the experimentation learned in reading contemporary literature with the demand for a space where collective memory unregistered in books can express itself. This dual heritage of *One Hundred Years of Solitude* is best symbolized, and indeed culminates, in the last image of the book: the text that the final Buendía is reading is his own history, the personal and collective history already written by the gypsy Melquíades but also by every one of the men and women of his family—and simultaneously—the printed literate words in the artifact we are consuming, an artifact that has itself been fabricated, printed, distributed, bought. For an instant, the last instant, we are the Buendías—except that we as readers survive in order to change the way we live, to tell and live, one would hope, our existence in a different manner.

Essential to the structure, themes, and language of *One Hun-*

dred Years of Solitude is the freedom to narrate from within the world of a family historically determined and condemned to extinction and failure, and yet at the same time to find a perspective outside that history so that the telling itself is not so determined or condemned, so the telling does not become entangled in the very forces that destroyed the chances of the Buendías to succeed and prosper.

This freedom explains, to begin with, the capacity of Macondo to be both a place which is tied to specific historical situations it cannot escape (no matter how hard its inhabitants try) and yet simultaneously a metaphor for other human realities. One can trace the evolution of Macondo quite clearly in Colombian history: founded at the beginning of the nineteenth century by José Arcadio Buendía, it is not allowed to live in embryonic isolation but is linked to the larger institutions in the nation when civil and ecclesiastical authorities arrive. It later suffers the sorrows of the prolonged civil wars between liberals and conservatives with one of its citizens, Colonel Aureliano Buendía, serving as commander-general of the revolutionary forces, who, after many battles and years have passed, finally signs a peace Treaty at Neerlandia. The period of prosperity which ensues does not last long. With the first railroad the North Americans arrive—and all too soon the banana company begins to squeeze the town dry. Its reign ends with the aforementioned massacre of the workers who have promoted a strike. This is followed by a torrential rain, the equally devastating drought, and the slow erosion of Macondo until a wind erases the town from the face of the earth. If Macondo's evolution parallels that of Colombia and, beyond it, that of Latin America, its beginning and its end are more metaphoric. The founding act apparently coincides with the start of the nation itself, just after the Wars of Independence, but it also subsumes and represents the previous discovery, conquest, colonization of the continent. José Arcadio, whose son fights the wars of the nineteenth century, is a Renaissance man of the sixteenth and seventeenth centuries, a dreamer of new horizons, fueled by the feverish desire for Eden and Utopia, the search for gold and the opening of new lands which characterized the expeditions of Columbus, Pizarro, Cortés, Pedro de Valdivia. As for the hurricane that sweeps Macondo away, one can sadly read in it the disappearance of these southern lands from the globe, their insignificance and irrelevance in the grand design of history. Perhaps it is a foreshadowing of an apocalypse that awaits our entire species, just as the original days of Macondo, when everything was so new that it hardly had a name, reminds us of the nostalgia every human seems to feel for some form of paradise.

Why does it have to end this way? Why is destruction the final destiny of the Buendías?

One answer is, of course, that the conclusion has already been written when García Márquez begins to tell the story, that he is looking back and seeing that these hundred years have led to disasters and loneliness instead of expansion and joy—in other words, he cannot invent a solution that people in history have not yet found by themselves. Melquíades (whoever he really is) has already written the story of the Buendías—they are trapped in a past that cannot ever be changed. And yet, when we open the novel, though the signs are everywhere, the terrible consummation does not seem that foregone. On the contrary, what has undoubtedly drawn readers to *One Hundred Years of Solitude* is its exuberant vitality, its sense that life was made for laughter and love, each generation renewing its pledge of innocence and youth as if the stagnation and futility awaiting their descendants were mere illusions.

When each new Buendía believes he or she can start anew, unburdened by the past, they are unconsciously imitating the founders of the dynasty, José Arcadio, his wife Ursula, and their friends, who created Macondo as a place outside time and history and violence, a place with no cemetery. And when their lives end up twisted, crossed by repression and solitude, they are prefiguring the final fate of Macondo, which will be nothing other than a vast burial ground where everyone is finished, past, dead, where the only act allowed to the last Buendía will be to passively read his death in the mirror of the narrator's words.

Two dread events—they might almost be called structures—haunt the family in Macondo, one from the past and the other from the future. The first is a terror that may come to pass—and eventually does. It has been foretold that if relatives such as José Arcadio and Ursula marry, their offspring will be born with the tail of a pig. It is Ursula's refusal to bed her husband which leads to the second terrible event: when his friend Prudencio Aguilar mocks him, José Arcadio's macho instinct, his sense of honor, his need to exercise his virility, explodes. He murders his friend and rapes his wife and then, when the ghost of Prudencio will not leave him alone, sets out to found a new village where sex does not lead to death. Though Macondo originates, therefore, in the twin sins of incest and fratricide, it will ultimately be unable to avoid them. In each generation, war among brothers devastates and divides the land, and in each generation the Buendías stage approximations and dress rehearsals of incest, sons desiring mothers, a brother marrying his adopted sister, a woman beloved by her nephew first and then her great-nephew, multiple uncles madly in love with their irremediably beautiful niece. The violence will culminate in the great massacre, a Colombian army killing Colombian workers; the sex will culminate in a final violation, that of the last male Buendía, Aureliano, of the last woman Buendía, Amaranta Ursula, and their child will be born with the tail of a pig and be devoured by the ants.

It is easy to proclaim that this inevitable fate is the consequence of outside factors which define the Buendías. The fact that the story, even before José Arcadio and Ursula set out, has been written—quite literally—for them, symbolizes the iron net that awaits them, the boundaries that hold them in. In order to flee from the incest, the endogenous isolation, they are impelled to open up to the external world; but each time they do so—and the novel is full of such escapades—what is brought back from those outer dominions invariably makes things worse. From the political and particularly the economic point of view, there are already powerful, technologically advanced empires out there that will thwart any effort at independence or self-sufficiency. These empires are a given of history: progress will come to Macondo, as in the rest of Latin America, in order to impoverish the people there, taking from them the control over their own existence. No wonder each expansion towards the vast territories beyond Macondo ends up in an almost fetal withdrawal and retreat, the mysterious return to the home as magnet and refuge, a womb which, familiar and repetitive, at least does not seem to pose a threat of extermination. The Buendías have arrived late—and there is nothing they can do about it.

This sense of doom, therefore, arises quite naturally from their dependent and secondary status in the world, living on its periphery, left outside modernity, and is expressed, at the literary level, in the feeling that these men and women are poor underdeveloped incarnations of faraway resonances of biblical or Greek classic myths, pale imitations of archetypes created elsewhere. But to see their lives only as a feeble, useless attempt to avoid the encroachment of an external power—be it literary or be it socioeconomic—is to forget that they have come to us because autochthonous versions of those lives did manage to find their way into the future, that they are not merely degraded heirs to a Western literary tradition that is being applied to them from without. The corollary of this idea, its almost inevitable consequence, is that there must be internal factors that have led to that disastrous outcome, choices that the Buendías made or did not make. If these are inscribed in the way they organized their existence, in a history of their own embedded with reasons that did not allow them to break out of their solitude, those reasons and mistakes could be indeed understood by readers in the hope that they will not be repeated.

If incest will destroy the family, if the females attract their relatives with the kiss of death, if most of the Buendía women are associated in one way or another with self-destruction and doom, anticipating the final storm that their sexual relations with their male family members could engender, it is worth our while to examine the problems encountered by these men and women as they try to marry outside and bring in new blood. The Buendía men are constantly fascinated by women from "lower" classes and—though it is not spelled out—of another (black) race. But a permanent, public alliance with these women of the people, Pilar Ternera, Petra Cotes, Nigromanta, is unacceptable, as is the coupling of Meme with the mechanic Mauricio Babilonia. When a marriage is consummated, as with the hard-working, long-suffering Santa Sofía de la Piedad, the woman is totally ignored, treated as a servant. To have crossed and transgressed the invisible, almost unstated, frontiers of their class and race prejudices, indicates a possible direction that the family never allowed itself—made all the clearer by the fact that the one woman who does come from outside and is received with all solemnity is the glacial, repressive, and aristocratic Fernanda. What could signify better the way in which the Buendías are limited by the claustrophobic cultural barriers that they hardly see then the madness of forging an alliance with a faraway figure from the Spanish Inquisitional past rather than with the invigorating sensuous wise lovers carousing in the prodigious backyard?

Something similar could be said about the fratricide which takes over Macondo. The two Buendías who try to change circumstances significantly, who want to be the agents and actors of history instead of its objects, will fail miserably, though for diametrically opposite reasons. Colonel Aureliano Buendía illustrates the danger of recurring to violence, even in the noblest of causes. In a society where there is no democracy, where there is no popular participation, where the military are a law unto themselves, the irrevocable logic of power will isolate even the most decent human beings from reality. Struggling against injustice, the Colonel will end up embracing the violence he supposedly wants to stop, a captive of the macho mentality that decades ago led to the murder of Prudencio Aguilar and many decades later will lead to the murder of the three thousand workers that José Arcadio II witnesses. When they fail, both the Colonel and José Arcadio II retire from the world—a symptom of their initial loneliness, their incapacity to really be part of a movement of innumerable others, a collective where they could have found a meaning, a direction, a superior sense, to their lives. What they found in history is, ultimately, nothing more than a reflection of their basic solitude, their own image mirrored back at them.

The failure of Aureliano Buendía is particularly emblematic because he was the first human being born in Macondo—and as such his life will turn out to anticipate the village's future. And it is all the more heartbreaking because he had in him the possibility of dominating the unknown through other means than violence; born "with his eyes open," looking at everyone with "a curiosity lacking any note of surprise," he is able, through lacerating visions and lightening premonitions, to foretell the future—in other words, to step outside the grinding track of history and see a moment which will come to pass as if it had already happened.

This is an extraordinary faculty in a world that is, of and in itself, quite extraordinary. It is, of course, the most remarked upon feature of Macondo that its inhabitants live innocently immersed in the marvellous. Objects are often magically animated, animals proliferate beyond belief, people levitate, the seventeen sons of the Colonel converge on the village from the most distant corners of the land without prior agreement, not to mention the ghosts, prophetic dreams, fortune-telling cards, precognitions. For the Buendías this incessant presence is treated with matter-of-fact complacency: it is as much a part of their world as breathing, as yellow butterflies fluttering around a poor mechanic. What seems strange and impossible to the people of Macondo are the inventions that come in from abroad, the capacity to transform nature through the use of technology; whereas the readers, watching from the end of this supposedly rational and scientific century, taking those achievements for granted, are amazed at the wonders of everyday life in the remote premodern Colombian village.

This presence of the marvellous is—like the language of the novel itself—not an artificial addition or injection into reality—which is why I object so much to the term "magical realism." That term attempts to explain what happens in novels such as these as a merely literary strategy rather than a cultural experience that comes from the way people in Latin America cope with their existence. Things are marvellous in Macondo because along with living their hard, incontestable, fact-ridden intractability, the villagers are simultaneously living the instantaneous retelling of those events, their conversion into legends, that which will be ledgered—read, registered. The immediate exaggeration of what is happening to us forces those circumstances into memory, ensures that they will not be forgotten, that a "plague of insomnia" will not attack our descendants and allow them to sidestep the relationship between things and their names. People in misdeveloped, twisted lands may not be able to dominate what really happens to them; but they can at least control the stories they tell about how they want what happened to them remembered. This does not quite make them masters of themselves. For that, they would have to go beyond mere flashes of clairvoyance, they would have to find a way of grasping permanently the knowledge which comes from seeing the entire sweep of their lives—a quality which only Melquíades, the narrator, and the last Buendía have attained, one at the beginning of the story, the other at its end. The final Aureliano achieves the totality the others—mad explorers of the possibility of omniscience—have been searching for during the whole novel. Catching glimpses of the future from time to time, that final Aureliano becomes the "spoken mirror" where reader and narrator are identical; what he enters is an absolute and useless freedom. On the other side of total knowledge is, of course, death, that point where everything is known because everything is already finished, a nothingness that contemplates what has been used up and can never happen again.

The last Buendía manages to do that which his forefathers (more than his foremothers) always desired: to go beyond a state of blind clairvoyance to a state of absolute cognitive dominion; but the price that must be paid is to die, to have all one's acts fixed and immutable and readable forever.

While they are alive, therefore, the characters have been able to communicate with the future, with Melquíades's version, with their own version told by their distant descendants, with a complete image of themselves, by means of the imagination, that faculty which is not yet omniscience because it embraces only the possible and reveals only one of many unnamed futures. The narrator knows all, and certainly more than his characters; and he knows it from the realm of aesthetic intemporality. The Buendías have managed, once in a while, to leap over the barriers of time, to see themselves beyond their immediate circumstance, to turn the walls into transitory openings. They can live for a moment what has already happened in the future, but they cannot persist in that magical order, because it would mean becoming static and immobile. If they were only able to see themselves completely while they live, if they were only able to write *One Hundred Years of Solitude* during the hundred years that Colombians suffered those forms of solitude, they would be saved. If they could only know without having to die—without having to fatalistically live all the steps and mistakes that lead to final extinction.

That is what Colonel Aureliano Buendía should have been able to do, was in some way specially equipped to do. He squanders his "pacts with death"—that is, the capacity for seeing things as if they were already past, had already been told, and were finished—by imposing death in the thirty-two wars he participates in. He cannot stand the uncertainty of life and so, instead of exploring it with his imagination, he turns it into something certain and death-like. His answer to his loneliness is to expand his ego, until nothing exists except his desires, until reality itself disappears and becomes a prolongation of his power, anticipating the machos of García Márquez's later novels, the tyrant of *The Autumn of the Patriarch* and, in a bizarre way, the Bolívar of *The General in His Labyrinth*. As for the Colonel, the revenge that reality inflicts upon him is devastating, one of the most moving descriptions of the effects of tyranny to have been written: reality begins to anticipate what he wants, becomes independent, interprets, and carries out his thoughts "before he conceived them." He wanted to control history so much, to make it identical to his thoughts and inner world, that it has acceded to his request, although perversely stripping him of his freedom. There is no longer any clash between his personality and the world. He is made of ice, the very ice that so fascinated him at the dawn of the novel—dead in life instead of running like the Edenic springs and waters of early Macondo. When he realizes he is trapped in a remote mirror he has just enough energy left to put an end to the fratricidal struggle and withdraw. He has tried so hard to determine the future through violence that he has, in fact, lost it, lost the reason why people want to know the future, lost the humanity they should be serving.

That is why the death of this character, the one who was touched most deeply by the marvellous, by the possibility of foretelling the future, is the only one that is narrated indirectly and does not include even the slightest hint of magic. All the other members of his family die in a special way, each of them marked by a miracle, a fantasy of words and events which are woven around the body in order to eternalize it in a characteristic pose, fix it in the popular imagination with an unmistakable funeral identity. Each Buendía freezes in death a surprising summary of his or her life, a categorical essentialization that can thereafter reverberate imaginatively in the memory of others. One dies as one has lived, and in the very act of being extinguished, the people of Macondo try to prolong their being into the outer limits of who they really were. Thus, in order to draw José Arcadio, who is full of dreams and projects, toward death, he must be trapped by illusion, forced to dream his death, led to believe that the unreal room of death is the real room of life. And the supernatural participates in his burial, objectifying the idea that the founder of the dynasty deserves a snowfall of yellow flowers, a live prefiguration of the yellow scrolls that will tell the story ultimately. The gigantism of his son José Arcadio is expressed in the prodigious thread of blood that explodes from his body when he is killed and which goes off in search of mother Ursula—who herself dies in such a prolonged and centenary way that it almost seems more like a resurrection than a disappearance. One could go on and on—Amaranta's announcement that she would carry letters to the next world, the ethereal flight of Remedios la Bella merging with nature, the twins dying at the same moment in separate rooms, and so on and so forth, all of them personifying in one last act the purified version of what they really were.

Colonel Aureliano Buendía's death is not narrated at all, but merely implied in absentia. If he tries to erase all signs that he passed through this world, it is because he has given up the hope of narrating himself at all; he considers it all futile. His frozen emptiness, his passive and involuntary death in life, his desire to be forgotten is the foreshadowing of the final destiny of the family, that cosmic frozen nothingness, without even the myth that could give a meaning to their destiny. Like the other military figures in the novel, he cannot see the immaculate purity of the room where Melquíades's manuscripts are lodged: he can only see the implacable ruin, the way that room will be when the hurricane blows into Macondo, the destruction that will descend upon Latin America precisely because the many Colonels severed their link with the imagination.

This may be the reason why the Colonel is the only existential character in the novel. All the others may be suffocated by some form of sadness, but they are tragic only inasmuch as they are part of a collective that is doomed. In the case of the Colonel, one feels that it is his own personality—which could have somehow chosen differently—that contains the naked seeds of ambivalence and tragedy, his involvement in an ethical dilemma that will fatally lead him to annihilation. The difference becomes visible if we contrast him with the other characters: his life never produces a smile; his errors are not laughable; and his solitude ends up being a terrifying and compassionate lesson.

Despite this difference, the Colonel shares with the other char-

acters, as one would expect in a novel that is such an example of
flowing unity, certain basic laws. Everyone in *One Hundred Years
of Solitude* is endowed with a stubborn loyalty to his or her own
inner self. Their actions are outlined sharply, unambiguously, unfolding in a uniform, constant, clear line. Their journey inward is
brief and savage: they quickly discover in their inner limits a sense
of who they are and spend the rest of their life expanding those
traits. "Ursula always tried to go farther"—words that could be
applied to the steps all of them take, each more intense and more
complete than the one before.

Adolescence is the critical moment, the period when sex—
copulation that tends to be, although not always, brutal, fleeting,
tangential—makes them confront another human being and, at
the same time, reveals the impossibility of escaping from their im-
pregnable egocentrism. Rather than lose themselves in the other,
they will hasten to shape in the outer world the stubborn, definitive, absolute being they have glimpsed inside. The way to make
that inner being visible to other eyes is to project it onto the world
with decisive gestures and attitudes. And what is meant for those
who surround and survive us, will eventually reach, of course, the
narrator, will force their way into the text that we are reading.
In a world which threatens to forget everything, where all traces
will be erased, human beings exaggerate the power of their own
extreme egos as a means of establishing some permanence, incorporating themselves into the secret structure of what is marvellous
and also real at the same time. The basis for Melquíades's ability to
tell their story is that they found a way to tell it obsessively. The irrevocable actions which they repeated as a way of possessing their
potential unity also created a thread of echoes and cycles in their
existence that makes it tangible and imaginable.

If this struggle against death gives the family its dignity, guarantees it a space in memory, it also seals the family's fate. Because it
is precisely this enclosure in implacable activity, this refusal to see
everyday reality in order to forge the epic adventure of a destiny
apart from others, which assures the clan's destruction, their excess
of self-suffocation, their lack of self-knowledge. They can unconsciously, through their actions and their words, narrate themselves
but they cannot narrate others.

This conflict between the self and the surrounding world had already been developed in García Márquez's earlier works, where men, rotting alive in a hot, impoverished, fatigued reality, only can defy death and differentiate themselves from their environs by making some lonely, brave gesture. This happens principally to persons of the male sex—those who try to dream up some heroism in a degraded world. The male character, faced with a history that would subjugate or devour him, first takes refuge in the whimsical bubble of his personality but will later try to impose his very individual dream upon the overwhelming external reality. In that attempt, he may be destroyed, it is true; but he may also have succeeded in breathing a hint of fresh air, a sense that he will not let the lethargy around him win the battle. The Colonel, for instance, in *No One Writes to the Colonel*, seems pathetic in his blindness, his inability to measure what is real; but to the extent to which he manages to draw from that illusion the energy to overcome his demonically trivial waiting for a letter that never arrives, his figure may touch upon a certain majesty. That inner world, hidden from others, which can make him do ridiculous or foolish things, can also be the source of his pride in himself, the only basis for moral affirmation in a society that has betrayed him. Just like the characters in *One Hundred Years of Solitude*, he needs to find at least one gesture or word—which he pronounces, at the end of the novel—where his inner and external self will be reconciled, where he can be "pure, explicit, invincible." Something similar happens in *Leafstorm* and many of the stories by García Márquez: a final defiant gesture as the result of years of premeditated, but also unexpressed, rebellion. What was subjective, concealed, unable to reach others, finally becomes objective, proves itself in the social reality where it can be seen by all, where the intuition of what we were can be verified publicly. Their imagination has always secretly murmured to them what they should do. The challenge for them is to go beyond conjecture and anticipation, to mold their pre-visions of themselves into inspired and inspiring actions.

These characters do not, nevertheless, reach a mythic state. Their lives are too inconclusive. As readers, we are not given the knowledge of what, finally, happens to them. Volkening has drawn attention to the fragmentary condition of this early world of García Márquez: the story ends at the moment before the victory or the defeat of the characters, when they are about to combat the established norms of society, when they confront the supreme test of their own reality. But for a myth to be born, it is necessary that the figures not be subject to doubt and inadequacy, that they be well-rounded, perfect, memorable—as they are in *One Hundred Years of Solitude*.

In these earlier works the imagination exists only in each human being, sucked out from an enclosed interior life in order to confront adversity, but it still does not have a parallel world at its disposal, the existence of the marvellous text of Melquíades's that accompanies the Buendías, the sign that there is indeed some collective narration that, if we could only gain access to it (read it and live it at the same time), would give us an intimation of a totality.

Before that vision of *One Hundred Years of Solitude* could be fully expressed, García Márquez needed, in the novel *In Evil Hour*, to explore the possibility that a collective could, in fact, establish a parallel sphere of the imagination where words could take on a mysterious semiautonomy. In a town dominated by fear and corrupted by political oppression, where church and government, mayor and priest, insist on affirming that no problems exist, everybody has retreated into the intimate life of their own. But just as the mayor's jaw begins to rot from a dead tooth, and the town's atmosphere is polluted by the smell of a dead cow decomposing beneath the river, posters filled with words will begin to appear on the walls, belying and undermining the false official peace and truth. In these anonymous sheets of paper the private life of each citizen is commented upon, what they gossip about or dare not declare are revealed in the full light of day. These words emanate from the entire town and from no one in the particular: they are the sublimation of its strangled political energy, the collective folklore that each one would like to objectify and cannot. The posters confront the private world of each one with the objective world of the others. These clandestine thoughts go, therefore, beyond the individual acts of the colonels and characters in the earlier works. Those words will end up being more real than the paper on which they are printed or the wall upon which they are nailed. This annihilation of the official truth through linguistic subversion anticipates *One Hundred Years of Solitude*.

This excursus may have helped us to realize that incest and fratricide are structures that shut the Buendías—the Colombians, the

Latin Americans—off from the imaginary that is their real heritage, the text that they have been writing but cannot read. Incest which shuts the men inside the boundaries of their own women-mothers-daughters, unable to love anyone else; fratricide which is the way in which men finally end up contacting other men, under the guise of death and violence. Blessed though they may be with creativity, vitality, exuberance, tenderness, humor, none of it will manage to save them from ultimate destruction.

Why not?

Because the Buendía men are unable to grow up—which means to learn from their experience, to assume responsibility for the world as they found it. Like children, their imagination can run rampant but cannot be applied to the community, can give them a glimmer of themselves but cannot serve as a way to contact the others with whom they must build the story of their lives. The incest shuts them in and the violence excludes by killing it the objective look from the other, from outside—and so they find themselves caught in a never-ending, ever-repeating cycle, generation after generation, unable to decipher the manuscripts of their own lives, to write reality as they live it.

One Hundred Years of Solitude situates itself in the impossible middle between what is inside and outside, between life and death, between history and imagination. This means that the reader, ultimately, gets to choose. He or she can stay inside the text, like the last Aureliano for whom it is already too late. He must die as the closing act of a tale of love and extinction because his whole contradictory reality, like Remedios la Bella herself, "stagnated in a magnificent adolescence." Or the reader can leap outside that ambiguous relationship with death and, deciphering the repression, reading its causes and its loneliness, manage to take the fiction back into reality, make it historical, try to make sure that the next hundred years will not end in the same way.

The second path is not meant to turn away from the past but to surpass it by looking it in the face. If the readers—as well as the author and his characters—are urged to take this path, it does not require an epic commitment on their part but rather the need to relive the sources of their present circumstances.

García Márquez has, in fact, provided a model for how this might possibly be accomplished in the everyday existence of us all in another of his masterpieces, *Chronicle of a Death Foretold*. If it took at least a century to create the conditions for *One Hundred Years of Solitude* to exist, *Chronicle*, which I interpret as its complement, is the product of a more modest thirty-year period. A symbolic return perhaps to that smaller, less grandiose, dimension of Isabel merely watching the rain go down during a week in Macondo instead of the long years of deluge.

Early one morning in 1951 one of García Márquez's best friends, Cayetano Gentile, was hacked to death by two men in front of his house in Sucre. They were the brothers of a woman married the day before who, having been returned by the bridegroom on their wedding night because she was not a virgin, had falsely named Gentile as her secret lover. The brothers had washed their family's honor with his blood.

Behind the superficial sensationalism of the crime, the sort that drip from the pages of yellow journalism the world over, the Colombian novelist sensed a deeper drama, where the forces of history and myth that have incessantly obsessed him were apparently again at work. How could such savagery erupt, almost unpredictably, in the midst of a peaceful celebration? Where had it come from? And how was it possible that the whole town, which knew that the crime was about to happen, had been unable to prevent it? In a sense, the question he was asking was similar to the one central to all his previous work: Is Latin America doomed to this sort of everyday civil war on its streets and in its bedrooms, does violence narrate us over and over again, whether in our relations with one another or with our rulers?

As if he were one of his own characters, so near to the events and their overwhelming madness, García Márquez could not find right away the form, or the formula if you will, for answering those questions—which is like saying that it took him many years to figure out how a place so familiar could abruptly be transformed into Hell. And at the same time he had to discover how to turn the facts into a fiction that would reveal the concealed and more profound structure of truth.

We have seen that *One Hundred Years of Solitude* depends, for its narrative, on the author's acting as a channel for the oral tradition that is the foundation of that world, presenting without any gnawing doubts the version of people who have re-elaborated their experience, who assume themselves to be the final authority, believing that history and legend are one, and that memory and fact are inseparable. In order to construct the *Chronicle* García Márquez had to, for the first time, submit that popular oral tradition to a test, questioning his own voice. The narrator himself—a journalist—will appear before us researching the event, attempting its reconstruction, from the dozens of fragmented and contradictory accounts, where time, place, weather, and motives shift and lose their anchorage. By blending journalism, so dependent on immediate evidence, with the imaginary, which expands freely according to its own creative laws, the Colombian writer grounds the incredible murder in everyday detail.

As I have argued insistently in these pages, these two forms of communication are not incompatible and, in Latin America in fact, would seem to be almost inevitably symbiotic. I remember the almost childlike joy of García Márquez when he told me—he had just completed the manuscript and we were spending a week together as members of a literary jury in Mexico in 1980—that the coroner's autopsy of the real victim's wounds confirmed his imagined version. "The only [wound] he had in the back, at the level of the third lumbar vertebra, had perforated the right kidney," García Márquez said. That synthesis of what can be seen and what can be envisioned seemed to be proving his *Chronicles* to be a prolongation of the original *Crónicas de Indias*—those wild, eyewitness testimonios with which the first conquistadors recounted the real—and simultaneously fabulous—story of the New World.

In this case, García Márquez invented a narrator who acts as a newspaper reporter would, interrogating during twenty-seven years everyone connected with the crime, trying to make sense out of the chaos in the witnesses' throats, trying to pinpoint how each person who could have avoided that death ended up contributing to it. Those spectators, however, are not allowed to take over the proceedings. Their testimony is rigidly organized within a time frame that lasts exactly one hour and a half. The first sentence tells of the awakening of Santiago Nasar (the name given to Gentile) at 5:30 in the morning of the day he is to die; the book closes, a scant 120 pages later, at 7 o'clock, when he collapses and breathes no more.

Till the very end, we have certainty that the murder could have been prevented. The two killers did everything to force someone to stop them. They bragged of their intentions in the hope that they would be dissuaded or jailed. In fact, they waited in front of the one door that their victim was sure not to approach the whole day. But that day, Nasar disrupted his habitual itinerary and went through that door. And his mother, on the other side, was putting up the bar to shut it, believing that he had already entered the house. This confusion is typical of all the events that accumulate like foul rising water and slowly drown Nasar.

It is as if all the people in town were doors that might lead to life and instead lead to death. Those who rushed after the victim to warn him were unable to find him. Those who could have warned him did not do so for a variety of reasons. We watch the community do the wrong thing and then we watch the swamp of their justifications, their excuses, their pretexts.

The readers, confronted by the double clockwork of the novel— the wizardry of the author and the chain of coincidences and blunders whereby the right doors were being closed while the wrong ones were being opened—could end up bedazzled, succumbing to the illusion that what we are submerged in is the working out of a destiny that no man can control.

And yet I would suggest that this is not what the novel is really telling us. It is, on the contrary, a political parable that hints at the ways in which the cyclical wheels of copulation and violence that have determined Latin American history up till now can, in fact, be escaped.

When I first reviewed the novel in English (in *The Philadelphia Inquirer*), while praising Gregory Rabassa's precise and hallucinatory translation, I disagreed with its title. Rather than "foretold," which admittedly does sound better, but that smacks of a fatal, delphic, solemn irrefutability, the original *anunciada* (announced) would more reliably indicate that the *Crónica* (the story as it materialized in *chronos,* time) was on everybody's mind, near everybody's tongue, but never was uttered to save the victim.

If Santiago Nasar is doomed, it is not because his life is a circle that an oracle has pronounced complete, finished. He will die because of the sum total of rituals, habits, misconceptions, and prejudices that crisscross and corrupt society like shadows. As García Márquez has pointed out in an interview, most people back in 1951 did not intervene because they felt that this was a social rite—the taking back of honor spilled, the death of the violator—with which they agreed.

The concatenation of misunderstandings and hesitations that spun Nasar's death are only apparently expressions of a culture that needs, expects and creates that death, and that stands by passively while it is enacted. The real cause of the murder is the unproclaimed law of war between men, of machismo. Nasar is foretold only by his own code. Though he is innocent of having despoiled the bride, he is guilty of sharing the same preconceptions that his murderers will use to justify their act.

It is a network of minds that has set the trap for the victim. The closed blind alley minds, marooned in their solitude and unable to imagine a different interpretation of what they see and should do, sentence Nasar to his extinction and themselves to their guilt.

Just one door opening, just one person standing up and shouting what had been announced in murmurs by all, would have been enough to turn tragedy into peace. *Chronicle* is the story, as is *One Hundred Years of Solitude*, of a collective failure and it is, at the same time, a challenge to create a collective difference, a story that asks us to open the doors behind which we hide.

If we dare, we may just have the time—and it is García Márquez himself who said so in his Nobel prize acceptance speech—to give the races condemned to one hundred years of solitude a second opportunity on this earth.

It is a matter of discovering the real story inside each falsehood we have been told.

In this sense, one might almost accuse the prodigious García Márquez of not exaggerating enough.

Two hundred wagons, after all, hardly seem sufficient to transport the bodies of all the workers who have been murdered in Latin America—and in the world—to the funeral humanity is preparing for them in the future that must be written by us right now in order to exist.

1990

Men of Maize: *Myth as Time and Language*

1   It is worthwhile to briefly outline reactions to the novel.
    Seymour Menton, who has written the best analysis that I know of, *El señor
    Presidente*: "La novela experimental y la república comprensiva de Hispano-
    américa" (*Humanitas*, Anuario del Centro de Estudios Humanísticos Univer-
    sity de Nueva León, 1, 1:409–64), is mistaken with regard to *Hombres de maíz*
    in his *Historia crítica de la novela guatemalteca* (Guatemala:Editorial Univer-
    sitaria, 1960), mentioning "el método artificial que emplea el autor para atar
    todos los cabos sueltos, o mejor dicho para entrelazar con hiedras los distintos
    troncos individuales" ("the artificial method used by the author to tie up all
    the loose strings, or to put it in a better way, to weave together with ivy the
    different individual trunks"), suggesting that Asturias threw away "una mag-
    nífica antología de cuentos y de folklore maya" ("a magnificent anthology of
    Maya stories and folklore"), due to the fact that "desgraciadamente . . . insis-
    tió en revestir el libro de forma novelesca" ("unfortunately . . . he insisted on
    dressing the book up in novelistic form"). This opinion, which is shared by,
    among others, Anderson Imbert and Zum Felde, finds its maximum expres-
    sion in the attitude of Francis Donahue, who in "Miguel Angel Asturias: su
    trayectoria literaria," *Cuadernos Hispanoamericanos* 186 (June 1965), in an essay
    of some twenty pages devotes only four lines to *Hombres de maíz*.
    We could compile a long list of similar judgments, which speak of "ininteli-
    gibilidad" ("unintelligibility"), "falta de solidez arquitectónica" ("lack of
    architectural solidity"), "un alto en el camino novelístico" ("a halt in the novel-
    istic journey"), but this example from an essay by José Antonio Galaos, in
    "Los dos ejes de la novelística de Miguel Angel Asturias," *Cuadernos Hispano-
    americanos*, 154 (October 1962), should be sufficient: "Pertenece al género
    novelístico, porque es en éste donde se sitúa cuanto en literatura es inclasi-
    ficable. Unas veces semeja una serie de relatos unidos entre sí por el simple
    vínculo geográfico y étnico; otras, meras evocaciones de esos personajes y esas
    gentes . . . , es una enorme retorta donde se han mezclado cosas tan dispares
    como la poesía y el más insoportable prosaísmo" ("It belongs to the novelistic
    genre, because that is where everything in literature that can't be classified is

placed. At times it resembles a series of stories linked by a simple geographic and ethnic bond; at other times, mere evocations of those characters and those people . . . , it is an enormous pie where things as disparate as poetry and the most unbearable prosaism have been mixed").

There are also defenders. Fernando Alegría, in his *Breve historia de la novela hispanoamericano*, (Mexico City: Ediciones Andrea, 1959), considers it the work of "mayor envergadura" ("greatest breadth") of Asturias, but he has not proven his judgments by a detailed analysis of the novel. Bellini, *La narrativa di Miguel Angel Asturias* (Milan: La Golliardaca, 1966), affirms that the plot is less important than the atmosphere and "Ciò che ad Asturias interessa e rendere in sostanza lo spirito del Guatemala, la sua consistenza fenomenica, ma sopratutto la sostanza spirituale, che lo rende entità permanente nel tempo. Perciò egli situa la sua vicenda in un succerdersi diluito de eventi, i quali sono unicamente un pretesto per raggiungere il fine indicato" ("What interests Asturias is to present the substance of the spirit of Guatemala, its phenomenological consistency, but above all its spiritual substance, what makes it a permanent entity in time. Therefore he situates his action in a diluted succession of events, which are only a pretext to achieve the indicated end"). That is, he accepts the disorder as necessary, adding in addition that the fifth episode (María Tecún) "presenta tenui legami con la trama centrale del libro" ("presents tenuous connections with the central plot of the book"). In spite of these limitations, his study is the best that has been published about *Hombres de maíz*, understanding the novel as a superannuation of an antiquated way of seeing reality. Atilio Jorge Castelpoggi, in *Miguel Angel Asturias* (Buenos Aires: Editorial La Mandrágora, 1961), who has done the only serious analysis of the Banana Trilogy, demonstrating the quality that so many critics had denied them, finds the unity of *Hombres de maíz* in the last chapter, which he considers a synopsis, a gloss of the previous chapters. But he does not examine the entire text and he does not explain the character of this "notable unidad" ("notable unity"), although he does have very accurate judgments ("El libro de Asturias vive de esta confrontación de lo invisible y de lo presente, de la magia y de la realidad." Juan Carlos Ghiano, cited by Castelpoggi (*Asturias*, 71)—"Asturias's book lives from this confrontation of the invisible with the present, of the magical with the real." He affirms that the book is "menos que epopeya, más que novela" ("less than an epic, more than a novel"), which adds very little to our knowledge. Orellana Riera, in an unpublished dissertation, "Miguel Angel Asturias, *El señor Presidente* y otras obras" (Santiago de Chile, 1954), indicates that *Hombres de maíz* "es un profundo poema sinfónico, donde no se excluye ninguna nota del pentagrama nativo; así, es una novela folklórica por lo colorido de las descripciones de costumbres típicas, de tradiciones religiosas, por el empleo de giros lingüísticos de acentuado sabor popular; novela social por el cuadro sórdido del indígena, y el perfil áspero de su explotación; novela mitológica por la sucesión de hechos fantásticos, trabados en una línea de exaltación legendaria y mágica" ("is a profound, symphonic poem, where not a single note of the native pentagram is excluded; thus, it is a folkloric novel because of the colorful descriptions of typical customs, of religious traditions and because of the use of linguistic expressions of a strong popular flavor; a social novel because of the sordid portrayal of the Indian and the harsh profile of his exploitation; a mythological novel because of the succession of fantastic events, unfolded in a line of legendary and magical exaltation.") Ray Angel Verzasconi's analysis, in an unpublished doctoral thesis, "Magical Realism and the Literary World of Miguel Angel Asturias" (University of Washington, 1965), is an attempt to find unity in something within the text, in the characters and their problems, and not in an impalpable and vague entity: the struggle between revenge and fertility, the union of the characters around a psychological conflict which gives meaning to the apparently disorderly development of the actions. The principal theme of the book would be the struggle between the land and the corn, the reiterated creation, the generation that dies in order to live again, the conflict between man and woman ("On the one hand, the male is moved by his instinctual desire to propagate his race—the 'hombre de maíz' is the symbolic fertile kernel of corn. On the other, the female stimulates her partner's instinct, but at the same time, she acts as a barrier against unlimited procreation. Gaspar, Piojosa, Machojón, Tomás Machojón, María Tecún, Goyo Yic, and Nicho Aquino are all involved in this life and death struggle"). These Freudian explanations do not seem very convincing to me.

The best defender of *Hombres de maíz* turns out to be the author himself, who on two occasions has pointed out the route that must be followed by anyone who wishes to understand his book. "Toda mi obra se desenvuelve entre estas dos realidades: la una social, política popular, con personajes que hablan como habla el pueblo guatemalteco; la otra imaginaria, que les encierra en una especie de ambiente y de paisaje de ensueño" ("My entire work moves between these two realities: the one, social, popular politics, with characters who speak the way the Guatemalan people speak; the other imaginary, enclosed in a kind of dream-like atmosphere and landscape"); quoted by Claude Couffon, "Miguel Angel Asturias y el realismo mágico," *Alcor*, Asunción, March–June, 1963. And "Una novela en la que presento como aspecto social de la vida americana el hecho tan corriente entre nosotros, y que todos hemos vivido, de sucesos reales que la imaginación popular transforma en leyendas o de leyendas que llegan a encarnar acontecimientos de la vida diaria. A mí me parece muy importante en el existir americano esa zona en que se confunden, sin límite alguno, la irrealidad real, como diría Unamuno, de lo legendario con la vida misma de los personajes" ("A novel in which I present as a social aspect of American life the fact that is so current among us, and that all of us have experienced, of real events which the popular imagination transforms into legends or of legends that come to incarnate events in daily life. In my opinion, that zone in which the real unreality of the legendary is mixed, without any limit, as Unamuno would say, with the real life of the characters is very important to American existence"); from an interview reproduced by Ricardo Triqueros de León, *Perfil en el aire* (El Salvador: Ministerio de Cultura, 1955).

2 "Il confine tra realtà leggende è così tenue che i piani dell'una si fondono con quelli dell'altra, fluttuando continuamente," Bellini, *La narrativa*, 71. ("The

boundary between reality and legend is so tenuous that the planes of one merge with those of the other, continually fluctuating.")

3   "Il quale, in sostanza, non canta che un unico grande tema, la libertà . . ." ("Which, basically, has only one great theme, freedom . . ."), ibid., 13; "su tema novelístico es la libertad" ("its novelistic theme is freedom"), Galaos, "Los dos ejes," 126.

4   "La leyenda que no muere, porque oralmente, por la intuición que transmite la sangre, sigue a través de lo popular." ("The legend does not die, because orally, by the intuition which is transmitted by blood, it goes on by means of what is popular.") Castelpoggi, *Asturias*, 68–69.

5   Asturias himself has said concerning American language: "Este lenguaje no es el uso del modismo simplemente. Es la interpretación que la gente de la calle hace de la realidad que vive: desde la tradición hasta sus propias aspiraciones personales" ("This language does not consist just of the use of the idiom. It is the interpretation that the people in the street make of the reality they are living: from the traditional to their own personal aspirations"), words that Salvador Cañas reproduces in "Homenaje a Miguel Angel Asturias," *Repertorio Americano* (March 1950):82.

6   Verzasconi, "Magical Realism," 155–60, links this episode with the rest on the basis of the theme of fertility and in the parallelism with La Piojosa Grande, using both the Popol Vuh and Judeo-Christian tradition. It is the only interpretation which tries to relate this chapter with the rest of the novel.

7   "Quando il cieco Goyo Yic recupera la vista perde ogni possibilità di comunicazione con il mondo che sta oltre le aparenze della realtà, l'unico vero, a contatto del quale era vissuto fino allora, in intima comunicazione, proprio per la dua desgrazia" ("When the blind Goyo Yic recovers his vision, he loses all possibility of communication with the world that is beyond the appearance of reality, the only true one, in contact with which he was seen until now, in intimate communication, really by the double misfortune"), Bellini, *La narrativa*, 71–72.

8   Ricardo Navas Ruiz has analyzed the phenomenon in *El señor Presidente* ("Tiempo y Palabra en Miguel Angel Asturias," *Quaderni Ibero-Americani* 29 (1963), although with a different focus.

9   Of special interest is Wolfgang Kayser, *The Grotesque in Art and Literature* (Bloomington: Indiana University Press, 1963). See in particular 34–37 and 184–89. Kayser separates the grotesque from the Surrealist movement, which could lead to rethinking the relationship of Asturias with that European movement.

10   Later, Hilario thinks about how he will relate the appearance of the coyote: "que alcancé a ver al correo Aquino en forma de coyote, aullando (esto ya sería arreglo mío)" ("that I happened to see the mailman Aquino in the form of a coyote, howling (this would be my own version)"), and with those words, "esto ya sería arreglo mío," we are witnessing the transformation of every-day event into myth and its approximation to the truth that stirs beneath appearances: the nahual *is* the man. The lie would be, involuntarily, imitating reality.

Borges and American Violence

1 Ana Maria Barrenechea, *Borges, the Labyrinth Maker* (New York: New York University Press, 1965; expanded version of *La Expresión de la irrealidad en la obra de Jorge Luis Borges*, published by El Colegio de México). This work, one of the best on Borges, is devoted exclusively to irreality, affirming that there is no narrative substance and that the ideas in themselves are the only adventure in that world. This unilateral quality is found in almost all the essays on Borges.

2 There are some stories in which this does not occur: *Pierre Menard, Author of the Quixote*, and *Examination of Herbert Quain*, which, nevertheless, are written in the form of obituary notes; *The Library of Babel*, *The Sect of the Phoenix*, *Tlön, Uqbar, Orbis Tertius*, which are dislocated metaphors that comment upon reality and that lack a protagonist and can scarcely be considered short stories, since they have no characters nor plot development, nor do they carpet a concrete, daily world with situations involving tension and relaxation of tension; they also do not manage to weave an action that leads somewhere (none of which is intended to detract from their quality). They must be valued more as poetic visions, allegories of our reality, than as incarnations of the cosmic life of some human being; they are rather the crypto-history of all of humanity, a secret humanity parallel to our own, reflection of our essence but not of our existence.

3 The exceptions are *El inmortal* and *Funes el memorioso*, where the protagonists die "natural" deaths, although we could well argue that Joseph Cartaphilus (Marco Flaminio Rufo, Homer, etc.) commits suicide (see, for example, "Commentaire de l'inmortel" by Jacques Réda in *Cahiers du Sud*, no. 370 (February–March 1963):435–55). Even the case of Funes could be considered as one of self-destruction, an idea suggested by Robert Lima, "Internal Evidence on the Creativity of Borges," *Revista de Estudios Hispánicos* 1, 2 (November 1967, University of Alabama Press): 129–56.

4 *El muerto, Los teólogos, Biografía de Tadeo Isidoro Cruz, Emma Zunz, La otra muerte, El milagro secreto, Deutsches Réquiem, La espera, Tema del traidor y del héroe, Historia del guerrero y de la cautiva, El Sur, El hombre de la esquina rosada, Las ruinas circulares, El jardín, La muerte y la brújula, El fin, La casa de Asterión, El acercamiento a Almotásim, Abenjacán, El hombre en el umbral, El espejo de tinta*, almost all the episodes of *Historia universal de la infamia*, several stories that he has written in collaboration with Bioy Casares, as well as the screenplay *El paraíso de los creyentes*, "Un Problema" (a short story about Don Quijote that appeared in *El Hacedor*), and *Encuentro con el enemigo*, published in *Indice*.

5 See "Borges et les ancêtres," in *Jorge Luis Borges*, L'Herne (Paris, 1964), 151–55.

6 As an example: "Lo que más me emociona en la literatura es lo que es épico. Por ejemplo, sólo he llorado en el cine gracias a un film de piratas, de gangsters . . ." ("What moves me most in literature is the epic. For example, I have only wept in the movies during pirate or gangster films . . .") ("Entretiens avec Gloria Alcorta," L'Herne, 404).

7 Making a classification (a falsification), we could point out different types of

revelations on death: the revelation of one's self-identity or of a meaning in the universe at the moment of death (*El muerto, La otra muerte, El milagro secreto, La espera, Historia del guerrero y de la cautiva, El Sur, Tema del traidor y del Héroe, El espejo de tinta, Las ruinas circulares, La muerte y la brújula, Los teólogos* (after death), *La casa de Asterión, Poema conjetural, Isidoro Acevedo*); the revelation of one's self-identity or of a meaning in the universe at the moment of killing (*El fin, Emma Zunz, Deutsches Réquiem, Un problema, El jardín*, and at the moment of surrendering to violence, *Biografía de Tadeo Isidoro Cruz*; the revelation to a witness of a meaning hidden until that moment (*Abenjacán el Bojarí, Muerto en su laberinto, El hombre en el umbral, El hombre de la esquina rosada, La forma de la espada*, in the case of the two latter works, with Borges or the reader as witnesses).

8   Horst, in "Intention et Hasards dans l'oeuvre de Borges," L'Herne, 218–23, in order to try to show why at the moment of his death "l'homme comprend la loi de son existence: n'être personne et immortel et être le rêve d'un dieu" ("man comprehends the law of his existence: not to be a person and immortal and to be the dream of a god"), points out that "un moment d'intelligence et de liberté divines brise la chaîne de ses palingénesis ou de ses réincarnations. Voilà dans quelle mesure le rêve profond de la conscience se fait reconnaître en tant que rêve par des moments de révils rapides comme l'éclaire" ("one moment of intelligence and of divine freedom breaks the chain of his palingenesis or of his reincarnations. Here we see in what measure the deep dream of consciousness makes itself known, as a dream in moments of revelation as sudden as a flash of lightening"). Although Thorpe Running, in "The Problem of Time in the Work of Jorge Luis Borges," *Discourse* 9, 3, (Summer 1966): 296–308, does not examine the problem of revelation, his analysis of the two types of time in Borges's work (man is a tiger of time creeping through a nontemporal universe) helps us to understand this possibility of abolishing time. Another who has recognized the importance of this final instant in Manuel Durán, "Les Deux Borges," L'Herne, 237–41, speaking of "le moment décisif où l'homme affronte, sous une forme tranchante et définitive, une vérité généralment déagréable, mais qu'il accept pour toujours" ("the decisive moment when man confronts, in a sharp and definitive way, a generally disagreeable truth, but one that he accepts forever") and he adds that "Borges accorde à ses personnages une seconde—ou une éternité hors du temps—pour se comprendre et s'accepter." ("Borges grants his characters a second—or an eternity out of time—to understand and to accept themselves.") Durán believes, and rightly so to a certain extent, that Borges does this in order to destroy the Romantic tradition of the hero, which has predominated in Argentine narrative, and to stabilize the sentimentalism by means of the attitude of rational serenity confronting nothingness. But Borges, as we shall see, embraces this same heroic tradition. In *El muerto*: "Así nosotros, también el hombre que entreteje estos símbolos, ansiamos la llanura inagotable que resuena bajo los cascos" ("Thus we, also the man who weaves these symbols, long for the endless plain that resounds beneath the hoof beats"). Jacqueline van Praag-Chaintraine, in "Jorge Lues Borgés ou la mort au bout du labyrinthe," in

Synthése, 236–37 (January–February 1966): 117–26, also affirms, without any further analysis, that "arrivés au seuil de la révélation, les créatures de Borges son frappées de mort . . ." ("Whenever they reach the threshold of revelation, Borges's characters are struck down by death . . ."). Barrenechea, *Labyrinth Maker*, 70, has mentioned, in passing, that Borges wants to "mostrar al Hombre en ese instante de su vida cuando se le confronta con la revelación," but she gives no further details. David William Foster, in Borges, "El Aleph— Some Thematic Considerations," *Hispania* 47, 1 (March 1964): 56–59, analyzes the loss of personality and its recuperation ("individual self-assertion") at the last moment. Frances Wyers Weber, in a recent study, "Borges's Stories: Fiction and Philosophy," *Hispanic Review* XXXVI, 2 (April 1968) attacks Horst's idea that the labyrinth has a center and its ramifications a basic law: "One is never master of the labyrinth and it is impossible to formulate its law . . ." The study, which, in my view, confirms this procedure on the part of Borges, is that of Jaime Alazraki, "Las figuras de contigüidad en la prosa narrativa de Borges," *Revista Iberoamericana* 34, 65 (January–April 1968), which constitutes a sharp stylistic analysis of Borges's stories, demonstrating his preference for figures of continuity rather than the metaphor. The theme of the last moment as a synopsis of the entire previous life and as a representative segment of it, is thus supported upon the metonymic structure or the structure of synecdoche of his prose, where totality is avoided and the part is emphasized.

9 Borges constantly identifies understanding with light. But there is a light which especially fascinates him: it is the twilight, the last light of the day. This motif is related to that of revelation at the moment of death, death as an instant of sparkling immortality. Obsessed by sunsets ("la claridad que ardió en la hondura," "the clarity that burned in the deep," in *Ultimo sol en Villa Ortúzar*, "Los tumultuosos ponientes," "the turbulent sunsets," in *El Hacedor*, and its repeated appearance in so many poems, *Buenos Aires*, *Ultimo resplandor*, *Atardeceres*, *Campos atardecidos*, etc.), death is also described in terms of light: Albert's disappearance as a "fulminación" ("fulmination"); Lönnrot's as "hacer fuego" ("to fire") (an excellent analysis of the symbolism of the color red, in Marcial Tamayo and Adolfo Ruiz-Díaz, *Borges, enigma y clave* (Buenos Aires: Editorial Nuestro Tiempo, 1955); the same thing occurs in *El muerto*, "Suárez, casi con desdén, hace fuego" ("Suarez fires, almost with disdain"); in *Los teólogos*, Juan de Panonia is burned at the stake, "y es como si un incendio gritara" ("and it is as if a fire screamed"), while years later, "un rayo, al mediodía, incendia los árboles, y Aureliano pudo morir como había muerto Juan" ("a lightening bolt, at midday, set the trees on fire, and Aureliano was able to die as Juan had died"); in *Las ruinas circulares*, "el mago vio cernirse contra los muros el incendio concéntrico . . . Caminó contra los jirones de fuego" ("the magician saw the concentric flames engulf the walls . . . He walked against the flames"); in *La casa de Asterión*, "el sol de la mañana reverberó en la espada de bronce" ("the morning sun reverberated on the bronze sword"); in *Historia del guerrero y de la cautiva*, "bruscamente lo ciega y lo renueva esa revelación" ("Suddenly that revelation blinds and renews him"). Also in *Biografía de Tadeo Isidoro Cruz* that night is mentioned as "lúcida" ("lucid"),

adding that "amanecía en la desaforada llanura" ("dawn was breaking on the vast plain"), in contrast to the previous image that "la tiniebla era casi indescifrable" ("the darkness was almost indecipherable"). The realm of the divine is also described with light imagery: "una pequeña esfera tornasolada, de casi intolerable fulgor" ("a tiny, iridescent sphere, of almost unbearable brightness"), and "ahí estarán todas las luminarias, todas las lámparas, todos los veneros de luz" ("There will be all the lanterns, all the lamps, all the sources of light") (*El Aleph*), as in *La Escritura del Dios*, where he speaks of seeing "Dios en un resplandor" ("God in a blaze of light") and of glimpsing "los ardientes designios del universo" ("the burning designs of the universe").

10   Alazraki, "Las figuras," p. 49, suggests the stylistic reasons for this kind of transfer or substitution.

11   Tamayo and Ruiz-Díaz, *Borges, enigma*, 41–42, have analyzed this identification very well: "Los destinos de ambos participan de una dimensión común, colaboran en la realización de la serie de crímenes desde sus respectivas entidades . . . Entendidos desde su causa final, el asesino y el destino. Las recíprocamente implicadas participaciones consignadas hacen de Scharlach y Lönnrot un ente bifronte cuya constatación propicia Borges colocando en la quinta de Triste-Le-Roy una estatua de Hermes-Jano" ("The destinies of both have a common dimension; they share in the realization of a series of crimes from their respective entities . . . Understood from the perspective of their final cause, murder and fate. The reciprocally implied participations imputed to them make of Scharlach and Lönnrot a bipartite entity whose presentation Borges offers placing a statue of Hermes-Janus in the park of Triste-Le-Roy").

12   We also find in the poems this encounter with the other, with the self, past or future, in death. We have already commented upon *Poema conjetural*. In *Isidoro Acevedo*, Borges narrates the way in which Acevedo, is relegated to a miserable old man's bed:

hizo leva última,
congregó los miles de rostros que el hombre sabe sin saber
después de los años;
caras de barba que se estarán desvaneciendo en daguerrotipos,
caras que vivieron junto a la suya en el Puente Alsina y Cepeda.
. . .
juntó un ejército de sombras porteñas
para que lo mataran.
Así en el dormitorio anochecido que miraba a un jardín
murió en milicia de su convicción por la patria.

(he weighed the last anchor,
congregated the thousands of faces that man knows without knowing
after all the years;
bearded faces that will be fading on daguerrotypes,
faces that lived next to him on the Alsina y Cepeda Bridge.
. . .
he brought together an army of the Port's phantoms
so that they would kill him.

So it was that in the night-dark bedroom that overlooked a garden
he died dedicated to his conviction for the Fatherland.

13 It is worthwhile to analyze one story in detail, for example *El sur* (*The South*),
in order to demonstrate this structure more closely.

In *El sur*, Dahlmann (like Borges, the product of two lineages; with heroic
ancestors; "secretario de una biblioteca municipal," "secretary of a municipal library") suffers an accident and is admitted to the hospital (just as also
happened to Borges, and with the same illness). There, it seems, he has been
cured, but he has lost his dignity as a man. It is implied that this is the consequence of living in the city, far from the mythic and glorious past, far from the
wild land: "en cuanto llegó, lo desvistieron, le raparon la cabeza, lo sujetaron
con metales a una camilla, lo iluminaron hasta la ceguera y el vértigo, lo aus-
cultaron y un hombre enmascarado le clavó una aguja en el brazo. Se despertó
con náuseas, vendado, en una celda que tenía algo de pozo, y en los días y
noches que siguieron a la operación pudo entender que apenas había estado,
hasta entonces, en un arrabal del infierno. El hielo no dejaba en su boca el
menor rastro de frescura. En esos días, Dahlmann minuciosamente se odió;
odió su identidad, sus necesidades corporales, su humillación, la barba que le
erizaba la cara . . ." ("as soon as he got there, they undressed him, shaved his
head, tied him to a stretcher, shown lights on him until he was blinded and
dizzy, auscultated him and a man with a mask jabbed a needle into his arm. He
awoke with nausea, bandaged, in a cell that resembled a well, and in the days
and nights that followed the operation he grew to understand that he had
hardly been in a suburb of Hell up to that point. Ice didn't leave in his mouth
even the slightest trace of its coolness. In those days, Dahlmann hated himself
minutely; he hated his identity, his bodily needs, his humiliation, the beard
that stood up on his face . . ."). He travels to a ranch that he inherited years
earlier and which he has still not seen, a return to the past or to his ancestry.
Dahlmann is insulted in a store. At first he believes that it is an accident, but
when they recognize him and call him by his name, the incident assumes more
gravity: "Antes la provocación de los peones era a una cara accidental, casi a
nadie; ahora iba contra él y contra su hombría y contra su nombre y lo sabrían
los vecinos" ("Before, the provocations of the peons appeared to be directed
casually, to no one in particular; now they were directed at him and against
his manhood and his name and the neighbors would know that"). With his
manhood wounded, he confronts the peons, not as a convalescent or a man
from the city who has come for a rest, but as one accustomed to violence, a
man of the land, who knows how to attack and to defend himself.

It will be El Sur (the figure of El Sur) who will urge him to fight ("Era
como si el Sur hubiera resuelto que Dahlmann aceptara el duelo," "It was as if
el Sur had resolved that Dahlmann should accept the duel"). It is understood
implicitly (and Borges himself has confirmed it in his interview with James
Irby) that we witness (a) his real death, after the hospital stay, which restores
his dignity as a man who has been insulted; or (b) his death in a dream, which
takes place in the middle of the operation (to free himself of that humiliation he dreams another death as his consciousness fades in that glacial and

inhumane hospital). In any case, we see here a violent act that justifies the man, rescuing for the Argentinian his alienated past, and his dignity, which has been wounded in the labyrinthine hallways of the hospital. Fate (whether in reality or in a dying man's dream) offers him another opportunity to die, as a brave man; his death is a solution, an escape from the meaningless state in which he finds himself. In that courageous death, Dahlmann understands, but the reader understands even more, that there is an order in the world, that through the fulfillment of that fate decided long ago by "la lotería de Babilonia" and by secret desires (the heroic dream that has accompanied him since childhood) and by the hidden law of the universe, Dahlmann becomes a man (he is no longer a man-doll, as his name suggests) and recovers his lost being, reintegrating himself, he becomes a proud descendant of his ancestors:

"Salieron, y si en Dahlmann no había esperanza, tampoco había temor. Sintió, al atravesar el umbral, que morir en una pelea a cuchillo, a cielo abierto y acometiendo, hubiera sido una liberación para él, una felicidad y una fiesta, en la primera noche del sanatorio, cuando le clavaron la aguja. Sintió que si él, entonces, hubiera podido elegir o soñar su muerte, ésta es la muerta que hubiera elegido o soñado." ("They went out, and if there was no hope in Dahlmann, there was also no fear. As he crossed the threshold, he felt that to die in a knife fight, in the open and attacking, would have been a liberation for him, a joy and a celebration, on that first night in the hospital, when they jabbed him with the needle. He felt that if he, then, had been able to choose or to dream his own death, this is the death he would have chosen or dreamed.")

"Dahlmann empuña con firmeza el cuchillo, que acaso no sabrá manejar, y sale a la llanura." ("Dahlmann firmly grasps [note the use of the verb in the present tense] the knife, that he may not know how to handle, and goes out onto the plain.")

Through death, real or dreamed, Dahlmann encounters his own being and that of all Latin America; he breaks (through imagination and courage) the ironclad laws of normal occurrence. It is violence, which he, like so many other Borges characters, knows ends in death, that brings him back to himself, destroying the labyrinth by transforming that riddle into something that man can understand and where man has, even though his ceremony of initiation may be the final one, a place and a meaning. Death for Borges, like the violence that one commits or suffers, is what defines the universe, fixing it in place, suddenly illuminating it in a howling, final conflagration, creating a momentary, permanent, disappearing and eternal light in the bewildering darkness. We should nevertheless note that the character's rebellion and his encounter is always solitary and individual. Social struggle and ideological orientation are rejected.

14   Most of the "violent" stories (besides *Poema conjetural*, 1943) were written between 1941 and 1952, that period which he calls "época irreal" in *El Hacedor*, and which coincides with Peronism in Argentina, with its political persecution and with the imprisonment of his mother and his sister. The volume *El jardín de los senderos que se bifurcan* will be written between 1939 and 1941 and

contains only two *violent* stories (*El jardín* and *Las ruinas circulares*), which are the only ones of that series of eight fictions that have characters and plot development. Thus, his production of short stories with a concrete world cohabits with Peronism, in which Borges implacably suffered Latin American reality. This does not mean an inevitable relation between biography and literature, but Borges himself would be the first to affirm that all coincidence is significant and cannot always be attributed to chance.

15 Borges's anti-Latin Americanism has been discussed for over forty years (to be exact, since July 25, 1924, when Mariani started the Boedo-Florida polemic). Boedo's group criticized his distance from his native continent, his lack of political commitment, his intellectual exoticism, his metaphysical escapism, judgments repeated by the "parricida" generations, to use the terminology of Rodríguez Monegal. Those who wish to read the most brilliant and well-founded of the attacks can consult H. A. Murena's essay, "Condenación de una poesía," in *Sur* 164–65 (June–July 1948): 69–86, as well as the book by the same author, *El pecado original de América (Original Sin in America)*. Some of these affirmations have been repeated in recent years; for example, Antonio Regalado, Jr., in "Le Refus de l'histoire" ("The Denial of History"), L'Herne, 352–61, affirms that Borges is afraid of history, of the nation, and Mario Benedetti, in *Letras del continente mestizo (Letters of the Mestizo Continent)* (Montevideo: Arca, 1967), 40–46, considers that Borges "no ha podido ver la Argentina desde dentro" ("has not been able to see Argentina from within"), and that the themes that relate to the La Plata region represent "la visita de un turista" ("a tourist visit").

Nor has there been any lack of Borges defenders since 1924. There are those who, like Néstor Ibarra, in the preface of the French edition of *Ficciones* (*Fictions*, Gallimard, 1951), affirm that there is nothing South American about him, and who praise Borges precisely because he has been able to nourish himself from the great European source, thus raising himself above the amorphous mass of American writers. For these critics, among whom we could include Alicia Jurado, in *Genio y figura de Jorge Luis Borges* (Eudeba, 1965), Borges is saved by his independence and his intellectualism: he is a European writer. José Luis Ríos Patrón, in *Jorge Luis Borges* (Buenos Aires: Editorial La Mandrágora, 1955), sees in him only an orientalist, spiritualizing the author to the point of the ethereal, and emphasizes, like so many others, only one side of his work: his isolation from the world, his Berkeleyan abolition of the real, his idealist reconstruction.

On the other hand, others admit that his themes might seem to be enigmatic and difficult, but they point out, in the way of an explanatory smile, a bit ashamed of so much "metaphysics," Borges's fervor for Buenos Aires, his interest in what is local. With these compensatory arguments they in effect agree with their adversaries: Borges must be Argentine when he uses local color and customs and foreign when he writes of the infinite, of China, of Chesterton, and of eternity.

Other, more lucid, critics think that Borges is "universal" and that, by devoting himself to problems that are "esenciales y eternos acerca del Hombre y su destino en el universo" ("essential and eternal with regard to Man and his destiny in the universe") (Barrenechea, *Labyrinth Maker* 17), his human conception goes beyond what is merely American. Thus, also, Rafael Gutiérrez Girardot, *Jorge Luis Borges: Ensayo de una interpretación* (Madrid: Insula, 1959), recognizes him as Latin American "si por hispanoamericano se entiende el constitutivo universalismo con que Alfonso Reyes caracteriza la inteligencia americana, y no la vanidosa limitación provinciana" ("if for Hispanic American, we understand the constituent universalism with which Alfonso Reyes characterizes the American intellect, and not vain, provincial limitations"), words which Anderson Imbert and Paul Bénichou, among others, would subscribe to.

It is true that Borges is universal, but following this procedure we miss the major problem: In what way is Borges a product of Latin America? How do we, Latin Americans, find ourselves *specifically* in his work (and not just under the empty category of universality)?

People have been answering that question for at least ten years, although often in a vague fashion. Angel Flores, in "Magical Realism in Spanish American Fiction," *Hispania* 38, 2 (May 1955): 187–92, had pointed to Borges as the father of Magic Realism on our continent, but without analyzing his concrete world. Tamayo and Ruiz-Díaz, 170, point out that for Borges, "Buenos Aires no es sólo la convención metropolitana sino la sede de una profundizada experiencia" ("Buenos Aires is not just the metropolitan convention but rather the seat of a profound experience." Miguel Enguidanos, in "Le caractère argentin de Borges" ("The Argentine Character of Borges"), L'Herne, 131, understands Borges's work as a struggle between heart and intelligence, a thesis in part like my own, but with another emphasis ("Europa, símbolo esencial: el libro, el sueño, el mito. Buenos Aires, símbolo existencial: reflejo de una fatiga, melancolía, sudor, encaminamiento hacia la muerte"—"Europe, an essential symbol: the book, the dream, the myth. Buenos Aires, an existential symbol: reflection of a fatigue, a melancholy, sweat, movement toward death"). Federico Peltzer, in "Los Masques de Borges" ("Borges's Masks"), ibid., 179–84, believes that in this rootedness in Argentine themes there is a search for stability, for something solid and fertile. Also Emir Rodríguez Monegal, in his introduction to an interview by César Fernández Moreno with Borges in *Mundo Nuevo*, 18 (December 1967) and which was first published on August 30, 1967, in *Le Monde*, affirms that Borges's importance resides in having created a literary-linguistic space that holds up all current Latin American narrative. Multiplicity, without rootlessness, is another characteristic that "sólo puede lograr un argentino" ("only an Argentine could achieve"). Harss, in *Los nuestros* (Buenos Aires: Sudamericana, 1966), rightly affirms that "El 'europeísmo' es tan argentino como la pampa" ("'Europeanism' is as Argentine as the pampa"), but in his book he does not analyze how Latin America in Borges's world makes itself concrete.

This lengthy enumeration should demonstrate to us that Borges is Latin American or anti-Latin American, depending on the definition of America with which we begin.

Fathers and Bridges over Hell: Deep Rivers

1   José María Arguedas, *Los ríos profundos* (Buenos Aires: Losada, 1958); English trans., *Deep Rivers* (Austin: University of Texas Press, 1978). (Quotations from the text translated by George R. Shivers).

2   Roberto Armijo used a good expression, characterizing him as a "fugitivo de los blancos" ("fugitive from the whites"), in his article "La Reminiscencia de la Edad Perdida," in *Recopilación de textos sobre José María Arguedas,* edited with a prologue by Juan Larco, in the series *Valoración Múltiple* (Casa de las Américas, 1976), 252.

3   It is William Rowe who has examined the contours of this dilemma with the greatest clarity in his "Mito, lenguaje e ideología como estructuras literarias," in *Recopilación,* ed. Larco, 257–83.

4   Antonio Cornejo Polar goes so far as to affirm that, among other attitudes, Ernesto is characterized by confusion and ambiguity ("El sentido de la narrativa de Arguedas," *Recopilación,* ed. Larco, 61). Nevertheless, these traits are not offered again as significant ones in his fundamental work *Los universos narrativos de José María Arguedas* (Buenos Aires: Losada, 1972).

5   Concerning the romantic and heroic ideal of Ernesto, see Sara Castro-Klarén, *El mundo mágico de José María Arguedas* (Lima: Instituto de Estudios Peruanos, 1973), 101–03.

6   Mario Vargas Llosa, "*Los ríos profundos*: ensoñación y magia," in *Nueva novela latinoamericana,* ed. J. Lafforgue, vol. 1 (Buenos Aires: Paidós, 1969), 45–54.

7   In "La otra dimensión: el espacio mítico," José Luis Rouillon has analyzed the maternal and paradisiacal sense of this happy space (in *Recopilación,* ed. Larco, 148–49). Nevertheless this critic tends to sanctify spaces which, in my judgment, Arguedas was revealing as sources of a social dynamic. The appearance of the truly sacred ("paz de lo natural," "peace of what is natural") depends, as we will see later, on the struggle of human beings and in a definitive way on the strength and coherence of the social classes that represent *liberation* (the social equivalent of that harmonious natural world).

8   Rowe, "Mito," 279, relates this need for objectivity and universality to the subordinate position held by the indigenous culture which nourishes the child.

9   Some examples, taken at random: "su infierno" ("his hell") (p. 47); "callejones hirvientes" ("boiling alleys") (45); "el fuego del valle, . . . el camino era polvoriento y ardoroso, . . . el valle ardiente . . . sumergido como yo bajo el aire denso y calcinado" ("the fire of the valley, . . . the road was dusty and burning, . . . the burning valley . . . sunken like myself beneath the dense, calcified air") (67); "el valle cálido, el aire ardiente" ("the hot valley, the burning air") (51); "tierra tibia ("the warm earth") (50); "el sol caldeaba el patio. Desde la sombra de la bóveda y del corredor mirábamos arder el empedrado. El sol infunde silencio cuando cae, al mediodía, al fondo de estos abismos . . ." ("the sun heated the patio. From the shadows of the dome and the corridor we watched the stones burn. The sun instills silence as it falls, at noon, to the depths of these abysses . . .") (50); "las nubes iban quemándose en llamas" ("the clouds were burning in flames") (163); "ese valle angosto que empezaba

en el fuego e iba hasta la nieve y que en su región más densa, era caluroso con olor a bagazo" ("that narrow valley that began in fire and ended in snow and that in its densest area was hot and smelled of sugar cane") (187). Heat, confusion (45, 80, 82), and downward movement are ever-present.

10 This relationship of children-colonos is observed by Anne-Marie Metaillié in "Contenido social de *Los ríos profundos*," in a fragment anthologized in *Recopilación*, ed. Larco, 319. Ernesto "descubre, de golpe, que se puede impedir a un hombre convertirse en adulto . . . Los indios se han convertido en niños incapaces de rebelarse" ("suddenly discovers that you can prevent a man from becoming an adult . . . The Indians have become children, incapable of rebelling").

11 Arguedas himself alluded to this process on several occasions. The best summary of this vision is found in the book by Antonio Cornejo Polar already cited. Also, although along different lines, the interesting development explored by Gladys Marín in her *La experiencia americana de José María Arguedas* (Buenos Aires: F. García Cambeiro, 1973).

12 I have developed this theme in several essays, especially in "Inocencia y Neocolonialismo: un caso de dominación ideológica en la literatura infantil," *Cuadernos de la Realidad Nacional*, U. Católica de Chile, Santiago, no. 8 (June 1971). The most recent versions of this essay, and of others on the same theme, are found in *Sobre patos, elefantes y héroes*, (Ediciones de la Flor, 1985). See my *The Empire's Old Clothes* (Pantheon, 1983).

13 Yerko Moretic speaks of the lack of unity between the first chapters and the rest of the book in his "José María Arguedas y la literatura peruana," *Atenea*, Concepción, Chile (October–December 1964), 205–16. Sara Castro-Klarén calls attention to the dichotomous limitations to episodic unity in the novel, although she believes that it "se salva de un error que bien pudo ser fatal" ("it is saved from a mistake that could have been fatal") by rooting itself firmly "en el tema total de la lucha entre el bien y el mal" ("in the total theme of the struggle between good and evil") (*El mundo mágico*, 149–52). Vargas Llosa adds that the social sphere and the "íntimo-lírco" ("intimate-lyrical") are in opposition and do not fit together well (see "Ensoñación y magica" and his "Indigenismo y breves intenciones" ["Indigenism and Brief Intentions"] in *Nueva novela*, ed. Lafforgue, 30–36). On the other hand, Yurkievitch, while emphasizing the autonomy of the eleven chapters, believes that the book "tiene la estructura de una novela clásica" ("has the structure of a classical novel") (in "Realismo y tensión lírica en *Los ríos profundos*," in *Recopilación*, ed. Larco, 249). Although the most recent discussions of A. Cornejo Polar of *indigenismo* and its non-Western aesthetic canons (for example, the presence of story and myth and other oral forms within a narrative work whose tradition was born in Europe) casts this discussion of unity in a new light, I continue to think that *Deep Rivers* is constructed on the basis of a profoundly unifying criterion, even from the point of view of the norms and conventions of Western art.

14 Let us note that this chapter was published as an independent story in 1945

in the magazine *Las Moradas* (Lima), according to Yurkievitch ("Realismo y tensión," 250), eleven years before the novel was finished.

15   I called attention to these two categories of violence in the essay "La violencia en la novela hispanoamericana actual" in my book *Imaginación y violencia en América* (Santiago: Universitaria, 1970; 2d ed., Barcelona: Anagrama, 1972). Although I no longer believe its application to be as universal as it seemed at that time, in the case of this novel the differentiation still is singularly appropriate.

16   Angel Rama has studied the energy and flexibility of the inverse process, that of mestization, in his introduction to the selection of Arguedas's ethnographic texts, *Formación de una cultura indoamericana*, (Mexico City: Siglo XXI, 1975), ix–xxiv.

17   For another interpretation of the *Crucificado* (that is the pongo in opposition to El Viejo, who is the Antichrist), see the interesting study by Tomás Escajadillo, "Tópicos y símbolos religiosos en el primer capítulo de *Los ríos profundos*," *Revista de Crítica Literaria Latinoamericana*, Lima, V, 9, (1979), 57–68.

18   This is not just a problem of *cultural* dialogue, the necessity for which José María Arguedas never doubted, but rather it is projected in the idea, which is fundamental to his thought, of "la parte generosa, humana de los opresores" ("the generous, human part of the oppressors") (in "No Soy un Aculturado," published as an epilogue to *El zorro de arriba y el zorro de abajo* (Buenos Aires: Losada, 1971), 297), the only guarantee that the powerful (or a fraction of them) would listen and allow themselves to be enchanted by the "gran nación cercada" ("the great besieged nation"). E. A. Westphalen points out the same thing in his memorial note "José María Arguedas" in the homage to Arguedas published in *Amaru*, Lima (11 December 1969).

19   "Su rostro estaba como rígido" ("His face was rigid") (p. 146); "Nunca más se juntó con nosotros" ("He never joined us again") (146); "Nos pareció que sus ojos se habían hundido. Estaba pálido, casi verdoso" ("It seemed to us that his eyes had sunken. He was pale, almost green") (149); "Casi ha muerto ya" ("He's almost dead already") (154). "El Añuco, creo, agonizaba" ("Añuco, I think, was dying") (167). And on the night of his farewell, they see him "delgado, frágil, próximo quizá a morir" ("thin, fragile, perhaps about to die") (167).

20   Recently the mechanical application of Mircea Eliade to Spanish American literature has been so abused (I recognize that I have been guilty of it myself), that I am tempted not to quote him here. But the truth is that this magical and totemic ascension of "la opa" carries within it echoes of the sort of shamanism and of rebirth that the Romanian scholar has pointed out in his multiple texts.

21   Rowe says: "la capacidad de convertir el sufrimiento en voluntad de resistencia es el patrón dominante de *Los ríos profundos*" ("the capacity to turn suffering into the will to resist is the dominant pattern of *Deep Rivers*") ("Mito," 272), referring to the role of the *zumbayllu* and of the rivers in the book, more than to this incident.

22   Both read diverse motivations into the river: Antero sees there the furious element which is like him, that which tests his courage, but not any moral inspiration. This is important, because even that reality, the most permanent that exists, resembles whoever approaches it and contemplates it. The River is de-objectified, being less constant in its flow than Ernesto would like.

23   In an interview, when I asked him about this tendency to idealize woman, he did not explain why, but rather reiterated the terms of the question itself: "A través de mi infancia, sólo aprendí a temer o a adorar a la mujer" ("Throughout my childhood, I only learned to fear or to adore woman"). "Conversación con José María Arguedas," in *Trilce*, nos. 15–16 (February–August 1969), 65–70.

24   Sara Castro-Klarén refers to the two types of women (*El mundo mágico*, 184).

25   See "Entrevista a José María Arguedas," by Tomás Escajadillo, in *Cultura y Pueblo*, Lima, nos. 7–8 (July–December, 1965), 22–23.

26   Rowe makes this observation, "Mito," 279.

27   See Leonidas Morales, "José María Arguedas: el lenguaje como perfección humana," *Estudios Filológicos*, Universidad Austral de Valdivia, no. 7 (1971).

28   See Henry James, *The Art of the Novel* (New York, 1947), and Percy Lubbock, *The Craft of Fiction* (London, 1921). Also consult Wayne C. Booth, *The Rhetoric of Fiction* (Chicago, 1961), 149–63.

29   See his "La novela y el problema de la expresión literaria en el Perú," prologue to the Chilean edition of *Yawar Fiesta* (Santiago: Universitaria, 1968), the first version of which appeared in *Mar del Sur*, Lima, 9 (January–February, 1950), 66–72.

30   "Estos elementos son utilizados desde el interior y en función de la narración y no como agregados decorativos . . ." ("These elements are used from within and with a narrative function and not as merely decorative additions"), says Rubén Barreiro Saguier (*Le Monde*, December 20, 1969).

31   In "Poesía y Prosa en el Perú Contemporáneo," *Panorama de la actual literatura latinoamericana* (Havana: Casa de las Américas, 1969), 138–53. César Lévano was the first to note the meaning of this denouement, in his 1960 study, "El contenido anti-feudal de la obra de Arguedas," in his book, *Arguedas, Un sentimiento trágico de la vida* (Lima: sin ed., 1969): "¿Acaso sería forzar demasiado la exégesis si se viera en este episodio de unos ex-hombres vueltos a la vida por obra de la fe una como anticipación de lo que serán capaces los indios, en este caso, los siervos de las haciendas, cuando adquieran ese grado mínimo de conciencia y esperanza que se requiere para desafiar las balas y para apoderarse de una ciudad?" ("Would it perhaps force the exegesis too much if we were to see in this episode of some ex-human beings returned to life by dint of faith an anticipation of what the Indians, in this case, the hacienda peons, would be capable of, when they acquired that minimum level of consciousness and hope that is required to brave the bullets and to take over a city?") (p. 64).

32   See Arguedas's essay "Mitos Quechuas Post-Hispánicos," in *Formación de una cultura* (1975), 173–82.

33 *The Singing Mountaineers, Songs and Tales of the Quechua People*, 2d ed. (Austin: University of Texas Press, 1971), with an introduction by Ruth Stephan.

Sandwiched Between Proust and the Mummy

1 Alejo Carpentier, *Reasons of State*, Writers and Readers, 1977. Although Francis Partridge's translation is fine, once in a while I have been forced to offer my own renditions, when they clarify the pertinent text.

2 It is Carpentier himself who, in an interview with Miguel F. Roa, "Alejo Carpentier: el recurso a Descartes," in *Granma* (May 18, 1974), suggests that he has taken a typical "pícaro" or picaresque hero and turned him into a tyrant. The traditional lowlife ruffian casts a giant shadow in a giant continent.

3 Our dictator is strangely similar to . . . Jorge Luis Borges, at least in Roberto Fernández Retamar's interpretation of the need of intellectuals in underdeveloped backlands to know everything about what happens in the metropolis.

4 Graziella Pogolotti has analyzed the way in which uprooting and violence are the necessary corollaries of our anti-hero's "false cultural foundations" in "Carpentier Renovado," *Casa de las Américas* 15, no. 86 (September–October 1974).

5 Walter Benjamin, in his essay "The Image of Proust," in *Illuminations* (London: Fontana/Collins, 1977).

6 Thorstein Veblen, *Theory of the Leisure Class* (New York: Penguin, 1979).

7 Jaime Mejía Duque, "Los recursos de un novelista," in *Recopilación de textos sobre Alejo Carpentier*, Serie Valoracion Multiple (New York: Casa de las Américas, 1977).

8 For the term "residual," I am indebted to Raymond Williams's chapter, "Dominant, Residual and Emergent," in *Marxism and Literature* (Oxford University Press, 1977).

9 See Zeev Sternhell's chapter, "Fascist Ideology," in *Fascism, A Reader's Guide*, ed. Walter Laquer (New York: Penguin, 1979), 325–406. Also interesting is that in 1972, when Carpentier was writing the novel in Paris, two books on Barrès and fascism were published in France—and were reviewed extensively in the French press.

10 This possibility of one epoch standing in for another is used selectively by Carpentier in other works (for instance, in *El arpa y la sombra*, the description of post-independence Chile alludes simultaneously to Pinochet's dictatorship; or the eighteenth century opening of *Explosion in a Cathedral*, seems to the reader for many pages to refer to the early twentieth century), but it is only in *Reasons of State* that it underpins the whole creative process.

11 Noel Salomon suggests that this superposition of various historical times (as noted in his analysis of *Explosion in a Cathedral* in the essay "*El Siglo de las Luces*: historia e imaginación," in *Recopilación*, 395–428) is possible because of an "aesthetic of imprecision."

12 What Carpentier does with a country and a dictator, the Head of State himself seems to have incorporated as a way of perceiving reality habitually: the

dictator's way of constructing the world, for instance, as a "gothic vitraux," is strangely and disturbingly similar to Carpentier's.

13   See Stefan Morawski's introduction to *Marx-Engels, On Literature and Art* (New York, International General, 1974).

14   The fact that this Student is too saintly, rather stereotypical, rigid and unreal, indicates, perhaps more than Carpentier would have wanted, some of the not-so-hidden weaknesses of the revolutionary movement in Latin America. See the essay on the *testimonio* in this same collection.

15   This mythical construction is essential to the existence of both these rebels. The Student will physically appear only after he has been prepared for as a legendary presence. Miguel Estatua, that "Black Christ," is narrated as if from afar, as if future generations were already placing him in the world of the imagination. We even see this elaboration working in front of our very eyes. The Mayorala Elmira (herself black) remembers him twice, in Paris, as Pedro Estatua—forgetting his name, which is accessory, and recalling his creativity and almost divine talent, which is central. For something to be real and marvellous—as Carpentier's own preliminary essay on the subject in *The Kingdom of this World* establishes—popular and collective participation is crucial. To abstract and separate the "magic" from those who produce it with their words and bodies, the Latin American people, is to take these fantasies away from history and lodge them in some eternal, hypothetical Continent of the Mind.

16   I have looked at this tension between the spiral and the circle in Carpentier's work before *Reasons of State* in my "El sentido de la historia en la obra de Alejo Carpentier," in *Imaginación y Violencia en América* (Barcelona: Anagrama, 1972).

17   Clementine Rabassa has remarked upon the importance of the black element in this novel in her "The Creative Function of Black Characters in Alejo Carpentier's Reasons of State," in *Latin American Literary Review* 6, no. 12 (Spring–Summer 1978), 26–37.

18   Carpentier had already developed a similar structure in his short story "Voyage to the Seed." The critic Manuel Durán has shown how the final disappearance of the hero (who lives his life backward, "progressing" toward conception) is due to the fact that he wasted his existence, which symbolizes a colonial society about to disappear itself. See Durán's essay "Viaje a la semilla: el cómo y el porqué de una profunda obra maestra," *Asedios a Carpentier, selección y notas de Klaus Müller-Bergh* (Santiago: Editorial Universitaria, 1972), 63–87.

19   Since 1964 Plon has been publishing Proust's correspondence, edited by Philip Kolb.

20   I am indebted to the two volumes of George Painter's monumental and controversial *Marcel Proust, A Biography* (London: Chatt and Windus, 1965) for most of these observations about Proust's life.

21   Just to give an example, look at the parallel paths of Françoise (in *A la recherche*) and the Mayorala, both of whom make the everyday into art through their cuisine, both of whom go to the market in similar ways.

22   It seems probable to me that Carpentier's novel opens on November 13, 1913, the day when *Du côté de chez Swann* appears. I have been unable to verify this

probability by finding out if that day would indeed have been the Day of the Drags that year, but it certainly would have a nice joke on the Head of State who reads the newspapers without reading the criticism of a book to which he owes his whole existence.

23 This is a controversial point. My view on the matter coincides with those who, like Levin, Benjamin, Camus, see Proust as a social critic, a writer who, through his literature, is able to surmount and defeat the pervailing snobbishness.

24 My interpretation of this incident owes much to Harry Levin's point of view as exposed in *The Gates of Horn: A Study of Five French Realists* (New York: Oxford University Press, 1966).

25 I am reminded of a similar situation in *Le Père Goriot*, when the daughters dance as their father dies.

26 See J. Y. Tadié, *Lectures de Proust* (Paris: Armand Colin, 1971), particularly pp. 164–66.

27 Mejía Duque's article in *Recopilación*, 437.

28 Carpentier confessed as much to Klaus Müller-Bergh in "Talking to Carpentier," *Review* 18 (Fall 1976), 22.

29 T. W. Adorno, *Prisms* (London: Neville Spearman, 1967).

30 Roberto González-Echevarría, "On *Reasons of State*," *Review* 25–29.

31 P. Costil, "La construction musicale de *A la recherche du temps perdu*," *Bulletin des Amis de Marcel Proust*, no. 8 (1958) and no. 9 (1959).

32 See Gide's judgment in Tadié's book (*Lectures de Proust*, 30–35).

33 See J. Y. Tadié's *Proust et le Roman* (Paris: Gallimard, 1971), the chapter "Techniques du récit," 366–412.

34 Both in Proust and Carpentier to reconquer the past is not a matter of metaphor but an act of metonymy—in other words, an experience that radiates contiguously rather than analogically. This is what allows the "immense edifice" of memory to be built, as Gerard Ganette argues in his "Métonymie chez Proust ou la naissance du récit," in *Les critiques de nôtre temps et Proust, compilation de Jacques Bersani* (Garnier, 1971), 169–80.

35 See B. G. Rogers, *Proust's Narrative Techniques* (Geneva: Droz, 1965), the first chapter.

36 See Mario Benedetti's *El recurso del supremo patriarca*, (Mexico: Nueva Imagen, 1979).

37 See Carpentier's interview with César Leante, "Confesiones de un escritor barroco," *Revista Cuba* (April 1964).

38 In *Recopilación*, 17.

Political Code and Literary Code:
The Testimonial Genre in Chile Today

1 The first case of which we know is the pamphlet from the beginning of October 1973, *Testimonios de Chile* (*Testimonies from Chile*), Boletín de Solidaridad con la Lucha de los Pueblos Latinoamericanos (the Bulletin of Solidarity with the Struggle of the Latin American Peoples), brought out in Buenos Aires

by Noé Jitrik and Silvia Bermann. The books would not appear for several months more, but there were already four or five titles in Argentina by early 1974, the first being *Testimonio: Chile, septiembre 1973 (Testimony: Chile, September 1973)*, from Editorial Crisis, with a prologue by Ernesto Sábato.

2 We have emphasized these three books, which seem to be the most notable examples (Sun Axelsson, Brigitta Leander, Raúl Silva Cáceres, *Evidence on the Terror in Chile* (London: The Merlin Press, 1974); translation of the original Swedish, *Terror in Chile* (Stockholm: Sabén & Sjögren, 1974); Sergio Villegas, *Chile, El estadio, los crímenes de la Junta Militar (Chile, the Stadium, the Crimes of the Military Junta)* (Buenos Aires: Editorial Cartago, 1974); *Chili: le dossier noir (Chile: the Black File)* (Paris: Gallimard, 1974), by a Franco-Latin American collective), but the list is longer. For example, *Génocide au Chile (Genocide in Chile)* (Paris: Máspero, 1974) by Carlos Cerda combines the voices of many with the voice of the author.

3 The length of the present essay excludes the possibility of examining, even summarily, the structure of this type of reportage, which in the last decades has had special transcendence in America. To the well-known cases of Barnet (*Biografía de un cimarrón* and *La canción de Rachel—Biography of a Runaway Slave* and *The Song of Rachel*) and of Raúl Roa (*Aventuras, venturas y desventuras de un mambí en la lucha por la independencia de Cuba—Adventures, Fortunes and Misfortunes of a Black in the Struggle for Cuban Independence*), of Ricardo Pozas (*Juan Pérez Jolote*), Elena Poniatowska (*La noche de Tlatelolco—The Night of Tlatelolco*) and Oscar Lewis (*The Children of Sánchez*), one can now add the book of Bernardo Subercaseaux and Jaime Londoño, *Gracias a la vida (Thanks to Life)*, about Violeta Parra.

4 "El Estado y la creación intelectual: reflexiones sobre la cultura chilena de la década del setenta" ("The State and Intellectual Creation: Reflections on Chilean Culture in the Seventies"), lecture at the Colloquium on Intellectual Creation in Latin America, organized by the University of the United Nations and the National Autonomous University in Mexico City in May 1979; "Pequeñas alamedas: la lucha de la cultura chilena actual" ("Small Avenues: The Struggle of Contemporary Chilean Culture"), *Casa de las Américas* 20, no. 115 (July–August 1979), 60–75; "Literatura chilena y clandestinidad" ("Chilean Literature and Clandestinity"), *Escritura*, Caracas, 2, no. 4 (July–December 1977).

5 See José Joaquín Brunner, "De la cultura liberal a la sociedad disciplinaria" ("From Liberal Culture to a Disciplined Society") (mimeographed working draft), FLACSO, Santiago, Chile (1977) and, by the same author, "La cultura en una sociedad autoritaria" ("Culture in an Authoritarian Society"), (mimeographed working draft), FLACSO, Santiago, Chile (1979).

6 See the interview of Jorge Barudy with E. González Bermejo, "Tortura y exilio. Rehacer al hombre" ("Torture and Exile. Remaking a Man"), *Revista de la Universidad de México* 24, no. 3 (November 1979), 2–8.

7 We are refering to Jorge Montealegre, poet, and Carlos Lira. The latter, since the publication of his narrative of captivity, has published *Así vemos nuestro destierro (experiencias de tres años de exilio) (How We See our Exile [Experiences of Three Years in Exile])*, (Hamburg: Verlag Duenbostel, 1978).

8   Alejandro Witker, *Prisión en Chile*, with a prologue by Galo Gómez (Mexico City: Fondo de Cultura Económica, 1975); Rodrigo Rojas, *Jamás de rodillas (Acusación de un prisionero de la junta fascista de Chile)*, with a prologue by Volodia Teitelboim (Moscow: Nóvosti Press, 1974); Rolando Carrasco, *Prigué*, with a prologue by Luis Corvalán (Moscow: Nóvosti Press, 1977); Carlos Lira, *Der Gefangene Gefängnisdirektor, 26 monate erlebter Faschismus in Chile*, with a prologue by Antonio Skármeta (Hamburg: Verlag Atelier im Bauernhaus, 1977); Aníbal Quijada Cerda, *Cerco de púas*, (Havana: Premio Testimonio Casa de las Américas, 1977); Manuel Cabieses, *Chile: 11808 horas en campos de concentración*, with a prologue by Argenis Martínez (Caracas: Rocinante, 1975); Jorge Montealegre's account circulated in mimeograph under the editorial sponsorship of the Christian Left at the end of 1974, being published later in a shortened version in Ximena Ortúzar's *Represión y tortura en el Cono Sur*, prologue by Clodomiro Almeyda (Mexico City: Extemporáneos, 1977), with the title "Un torturado de la Izquierda Cristiana." Each time one of these authors is quoted, the corresponding page will be indicated, with the understanding that we are using the edition here designated.

9   Their ages go from 19 (Montealegre) to 55 (Quijada, whom guards and prisoners baptized as "grandfather"). Party membership and profession: Witker (socialist party, historian and professor); Carrasco and Rojas (communist party, journalists, the latter, a miner in his youth); Lira (MAPU—Worker-Peasant, a prison warden); Montealegre (Christian Left, student); Cabieses (MIR, journalist); Quijada (ex-PC, worker in the Social Security Service); with Rojas and Cabieses occupying high political positions (the Political Commission and the Central Committee of their parties, respectively), while the rest were simply activists. Montealegre, Rojas, Carrasco and Cabieses were arrested in Santiago; Lira, in Rancagua; Witker, in Concepción; and Quijada in Punta Arenas. Several of them spent a long time in the North, in the Chacabuco concentration camp.

10   Henri Alleg, *La Question* (Paris: Les Editions de Minuit, 1958).

11   See Fernando Rivas Sánchez and Elizabeth Reiman Weigert, *Las Fuerzas Armadas de Chile: Un caso de penetración imperialista* (Mexico City: Ediciones 75, 1976), especially pages 40–44, and Roger Trinquier, *Modern Warfare: A French View*, (New York: Praeger, 1974).

12   Alleq, *La Question*, 14.

13   Bruno Bettelheim, *The Informed Heart*, (Boston: The Free Press, 1960), and Albert H. Friedlander, ed., *Out of the Whirlwind: A Reader of Holocaust Literature*, (New York: Schocken, 1976).

14   Words of Galo Gómez, in his prologue to *Prisión en Chile*, by Witker, 12.

15   Ibid., 9.

16   See Miguel Rojas Mix, *Los dioses de Pinochet* (the book was unpublished at the writing of these notes, with two chapters published in nos. 2 and 5 of the journal *Araucaria*); Armand Mattelart, "Un fascisme 'créole' en quête d'idéologues," *Le Monde Diplomatique*, Paris (July 1974); J. J. Brunner, "La estructuración autoritaria del espacio creativo" (working draft), FLACSO, Santiago (1979) and "Educación y cultura en una sociedad autoritaria," *Revista Nueva Sociedad* (Caracas, 1977); Francisco Soto (pseud.), *Fascismo y Opus Dei*

en Chile (Estudios de literatura e ideología), (Barcelona: Avance, 1976); and Julio Silva Solar, "El Integrismo Católico-Fascista en la ideología de la Junta Militar," *Chile-América* 2, no. 1, Rome (January 1975), supplement, 1–13.

17 Hernán Montealegre, *La Seguridad del Estado y los derechos humanos* (Santiago: Academia de Humanismo Cristiano, 1979).

18 Hernán Vidal, "La declaración de principios de la Junta Militar chilena como sistema literario: la lucha anti-fascista y el cuerpo humano," lecture to a session of the Latin American Studies Association (April 1979), *Casa de las Américas*, has pointed out this aspect, besides the authors cited in note 16.

19 In Lira's original manuscript, which reached me, the author mentioned the jailers' foul-smelling mouths and reeking feet as if those characteristics, which both patriots and revolutionaries could have, diminished the torturers more than their acts.

20 David Rousset, *L'Univers Concentrationnaire*, (Paris: Editions du Pavois, 1946), 13.

21 Jaime Concha exemplifies this cognitive process in the analysis he makes of Witker in "Testimonios de la lucha antifascista," *Araucaria*, no. 4 (1978), 143.

22 Anna Housková has analyzed this "hombre identificado con el colectivo" ("man identified with the collective"), which is presented in Rodrigo Rojas, "La narrativa chilena de resistencia anti-Fascista," *Revista de Crítica Literaria Latinoamericana*, Lima, 3, no. 5, (first semester, 1977), 35–48.

23 We refer to "El aullido volador" in the journal *Plural*, Mexico City (second period, January 1977), which anticipates another work, *Sopla un sonido oscura*, which is, without any doubt, another title for what must be *Cerco de púas*.

24 In addition to the works cited in note 4, one may also consult "Chile. La resistencia cultural al imperialismo," *Casa de las Américas* 16, no. 98 (September–October 1976), 3–11.

25 See the chapter "Black Laughter," in Lawrence W. Levine's *Black Culture and Black Consciousness, Afro-American Folk Thought from Slavery to Freedom* (New York: Oxford University Press, 1977).

26 In the work cited, Levine emphasizes that humor, along with other functions, acts as a permanent system of informal education for the oppressed and minorities. C. V. Gruner accentuates that informal networks of communication can be more important than the persuasive ability of humor in his "An Experimental Study of Satire as Persuasion," *Speech Monographs*, no. 32, 149–53.

27 See my interview with Oscar Castro in *Conjunto*, no. 37 (Havana: Casa de las Américas, 1978), 3–35.

28 Rousset, *L'Univers*, 13.

29 The original title of Lira's work was not *El alcaide preso*, but rather *Lo vi, lo viví, lo escuché*.

30 Roberto Fernández Retamar, "Algunos problemas teóricos de la literatura hispanoamericana," *Revista de Crítica Literaria Latinoamericana* I, no. 1 (1975), 7–39; and, by the same author, *Para una teoría de la literatura hispanoamericana y otras aproximaciones*, (Havana: Casa de las Américas, Cuadernos Casa, 1975); Antonio Cornejo Polar, "Para una interpretación de la novela indigenista,"

Casa de las Américas 16, no. 100, (January–February 1977), 40–48; and my own "Níveles de la dominación cultural en América Latina: algunos problemas y perspectivas," in *Ideologies and Literature* 2, no. 6, Minneapolis, (March–April 1978), 52–89.

31   The review of Concha, in *Casa de las Américas* 16, no. 96 (May–June 1976), 142.

32   Walter Benjamin, "The Story-teller, Reflections on the Works of Nikolai Leskov," in *Illuminations* (London: Fontana/Collins, 1973), 83–109.

33   As Françoise Perus suggests in her provocative article, "De la possibilité d'une littérature prolétarienne en Amérique Latine," in the issue of *Europe* devoted to "La littérature prolétarienne en question" (March–April 1977), 90–102.

34   For an analysis of the limitations of this language, see my "Notas para una aproximación marxista a la narrativa chilena de los últimos treinta años," in *Casa de las Américas* 69 (1971), 65–83.

35   "Those who suffered," writes Chaim A. Kaplan, in his diary of the Warsaw Ghetto (*Scroll of Agony*, ed. Abraham I. Katah [New York: Macmillan, 1965]), "addressed one another."

36   Christine Buci-Gluckmann, *Gramsci y el Estado* (Mexico City: Siglo XXI, 1978).

37   See *L'appareil répressif et le prisonnier politique: le cas du Chile* (Paris: CIMADE, 1977).

38   George Steiner, *Language and Silence* (London: Penguin, 1969).

39   One example will be sufficient. The beginning of the *Diario de viaje* by Núñez. We read, in manuscript, the date: Friday, the third, five in the afternoon, and the month, May, has been added in the author's handwriting, with a different ink, months later, to situate the reader. Then these words: "Voy atravesando el espejo y mi voz ya no tiene sonido . . . Estoy ciego en el túnel. Meto los dedos en el té frío y me atemorizo." ("I am crossing the mirror and my voice now has no sound. I put my fingers in the cold tea and I am afraid.")

40   Read in Paris before the Council of UNESCO on September 18, 1975.

41   "For writing, by objectifying words, and making them and their meaning available for much more prolonged and intensive scrutiny than is possible orally, encourages private thought; the diary or confession enables the individual to objectify his own experience, and gives him some check upon the transmutations of memory under the influence of subsequent events." J. Goodey and I. Watt, "The Consequences of Literacy," in *Language and Social Context* (London: Penguin, 1972), 346.

42   It is true that the rigor in the chronological ordering of events will gradually diminish. Until February 19 everything is narrated with constraint, morning, afternoon, and night. However, once this regularity has been assimilated by the reader, and the protagonist himself lives it unconsciously, that is, beginning with the aforementioned date, Valdés proportions his own experience of time, narrating one part in the past, another in the present, presenting panoramic views or compendia, in which each day is organized around a certain person or incident. The imprisonment does not have the same pressure and urgency it had before, the prisoner's attention is relaxed, he is lulled a bit, and falls into habit. But when the day of his torture arrives, preceded by a day in which the only thing the author did was to reflect on his absolute solitude, he

returns us to the present, the time of the voices of his guards. These movements are one more indication, if there were need for more, of the way in which he carefully elaborates his material.

43   I cannot here even begin to discuss in detail this relationship between testimony and fiction, which I believe to be essential to a full understanding of the genre. See Miguel Barnet's appendix to *La canción de Rachel*, "La novela testimonio: socio-literatura," (Barcelona: Estela, 1970, 125–50); and my "La última obra de Truman Capote: ¿un nuevo género literario?" in *Anales de la Universidad de Chile* (1966).

44   Words of Roberto Díaz Castillo, "Testimonios de la lucha anti-fascista" in *Revista de Literatura Chilena en el Exilio*, Los Angeles, no. 9 (Winter 1979), 5.

45   "Whatever the method of torture used, it is generally accompanied from the beginning by a procedure intended to weaken the prisoners physically and psychologically; an attempt to systematically destroy the defenses which the victim habitually utilizes to maintain his morale. Semi-privation of food and medical attention, provoked illnesses, absence of hygiene, debilitating physical exercises, and the forced maintaining of certain postures, prolonged interrogations under conditions of extreme tension, isolation: these represent the backdrop which accompanies the imprisonment and interrogation of every political prisoner in Latin America," Barudy, quoted from an interview with E. González Bermejo, 4.

46   It is interesting to note that this technique, like so many others, is not used exclusively by Valdés, but also appears in the other accounts. What distinguishes the author of *Tejas Verdes* is that his use is conscious: he has refined, purified, and polished the techniques in order to better prop up the helplessness of the narrator-protagonist.

47   See R. Brown and A. Gilman, "The Pronouns of Power and Solidarity," in *Style in Language*, ed. T. A. Sebeok (Cambridge: MIT Press, 1960), 253–76.

48   Concha speaks of the "deliberately pre-reflexive, almost somnambulistic" level in "Testimonios . . . ," 146 and, earlier, on the same page, of "pre-political, animal brotherhood."

49   *Zoom* (Mexico City: Siglo XXI, 1971). All further quotes are from this edition.

50   Antonio Skármeta, "Tendencias en la más nueva narrativa hispanoamericana," *Separata* from *Avances del saber*, vol. 11 of the *Enciclopedia Labor* (1975), 763.

51   Another example: "You shut your eyes and you understand that it would be all the same whether you re-opened them in an hour or in a hundred years . . . Any change would only serve to give the sensation of immobility." *Zoom*, 67.

52   For the theme of liberalism as I understand it here, consult José Joaquín Brunner, "La organización liberal de la cultura" (working draft), FLACSO, Santiago (1979), especially 17–26.

53   Vidal, "La declaración de principios," 24–25.

54   David V. J. Bell has recognized, among four typological categories of resistance, one that, being nonviolent, is limited to an elite and is disorganized. Members of these groups do not see themselves as belonging to specific social groups (although they identify or sympathize with vast sectors of the op-

pressed) and, in the case of an internal war, have scant possibilities of survival. In his *Resistance and Revolution* (Boston: Houghton Mifflin Co., 1973).

55 The reports and analyses of the now dissolved Committee for Peace in Chile recognized these distinct phases.

56 It should be mentioned that in Valdés there are some (few) moments of plenitude, sensuality, liberty, which suddenly appear in the middle of the worst circumstances, relieving the text and providing a counterpoint to the suffocating imprisonment.

57 This is true to such an extent that Jaime Concha in his analysis of the antifascist testimonies makes great efforts, despite the fact that he recognizes Valdés's "subjectivism," to ignore or to diminish the "negative" aspect of his experience.

58 His conference on the Encounter of Latin American Writers in Copenhagen in May, 1978, his positions read on the radio in September of 1978 in a forum in Frankfurt, his article "Sobre la inhibición del intelectual" in *Testimonio Latinoamericano*, Barcelona 1, no. 2 (May–June 1980), 13–14.

59 Juan Armando Epple, in "Esa literatura que surge de un cerco de púas," *Revista de Literatura Chilena en el Exilio* 5 (Winter 1978), calls attention to the unnoticed tradition of testimony on this type of experience in Chile during the twentieth century.

60 Commentary by Jitrik on a lecture by Ana Pizarro, "Sur le caractère 'ancilar' de notre récit latinoaméricain," in the Centre Culturel International de Cérisy-la Salle, *Littérature Latinoaméricaine d'aujourd'hui*. Union Genérale d'Editions, Paris, 1980. Leenhardt adds his commentary to the commentary, suggesting that the addressee of both is different: denunciation has an interlocutor and a public in mind, testimony exists "almost without an addressee; it is the immediate word, still confusingly mixed up with the body that speaks.", 23.

61 See his articles "La discusión cultural chilena" and "¿Prudencia o desorientación para formular las bases de una política cultural?" in the anthology of essays of CEREN, *Cultura y comunicaciones de masa* (Barcelona: Editorial Laia, 1975), 12–22 and 33–46 respectively, and "Por una práctica cultural compometida" in the journal *Testigo* (Buenos Aires: January–April 1972), 3–16.

62 See Marcelo Coddou, "Narrativa Chilena en el exilio: notas de aproximación," in *Revista de Literatura Chilena en el Exilio*, no. 11; Federico Schopf, "Fuera de lugar," in *Araucaria* 9 (1980), especially p. 151; and Antonio Skármeta, a lecture at a workshop of the Wilson Center, "The Rise of the New Latin American Narrative, 1950–1975, in October 1979.

63 Benedetti, in his short story "Pequebú," responds to this idea, showing an intellectual dreamer who is as strong as or stronger than his tough, militant companions.

64 Umberto Eco, *Apocalípticos e integrados ante una sociedad de masas* (Barcelona: Lumen, 1977), fifth edition.

65 An example: "This is the place (Chacabuco) for us to build the Museum of the Revolution in the future. And we have to start soon" (Carrasco, 130).

About the Author

Ariel Dorfman is the author of numerous novels, works of
fiction, and essays in both Spanish and English. His most recent book of fiction in English, *My House Is On Fire* (1990),
is a collection of short stories. Dorfman writes regularly
for such magazines and newspapers as the *New York Times
Book Review*, the *Village Voice*, and the *Los Angeles Times*.
He currently divides his time between Santiago, Chile, and
Durham, North Carolina, where he is Research Professor of
Literature and Latin American Studies at Duke University.

Library of Congress Cataloging-in-Publication Data
Dorfman, Ariel.
Some write to the future : essays on contemporary Latin
American fiction / Ariel Dorfman ; translated by George
Shivers with the author.
Essays originally written in Spanish or English.
Includes index.
ISBN 0-8223-1130-5
1. Spanish American literature—20th century—History and
criticism.   I. Title.
PQ7082.N7D67   1991
863—dc20   90-24936 CIP